Antique Trader

VINTAGE CLOTHING
PRICE GUIDE

Edited By
Kyle Husfloen & Madeleine Kirsh
Contributing Editor Nancy Wolfe

©2006 Krause Publications
Published by

kp books
An Imprint of F+W Publications

700 East State Street • Iola, WI 54990-0001
715-445-2214 • 888-457-2873

Our toll-free number to place an order or obtain
a free catalog is (800) 258-0929.

Library of Congress Catalog Number: 2005935192

ISBN 13-digit: 978-0-89689-370-2
ISBN 10-digit: 0-89689-370-7

Designed by Wendy Wendt
Edited by Kyle Husfloen

Printed in China

A WORD TO THE READER

I have always found vintage clothing fascinating. I can even recall writing a paper about historic costumes back in high school. Through the years I have become the owner of a number of antique and collectible outfits passed down through the family, including the wedding vest of one great-grandfather, and the wedding dress and traveling suit of one grandmother (married in 1919), as well as a special "Indian maiden" outfit she made as a teenager. Also, being a bit of a hoarder, I've held on to a number of shirts and accessories: knit sweaters from the 1960s, disco shirts from the 1970s and so on. Just for fun, I'm including here a photo of yours truly wearing one of the "stylish" little outfits a grandmother bought for me back in 1952 at age 2 1/2 and a shot of the jacket, shoes and accompanying overcoat. I can't really claim to be a "clothes horse," but over the years I did receive some nice outfits. Maybe many of you have also preserved a few special outfits that you or your children wore. As you'll see in reading through our new *Antique Trader Vintage Clothing Price Guide*, many "old clothes" have become very choice collectibles today. Pieces don't have to be "haute couture" to have collector value since very often more "everday" pieces are scarcer, and children's and men's outfits are often even harder to find.

When I started working on this project I was very fortunate to hear about the firm of C. Madeleine's of Miami, a major marketer of quality antique and vintage apparel. Richard and Madeleine Kirsh were most enthusiast about assisting me with this project and they oversaw the selection and photography of hundreds of the pieces you'll see inside. They also asked Elizabeth Martinez to work directly with me and she labored with diligence and care to see that the many CDs of images and corresponding descriptions were sent off to me in a timely manner. I can't thank her enough for her dedication to this book and her willingness to go that extra mile. A special tip of the hat to Cindy Borjas of C. Madeleine's for her efforts also, especially in preparing the special "Glossary of Clothing Terms" you'll find at the end of the listings.

Although C. Madeleine's carries clothing from both the 19th and 20th centuries its main focus is on 20th century outfits. In order to offer a broader selection of Victorian and early 20th century items I was very fortunate to be able to call upon my friend, Nancy Wolfe. I have known Nancy for years and was aware of her fabulous collection of early clothing. So dedicated is Nancy that she displays some of her choicest outfits on mannequins throughout her house. She supplied me with a great variety of ladies' apparel from the early 19th through the early 20th century, but also provided some wonderful shots of early children's pieces and even some from fashionable men of the past. My sincere thanks to Nancy for her fantastic help.

Since I wanted to cover as many aspects as possible of historic clothing from the last 200 years, you'll find here a comprehensive selection of pieces from the 1830s through the 1970s. In addition to clothing itself, we were also able to include a wide variety of "clothing accessories" which I placed in a special section at the end of the regular listings. Featured there are "Hats, Caps & Bonnets," "Purses & Bags," "Shoes & Boots" and "Ties." For this last category I again was able to call upon another specialist in vintage apparel, Chander Erickson of The Frippery of Palm Springs, Calif. It turns out Chander's husband has been collecting quality neckwear for sometime and generously shared pieces from his collection.

As you will see by reviewing our "Table of Contents" I have arranged the contents of this guide in chronological order, broken down into various time frames. Within each section I have sorted the pieces by subcatories of "Children's," "Ladies'" and "Gentlemen's" clothing. Adding to the great appeal of this new price guide we have all the images printed in FULL COLOR. In many instances we have included several views of the same garment, front, back and close-up. This helps highlight the wonderful details of so many of this fashion treasures.

I don't think any other recent price guide has brought together the scope and detail of fashion history that you'll find in the following pages. To start you off in your study, Madeleine Kirsh was kind enough to prepare a special introductory feature on "Collecting Vintage Clothing" that I'm sure you'll find enlightening.

We all hope that you will find this book a delight to read, informative and eye appealing. If you're not yet a collector of vintage fashion, this book may launch you on a new career or at least get you to take a closer look at what may hang forgotten in the back of your closet or packed away in a trunk.

Enjoy!

Kyle Husfloen, Co-Editor

For More Information:

C. Madeleine's
13702 Biscayne Blvd.
North Miami Beach, FL 33181
(305) 945-7770

Chander Erickson
The Frippery
The Galleria
457 No. Palm Canyon Dr., #9
Palm Springs, CA 92262
(760) 861-9747

Kyle Husfloen all dressed up at age 2-1/2.

The vintage outfit is now part of Kyle Husfloen's vintage clothing collection.

COLLECTING VINTAGE CLOTHING GAINS POPULARITY

By Madeleine Kirsh

When Antique Trader Publications first approached us to co-edit this Vintage Price Guide we jumped at the idea. The popularity of wearing and collecting designs from the past has seen tremendous growth and acceptance since we opened C. Madeleine's Vintage Showroom in Miami, Florida in 2001. Besides helping thousands of customers develop their own fashion identity through mixing clothing and accessories from the past with more modern designs, the store also taught us to appreciate the superior quality of these garments compared to most mass produced items we find today. This book reveals the real value of a fashionista's collectibles. The prices can be a revelation.

An 1890s fancy lady's dress.

The history of fashion is a mirror to the future. Nearly every style has already been done in some form and is reproduced with variations today. The fabrication might be changed, new color combinations used or some other minor changes introduced, however the basic patterns come from the past. Every season we find many of the top design firms in the world coming to C. Madeleine's to shop for inspiration. They can spend hours searching for the right touches to serve as a muse to their collections. From a bias cut velvet skirt found in a 1930s gown to a great 1950s Lucite bag paired with a wonderful summer dress, the designers carefully choose pieces from the past which are then resurrected when the "new" designs are introduced on fashion runways in New York, Milan and Paris.

The popularity and demand for vintage pieces is growing so quickly because clothing and accessories are great collectibles that are also a good investment. Clothing reflects our own personality and style, and vintage pieces offer high quality and unique style. When we go to parties or events, we won't look like everyone else. Our fashion stands out. Whatever the reason; personal style, collectible compulsion, or just for fun, we know you will enjoy finding and wearing vintage treasures like the ones featured in this book.

The Vintage Price Guide is designed to help determine the value of items by providing an idea of the selling price of comparables items. Pricing vintage is far from an exact science. A dress that might sell for $1,000 in Los Angeles may go unwanted at a fraction of the price in Chicago. This is because many factors come into play when assessing value. When shopping vintage, keep the following in mind:

- Popularity. How well known the designer is affects the price. We have all heard of the big names such as Yves Saint Laurent and Coco Chanel, however, the real finds can happen when we come across a lesser-known couturier such as Norrell or Sant'Angelo.

- Condition. This is of prime importance. Usually in very old pieces there is some leeway on slight damage. Collectors tend to want the original design condition with no modifications or repairs. Any changes made can dramatically affect pricing.

- Relevance. The piece should be a meaningful representation of a designer's work. Just because you find a great label doesn't mean it has tremendous value. A story of label caution; a few years ago my husband found a vintage 1970s piece in excellent condition at a reasonable price from a very well-known designer. He purchased it and quickly drove back to our store to show me his new find. When I saw this "thing" I just started to laugh. Although it was exactly as advertised, it was the ugliest dress I had ever seen. Though the label had a designer's name, it was not a good representation of their work. Everyone has a bad day or season. Also, if a designer is known for creating fabulous gowns, their shoes may not have great value. You must research individual designers to know their strengths.

A 1950s skirt and sweater outfit.

- When you're hot you're hot. This statement also applies to vintage clothing. As a trend develops, it is shown in all the fashion magazines, and the original vintage pieces go up in value (and plummet when it goes out of favor). The release of a blockbuster movie or the premier of a popular television show can affect the vintage market. When the film "Titanic" was in theaters, the demand for period dresses was very strong. This faded as the movie's audience diminished.

- Location: Prices fluctuate from one geographic region to another. Last year we attended an auction in Colorado. In our spare time we visited several stores searching for hidden treasures and we found that Mexican circle skirts from the 1950's were readily available. Many of the fashion magazines were featuring these beautiful designs but they were hard to come by in South Florida. The auction was a bust but the skirts made the trip worthwhile.

- Value: The appeal of vintage items has greatly increased over the last few years. With more collectors and fewer older pieces available the prices have gone up. Our rule of thumb is to buy quality. There is only so many of each item, and although there will be fluctuation; the long term value is in the better quality items.

We at C. Madeleine's emphasize that there can be a large difference of opinion as to the worth of an item. We have carefully researched each piece in this book and combined that

Elaborate 1920s lady's tea gown.

information with our years of experience to determine a final value. There's no exact formula, but pricing is part of the game which makes the process of acquiring vintage challenging and so much fun.

This price guide can be used in many ways—to determine values of pieces you own or are thinking of buying, as an introduction into the world of vintage and the magnificent designs of the past, or to help you see the benefits you will derive in wearing these works of art and developing a look perfectly suited for your personality and life style. Whatever your reasons we hope you get as much pleasure thumbing through the pages of this book as we did putting it together.

A stylish 1970s dress.

ACKNOWLEDGMENTS

First and foremost I must thank my staff at C. Madeleine's for the hundreds of hours they dedicated to finishing this project. The effort was led by Elizabeth Kohen Martinez who put her heart and soul into the book. Thanks also to Elizabeth's family - Adam, Marcel and Paloma for giving us their spouse and Mom for so many months. Thank you to our incredible photographer Cindy Borjas and to Elisa Weil whose vast knowledge of vintage made our research so much easier.

Many others also contributed items as well as guidance for this project. They included Tish Ramgoolam, Howard Segelman Neil of the Neil Vincent Collection, Fran Thorpe, Maggie Tonjussen, Donna MacDonald, the estate of Rita Hohenberg and Kyle Husfloen of Antique Trader Publications. All of these people came to bat with a winning hit whenever they were asked to help.

Finally, there are three other people who not only played a large part in the completion of this book but are also instrumental in the formation and success of our store, C. Madeleine's. The first two are Virginia and Leslie Fiur, who had faith in a concept financed by fumes and have always given their support. A special thank you goes to my husband, Richard, who continues to make sacrifices to guarantee our success. Most people start with a small store and expand. He envisioned a fashion superstore dedicated to the styling of the past where I could use my talents to create a store unique to the industry. Thank you, Richard, for your continuous love, support and inspiration.

I hope this guide gives you as much pleasure as we had in helping to create it. If we are able to help increase your appreciation for the history of fashion through this book then the hours of work spent in creating it we will deem a success.

Fashionably yours,

Madeleine Kirsh

C. Madeleine's
13702 Biscayne Blvd.
North Miami Beach, FL 33181
(305) 945-7770

TABLE OF CONTENTS

Part I – Pre-1850 Clothing

Chapter 1:
Children's Clothing.. 11
Ladies' Clothing 11
Men's Clothing.. 13

Part II – Clothing – 1850-1920

Chapter 2: 1850-75
Children's Clothing.. 14
Ladies' Clothing... 16
Men's Clothing.. 23

Chapter 3: 1875-1900
Children's Clothing.. 24
Ladies' Clothing... 28
Men's Clothing.. 42

Chapter 4: 1900-1920
Children's Clothing.. 43
Ladies' Clothing... 46
Men's Clothing.. 58

Part III – Clothing – 1920-1980

Chapter 5: 1920-1930
Children's Clothing.. 62
Ladies' Clothing... 63
Men's Clothing.. 74

Chapter 6: 1930-1940
Children's Clothing.. 76
Ladies' Clothing... 77
Men's Clothing.. 97

Chapter 7: 1940-1950
    Children's Clothing.. 98
    Ladies' Clothing.. 98
    Men's Clothing 108

Chapter 8: 1950-1960
    Children's Clothing.. 111
    Ladies' Clothing.. 112
    Men's Clothing 132

Chapter 9: 1960-1970
    Children's Clothing.. 136
    Ladies' Clothing.. 137
    Men's Clothing 157

Chapter 10: 1970-1980
    Children's Clothing.. 161
    Ladies' Clothing.. 161
    Men's Clothing 182

Part IV: Clothing Accessories

Chapter 11: Hats, Caps & Bonnets 187

Chapter 12: Purses & Bags 232

Chapter 13: Shoes & Boots 250

Chapter 14: Ties 262

Chapter 15: Miscellaneous.. 266

Glossary of Terms... 271

PART I - PRE-1850 CLOTHING

CHAPTER 1

CHILDREN'S CLOTHING

Early 19th Century Child's Cotton Dress

Dress, white cotton w/tiny blue print, back drawstring closure, first quarter 19th c. (ILLUS.) **$75-125**

LADIES' CLOTHING

Ball gown, two-piece, gold brocade, w/detachable long sleeves, brass hook & eye back closure, 1836 (ILLUS. with and without the sleeves, bottom of page) **$500-800**

1840s Lady's Silk Fan-front Bodice

Two Views of an 1836 Gold Brocade Ball Gown with or without the Sleeves

Bodice, fan-front style w/sleeve caps, tan patterned silk, brass hook & eye back closure, ca. 1840 (ILLUS., previous page) **$100-150**

sleeves, reportedly used as a wedding dress, ca. 1815-20 (ILLUS. w/long sleeves) **$800-1,200**

1830s Lady's Cotton Corset

Corset, tan cotton embroidered overall w/blue thread, stiffening created by pulling tiny cords through channels sewn into fabric, laces up the back, ca. 1830s (ILLUS.) **$200-400**

Rare Early 19th c. Lady's Cotton Dress

Dress, short-sleeved cotton roller-print, brass hook & eye back closure, ca. 1815-25 (ILLUS.) **$500-750**

Very Rare Early Patterned Silk Dress

Dress, brown silk w/a pattern resembling embroidered flowers, bodice front in two pieces to be held together w/a brooch, tape ties at each side of skirt front wrap around & tie in back, comes w/detachable long

Early Black Silk Crocheted Mitts

Mitts, fingerless-type, crocheted black silk, ca. 1840-50, pr. (ILLUS., bottom previous page). **$35-45**

Early Embroidered Net Pelerine

Pelerine, white embroidered net, ca. 1830 (ILLUS.) **$100-150**

MEN'S CLOTHING

Early Small Blue & Red Velvet Vest

Vest, small man's or boy's, navy blue & red velvet, fabric covering worn off the three bottom buttons, ca. 1840 (ILLUS.) **$45-65**

PART II - CLOTHING - 1850-1920

CHAPTER 2

CHILDREN'S CLOTHING

1850-1875

Girl's Checked Wool Coat & Red Bonnet

Coat, black & white windowpane checked wool w/red tape trim, dropped shoulder style w/two-piece coat sleeves, a red crochet bonnet, ca. 1860-70, bonnet $50-80; coat (ILLUS. of both) **$100-150**

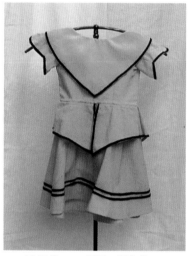

Light Orange 1860s Girl's Dress

Dress, light orange trimmed w/narrow bands of black velvet, late 1860s (ILLUS.) **$125-150**

Pair of Civil War Era Cotton Dresses

Red Plaid Dress Circa 1860

Dress, red plaid, comes w/a red velvet bonnet trimmed
w/white lace, ca. 1860, bonnet $50-75; dress (ILLUS.
of dress) **$85-125**
Dresses, white cotton, matching set probably belonging
to sisters, Civil War era, the pair (ILLUS., bottom
previous page) **$150-200**

1860s Boy's Silk Suit

Suit, boy's, striped silk, separate pants & skirt that
buttons to the bodice, trimmed w/brown velvet ribbons,
ca. 1860s (ILLUS.) **$120-200**

Victorian Boy's Blue Velvet Vest

Unusual 1860s Girl's Hoops

Vest, boy's, dark blue velvet, mid-19th c. (ILLUS.)
. . . . **$75-100**

Hoops, girl's, wire & cloth, ca. 1865 (ILLUS.) . . **$100-150**

LADIES' CLOTHING

1850-1875

Rare Victorian Lady's Belt with Photo of Queen Victoria

Belt, ribbon-type w/metal buckle enclosing a photographic portrait of Queen Victoria, mid-19th c., rare (ILLUS., top of page) **$250-350**

Bodice, ivory, orange & grey striped material, dropped shoulders & two-piece sleeves, ca. 1860s (ILLUS., bottom of page) **$125-150**

Bodice, red wool w/front & back points, laces up the back w/original lavender laces, shirred sleeves, ca. 1850 (ILLUS., below) **$125-175**

Burnous, made from one large uncut paisley shawl & lined w/grey polka dot fabric, false hood & tassel in back, ca. 1860s (ILLUS., previous column) . **$350-350**

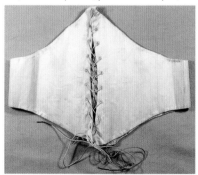

Burnous Made From Paisley Shawl

Victorian "Swiss Belt" Lady's Corset

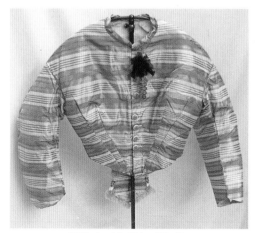

1860s Lady's Striped Bodice

Lady's Red Wool Bodice, Circa 1850

Corset, "Swiss Belt," laces front & back w/original laces, ca. 1860s (ILLUS., previous page) **$75-100**

Lady's Circa 1850 Print Day Dress

1850s Black Calico & White Print Dress

Day dress, black cotton calico w/tiny white flecks & three-leaf clover print, lined in back w/muslin, gathered bodice & shirt, hook & eye closure at waistband & down center front bodice, long sleeves w/buttons at cuffs, 1850-60, excellent condition, some discoloration to lining (ILLUS.) **$400.00**

Day dress, lightweight challis print w/pink silk ribbon trim & lace collar, small pagoda sleeves, bodice & hem lined w/white cotton, giving them the appearance of being a lighter color, ca. 1850 (ILLUS., top next column) **$300-500**

Colorful Cotton Day Dress, Circa 1865

Day dress, orange, red & green printed cotton, princess-style buttons down the front covered w/dress fabric, ca. 1865 (ILLUS.) **$400-600**

Scarce 1860s Brown Gauze Day Dress

1860s Day Dress in Printed White Cotton

Day dress, sheer brown gauze w/blue embroidered diamonds, lace collar, sleeve puffs & button skirt ruffles, side front closure, lined w/white chintz, ca. 1860s (ILLUS.) **$500-750**

Day dress, white cotton w/tiny red & blue print, round white buttons up the front, never worn, 1860s (ILLUS.) **$400-600**

Front & Back Views of a Striped Calico Dress, Circa 1860

Dress, brown calico w/floral print stripes, pointed lace collar, hook & eye closure at center front bodice & tightly gathered full skirt, long sleeves softly gathered at cuffs, self-fabric piping around shoulder seam & waist, bodice lined w/tan-colored cotton serge, one inset pocket at right center, lined in same fabric, good condition, discoloration around arms, bodice lining probably restored, restoration to collar, some small holes near hem, ca. 1860 (ILLUS. of front & back) **$500-750**

1859 Silk Wedding Dress

Dress, green & black silk w/black silk yoke & sleeves, wide embroidered ribbon belt, worn by an Illinois bride in 1859, some splits in the silk (ILLUS.) **$200-300**

Sheer Muslin Striped Dress, Circa 1850

Dress, purple, green & white roller-printed sheer muslin, gathered fan-front closure, ca. 1850 (ILLUS.)
.... **$350-550**

Lady's Circa 1850 One-piece Dress

Dress, one-piece, white windowpane check cotton, ca. 1850 (ILLUS.) **$300-500**

Fine 1860s Dress in Sheer Muslin

Dress, roller-printed red & blue design in sheer muslin, w/removable sleeves & pelerine, could be worn as a ball gown, 1860s (ILLUS.) **$400-600**

Dress, tan-colored cotton calico w/pinstripe of lighter beige, straight long sleeves unbanded at the cuff, hook & eye closure down center front, high sewn waist, self-fabric piping & inside thread used to pull fabric into tight gathers, modified full skirt tiered at mid-thigh, bodice lined w/tan-colored cotton serge, one inset picket at right center lined in brown cambric, good condition, discoloration to fabric, lining of pocket brittle & torn, ca. 1855 (ILLUS., left) **$300-400**

1860s Lady's Evening Headpiece

Headpiece, evening wear, composed of striped ribbon, ca. 1860s (ILLUS.) **$50-75**

1850s Tan Calico Dress

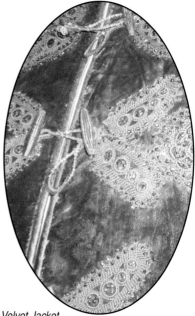

Front & Close-up Views of Blue Velvet Jacket

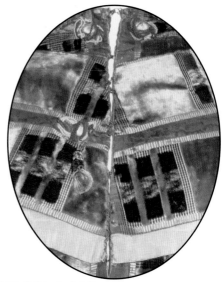

Front & Close-up Views of Silk Taffeta Jacket Cape

Jacket, deep blue velvet, collarless, modified bell-
shaped sleeves, frog & toggle closure, passementerie
w/jet beading, crochet & lace appliqués & braiding,
black taffeta piping, black quilted taffeta lining, good
condition, some wear to piping & lining, spot fraying on
trim & braiding, ca. 1870 (ILLUS. of front & close-up of
front, bottom previous page). **$1,000-1,200**

Jacket cape, moiré silk taffeta in shades of lavender
& black w/lilac velvet & black & white silk chenille
patchwork, lined in hand-quilted plum-colored
china silk w/inside pocket, modified pagoda-style
sleeves, box pleats in back, trimmings consist of two
decorative details on either side of center front of
lavender velvet-covered buttons w/tassels & cording
& several decorative button-like trimmings down back
sides made from lavender & black threads sewn in a
swirl design, hook & eye closure down center, good
condition, some decorative buttons missing on back
& some fabric discoloration, mainly in lining, some
hemline fraying, lining in upper neck reconstructed
w/purple cotton, ca. 1860 (ILLUS. of front & close-up,
top of page). **$1,500.00**

Fancy Black Cut Velvet Mantle

Mantle, black cut velvet, ca. 1870 (ILLUS.) . . . **$125-200**

Rare Mid-Victorian Maternity Outfit

Maternity outfit, two-piece, brown & blue wool brocade, long jacket over a very full skirt, ca. 1860s (ILLUS.)
. . . . **$500-750**

Red Quilted Cotton & Feather Petticoat

Petticoat, red quilted cotton stuffed w/feathers for added warmth, ca. 1860-70 (ILLUS.). **$125-200**

Scarce 1860s Lady's Morning Robe

Morning robe, orange, red, green & purple print corded cotton, dropped shoulders, w/two-piece coat sleeves & piping & purple silk trim & silver-covered buttons, ca. 1860s (ILLUS.) **$300-500**

Tea-Dyed Embroidered Petticoat

Petticoat, tea-dyed w/hand-done cutwork embroidery, ca. 1860 (ILLUS. of petticoat). **$125-200**

Classic Victorian Paisley Shawl

Shawl, woven paisley design, mid-19th c. (ILLUS.)
. . . . **$375-500**

MEN'S CLOTHING

1850-1875

1850s Man's Vest

Vest, black satin w/shawl collar, back in dark brown polished cotton w/lacing for size adjustment, lighter brown cotton lining, silk-covered button w/embroidered flowers, ca. 1850 (ILLUS. of front) **$100-150**

1864 Checked Silk Wedding Outfit

Wedding outfit, purple checked silk, ruched fabric on skirt & sleeves, belt w/bows front & back, petite size, from an 1864 wedding (ILLUS.) **$300-600**

Mid-19th Century Man's Velvet Vest

Waistcoat, voided velvet, mid-19th c. (ILLUS.)
. . . . **$85-120**

CHAPTER 3 -1875-1900

CHILDREN'S CLOTHING

Girl's Red Wool Melton-Style Coat

Coat, girl's, red wool Melton-style, ca. 1890-1900
(ILLUS.) **$100-150**

Boy's Plaid Wool Dress & Jacket Set

Dress, boy's, plaid wool w/vest-style bodice & matching
jacket, 1880s, the set (ILLUS.) **$95-150**

Girl's Burgundy Velvet Coat with Tam

Coat & hat, girl's, burgundy velvet coat w/rabbit fur trim,
cord frog closures, w/a white mohair lady's tam-style
hat, ca. 1890-1900, tam **$40-60**; coat (ILLUS.)
. . . . **$85-150**

Girl's 1870s Brown Plaid Silk Dress

Dress, brown plaid silk w/outside skirt pocket that was a
brief fad, ca. 1876-77 (ILLUS.) **$125-175**

Girl's Burgundy Wool 1880s Dress

Girl's Silk Dress & Peaked Straw Bonnet

Dress, burgundy wool w/plaid accents, ca. 1880s (ILLUS.) **$100-150**

Dress, grey silk plaid w/white lace collar, purple straw peaked bonnet w/plaid ribbon band & tiny flowers, ca. 1880, bonnet $75-125; dress (ILLUS.) **$125-150**

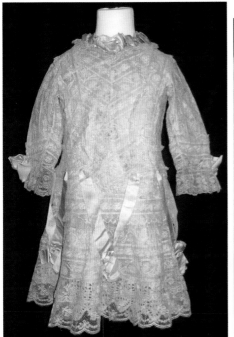

Two Views of a Lovely Lace Late Victorian Girl's Dress

1890s Girl's Jumper-Style Dress

Dress, jumper-style, tan wool, w/pink silk under blouse, ca. 1890 (ILLUS.) **$65-100**

Dress, lacy overlay over light blue satin, ruffled collar & light blue satin ribbon trim & details, late 1890s - early 1900s, excellent condition (ILLUS. of front & close-up of detail, bottom previous page) **$795.00**

Girl's 1880s Red & White Plaid Dress

Dress, red & white plaid silk w/lace-trimmed sleeves, ca. 1880s (ILLUS.) **$95-125**

Red Cotton Dress & Red Velvet Bonnet

Dress, red cotton w/white lace trim, a red velvet bonnet, ca. 1880-90, bonnet **$50-75**; dress (ILLUS.) **$85-100**

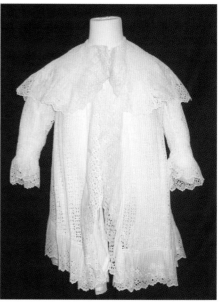

Fancy 1890s Girl's Eyelet Dress

Dress, white cotton eyelet w/oversized collar, long sleeves w/ruffled cuffs, ruffled flounce at hemline, excellent condition, ca. 1895 (ILLUS.) **$600.00**

Late Victorian Black Velvet Boy's Jacket

Jacket, boy's, black velvet w/cream satin brocade lining, excellent condition, late 19th - early 20th c. (ILLUS., above)
.... **$200.00**

Boy's Caped Jacket & Linen Knickers

Jacket & knickers, boy's, red wool caped jacket w/white braid trim & button, white linen knickers, ca. 1890-1900, knickers $30-50; jacket (ILLUS. of both)
.... **$80-120**

Late Victorian Lord Fauntleroy Suit

Lord Fauntleroy suit, boy's, beige silk shirt w/ruffled collar & placket, buttons to the brown velvet pants, mother-of-pearl buttons, good condition, silk shirt brittle & torn in places, velvet faded, late 19th - early 20th (ILLUS.) **$175-225**

1875-1900

LADIES'

Fabulous 1880s Victorian Ball Gown & a Red Flannel Petticoat

Ball gown, polonaise-style, the black velvet bodice trimmed w/red silk poppies, stomacher & cutaway skirt of lampas brocade, heavily gathered at hips & draped in festoons over a red satin skirt trimmed w/black velvet, red silk poppies at hemline, labeled "Mrs. Donovan, New York," ca. 1883, excellent condition (ILLUS. left with red flannel petticoat)
. . . . **$10,000-15,000**

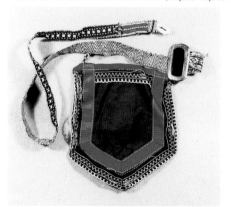

Victorian Lady's Belt with Purse

Belt, fabric belt w/attached purse to be worn on the outside of the skirt, rare, ca. 1870s (ILLUS.)
. . . . **$60-100**

1890s Brown Plaid Linen Blouse

Blouse, brown plaid linen w/large over-sleeves & cape trim, ca. 1890s (ILLUS.) **$95-120**

1870s Bolero Jacket with Trim

Bolero jacket, teal-colored velvet w/gold & silver brocade trim, gold & silver beads in a meandering design on the front, back & sleeves, paisley jacquard epaulets w/silk fringe, good condition, some fading to velvet, wear to inside lining, paisley fabric added later, 1870s (ILLUS.) **$475.00**

Black Net Cape with Braid & Lace Trim

Cape, black net w/wavy braid & lace trim, ca. 1890s (ILLUS.) **$85-150**

Black Brocade Cape, Circa 1880

Cape, black cotton brocade w/tucked & pleated black silk satin around the neck, a larger portion at hem, oversized alternating hook & eye closure at center front, lined in black silk surah, good condition, some fraying of hem trim & back of neck, ca. 1880 (ILLUS.) **$850.00**

Cape, black wool w/beaded, roped & silk chenille & tasseled passementerie trim, lined w/brown silk foulard, back gathered & tucked at lower waist w/black satin bow, fair condition, some slight damage to trim, few holes in wool, ca. 1880 (ILLUS. of front & close-up). **$300-450**

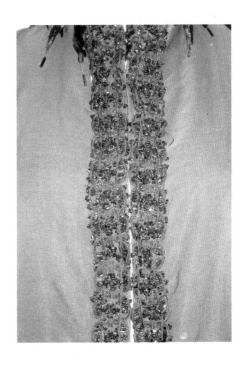

1880s Black Wool Cape & Close-up View of the Front

Pretty Blue Silk Faille Victorian Cape

Cape, bright blue silk faille w/chenille fringe & cord tie w/tassels, ca. 1880 (ILLUS.). **$95-150**

Brown Velvet Cape Lined in Teal Blue Satin

Cape, brown velvet lined w/teal blue satin, w/matching capelet, ca. 1890 (ILLUS.) **$100-150**

Front & Back Views of Elaborately Decorated 1880s Capelet

Capelet, black silk satin surah, lined w/cotton sateen, passementeries of multi-sized black faceted pieces, spheres, triangles, oblongs, very elaborate trimming on center pieces, w/center back extension for bustle, inwardly pleated & tucked, w/gros-grain strips as fasteners, hook & eye closures at neck, bustle extension & down center pieces, good condition, some beading loss, one side panel of lining replaced, ca. 1880s (ILLUS. of front & back) . . . **$1,800-2,000**

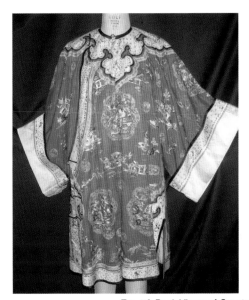
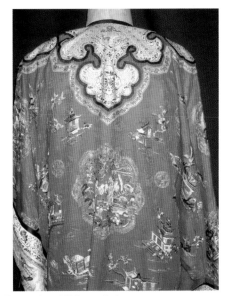

Front & Back Views of Ornate Embroidered Chinese Robe

Chinese robe, coral damasked silk w/metallic gold & bronze thread embroidery & embroidered appliqué curvilinear yoke & edging, further edged in black satin, extensive figurative embroidery throughout including courtship scenes, architectural elements, boats & foliage, two carved brass buttons & loop closure at neck from center to side & same three buttons & loop closure at bottom right side, slit at both sides, edged in black satin, lined w/lime green china silk, kimono sleeves w/exaggerated turn-back cuff, embroidery on white silk, good condition, some staining & small tears to brittle fabric, China, late 19th c. (ILLUS. of front & back, top of page) **$2,500-3,000**

Coat, dolman-style, purple silk, ca. 1880s (ILLUS.) **$125-250**

1870s Purple Taffeta Coat to Accompany Polonaise Dress

Coat, possibly original to 1870s polonaise dress ensemble, purple taffeta w/velvet details, satin bows down center front, hook & eye closure, center back faux pockets w/velvet & ribbon details, lined w/a brighter & smoother taffeta, near perfect condition, one front bow replaced, lining perhaps replaced (ILLUS. and shown with polonaise dress ensemble, page 33)

Purple Silk 1880s Dolman-Style Coat

"Sensible" Style Black Cotton Corset

Corset, "sensible" type, black cotton w/shoulder straps, ca. 1890s (ILLUS.) **$150-200**

1890s Lady's Nainsock Drawers

Drawers, white nainsock, yoke gathered at waistline, long legs w/bands of tucks & crochet inset at bottoms, single button closure at center back, excellent condition, 1890s (ILLUS.) **$250-275**

1890s Embroidered Cotton Day Dress

Day dress, fine white cotton heavily embroidered w/ sleeve puffs, ca. 1890s (ILLUS.). **$175-250**

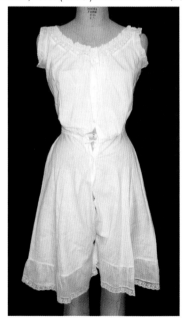

Young Woman's Combination Set

Drawers & bodice, for a young woman, cambric, bodice lightly tucked at crocheted yoke neckline, buttons down center front, lightly gathered at waistline of crocheted & ribbon insertion, attached drawers w/ flounce at bottom & lace edging, excellent condition, ca. 1890, the set (ILLUS.). **$250-350**

Prairie-style Blue Calico Dress

Dress, prairie-style, blue calico type, shown w/a detachable embroidered collar & hand-painted collar button, ca. 1900, collar button $10-15; collar $15-25; dress (ILLUS.). **$125-175**

Dress, dark brown silk w/bronze beaded appliqué & bronze buttons, worn in 1876 by a Minnesota bride, in the style of the late 18th c. w/side panniers, probably because of the U.S. Centennial (ILLUS., top next column) **$500-750**

Unusual 1876 Bridal Gown with Panniers

Dress, polonaise-style, two-part, jacket bodice of purple velvet & taffeta w/boning through tight-fitting bodice, lined w/dark-colored linen, silk & chenille fringe trim, satin bow & crocheted buttons, two low pockets (only one functions), long sleeves w/velt & ruffled details edged in black lace, back draped & full w/satin ribbon & bow detail, tape sewn to lining to control drape of bustle, silk twillstrap at waist, attached to back, labeled "R.H. Macy & Co., N.Y.," excellent condition, one button missing, some wear; matching skirt of purple taffeta w/blocks of same dyed purple cambric at hips,

1870s Lady's Polonaise Dress & Similar Coat

velvet & tucked & gathered details at flounced hem, dark glazed muslin footing, fair condition, cambric blocks w/some holes & slightly discolored in places, muslin footing brittle, shown w/similar coat, ca. 1875-1880, the ensemble (ILLUS. of dress & similar coat, bottom previous page) **$8,000.00**

Two-Piece Lady's 1880s Plaid Dress

Dress, two-piece, blue, brown & white plaid cotton, w/ bustle & apron, bodice buttons to the skirt, ca. 1880s (ILLUS.) **$225-350**

Petite Size Blue Silk Faille 1880s Dress

Dress, two-piece, blue silk faille, skirt & jacket edged in tiny pleats, jacket buttons up the front, brown cotton lining, petite size worn by a small woman or a teenage girl, ca. 1885 (ILLUS.). **$175-250**

Circa 1900 Lady's Two-Piece Dress

Dress, two-piece, brown checked wool w/lace yoke & pink silk ribbon & green glass bead trim, ca. 1898-1899 (ILLUS.) **$275-450**

1890s Two-Piece Cotton & Brocade Dress

Dress, two-piece, brown corded cotton w/silk brocade bodice & stand-up collar, brown silk skirt ruffle & wrist bows, ca. 1894 (ILLUS.). **$250-450**

1880s Lady's Two-Piece Dress

Dress, two-piece, green plaid silk, gathered skirt front, bodice front of ruched burgundy silk, ca. 1880 (ILLUS.) **$250-350**

Pretty 1870s Lady's Silk Dress

Dress, two-piece, rust-colored silk w/outside skirt pocket, ca. 1876-77 (ILLUS.) **$275-350**

Late 1890s Navy, Pink & Green Dress

Dress, two-piece, navy blue, pink & lime green silk print, pink silk yoke edged w/ruched lime green chiffon, late 1890s (ILLUS.) **$300-500**

Red Silk Dress with Appliqués

Dress & overdress, red silk dress w/beaded appliqués, ca. 1880, pr. (ILLUS.) **$350-550**

Lovely 1880s Satin Evening Dress

Evening dress, celadon green satin w/bodice front
& side skirt panel of matching silk brocade, bodice
buttons up the front w/crochet buttons, ca. 1885
(ILLUS.) **$350-550**

Fine 1880s Two-Piece Silk Dress

Evening or wedding dress, two-piece, tan & white-
striped sheer fabric over silk, rows of lace & ivory silk
ribbons, built-in bustle hoops. ca. 1885 (ILLUS.)
. . . . **$500-800**

Red Silk Victorian Lady's Long Gloves

Gloves, fingerless-type, red silk, w/original store tag, late
19th c., pr. (ILLUS.) **$25-35**

Lady's Jacket with Puffed Sleeves

Jacket, dark green silk & brightly striped ribbons, sleeves
w/small puffs at top, a precursor to larger leg-o'-mutton
sleeves, ca. 1890 (ILLUS.) **$150-200**

Late Victorian Jacket with Fancy Trim

Jacket, heavy navy blue wool, scoop neck, jacket front overlaps to button at center right, trimmed w/elaborate braid & embroidery at the front center & at the adjustable sleeves cuffs w/hook & eye closures, side vents edged in braid, blue & white brocade lining, red felt faces the neckline, lapels & cuffs, excellent condition, some minor stains to lining, late 19th - early 20th c. (ILLUS., bottom previous page) **$800.00**

Fine 1890s Lady's Velvet Winter Jacket

Jacket, tailored winter-type, chocolate brown plush velvet, made from nine panels, slight kick-up at shoulder, brown pile looped-frieze sleeves & same pile on shawl collar extending down edge of center front opening, vent at center back, button & loop closure, plum silk-lined, inside self-fabric embellished pocket lower right side, good condition, some wear to lining & sleeves, buttons replaced, 1890s (ILLUS.). . . **$800.00**

1880s Brown & Blue Silk Jacket & Skirt

Jacket & skirt, blue & brown silk, pleated brown silk trim, skirt gathered in front & back, pocket on outside back of jacket skirt, ca. 1880s (ILLUS.). **$150-250**

1880s Brown Cotton Print Morning Robe

Morning robe, brown cotton print w/black cotton gathered front panel, ca. 1880s (ILLUS.) . . . **$250-350**

Late Victorian Mourning Blouse & Skirt Outfit

Mourning blouse, blouse of black bombazine w/a pouter front, black silk & boned bodice, calico-lined, black lace neckline & trimmed cuffs w/self-fabric-covered buttons, hook & eye closure down center back well hidden by tapered tucks, good condition, some tears at lace trim, ca. 1890-99 (ILLUS. with matching skirt) **$300-650**

Mourning skirt, black taffeta, pleated & full, lined w/soft ecru fabric, hook & eye closure at center back, fair condition, some stripping to tucks & pleats, some holes along bottom seams, ca. 1890 (ILLUS. with mourning blouse) **$250-400**

Outfit, tan silk skirt, jacket & overskirt trimmed w/silk fringe, silver buttons w/blue glass centers, bustle-style back, ca. 1870s (ILLUS. of front & back, bottom of page). **$400-600**

Black Lace Overdress with Red Dress

Overdress, black lace w/crocheted buttons all the way up the front, pr. (ILLUS. over matching red silk dress) **$350-550**

Elegant Red Velvet Opera Coat

Opera coat with cape, wine red velvet, ca. 1890-1900 (ILLUS.) **$150-250**

Front & Back Views of Fine 1870s Silk Lady's Outfit

Petticoat, bright red flannel, brown glazed cotton waistband, quilling at hemline lined w/blue glazed cotton, excellent condition, ca. 1883 (ILLUS. right with 1880s polonaise ball gown) **$650.00**

Petticoat, cambric w/drawstring & gathered waist, ruffles & large flounce, consisting of lace & crochet under flounce for weight & fullness of white embroidered cambric, good condition, some holes to fabric near waist, a few holes in lace & flounce, ca. 1890
. . . . **$500-650**

Polonaise & skirt, flower print cotton polonaise w/side panniers, wateau back pleat & ruched green ribbon trim, over pale green silk faille tiered & trained skirt, ca. 1870s, skirt **$125-150**; polonaise (ILLUS.)
. . . . **$175-275**

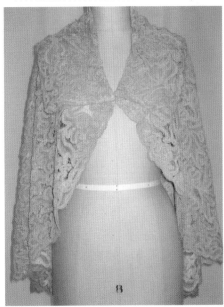

Lovely Late Victorian Pink Guipure Lace Shawl-Cape

Late Victorian Country-Style Bonnet

Poke bonnet, blue cotton w/small white polka dots, stiffened visor, self ties at back of neck, very good condition, some fabric fading, second half 19th c. (ILLUS.) **$375.00**

Shawl-cape, light pink Guipure lace w/a large swatch forming the collar, attached w/a hook & eye across the bustline, excellent condition, repair to closure, late 19th c. (ILLUS.). **$700.00**

Elegant 1890s Satin Shirtwaist-Blouse

1870s Lady's Polonaise & Skirt

Shirtwaist-blouse, light green satin w/surplice neckline w/self-piping & ruched, ecru lace insertions at the throat w/the high neck trimmed w/green satin piping & bows, ruched shoulderline w/draped bodice w/

wrapped buttons, elbow-length full sleeves heavily tucked & ruched, gathered green satin waist belt, excellent condition, ca. 1895 (ILLUS.) **$850.00**

Fancy 1880s Shoulder Cape

Shoulder cape, rust-colored velvet w/faceted jet beading & beaded fringed embellishments, lined w/black satin, gathered at shoulders, black ostrich feathers trimming around high wing collar, hook & eye closure, machine-made black lace reaching to mid-thigh, scalloped edges, three horizontal bands of black satin trim, good condition, some fraying to edges & wear to velvet, heavy wear to lining, ca. 1880-85 (ILLUS. of front & close-up of shoulder) **$2,000.00**

Blue Feather-Pattern Silk Skirt

Skirt, blue silk w/feather-patterned silk & solid blue silk ruffles, ca. 1890-1900 (ILLUS.). **$120-175**

Green Silk Taffeta Skirt, Circa 1890

Skirt, sage green silk taffeta w/center panel of deeper green satin w/woven damask swirl pattern, ecru lace trim, gathered flounce at bottom of skirt of deeper green satin, lined in beige cotton sateen, under flounce of same green taffeta w/sage green velveteen hem protector, fair condition, many tears overall, brittle, added snaps down back, ca. 1890 (ILLUS.)
. . . . **$300-400**

Victorian Lady's Cotton Stockings

Stockings, embroidered cotton, ca. 1880, pr. (ILLUS.)
. . . . **$50-75**

Lavender Silk Late Victorian Lady's Stockings

Stockings, lavender silk, ca. 1890s, pr. (ILLUS.)
. . . . **$30-50**

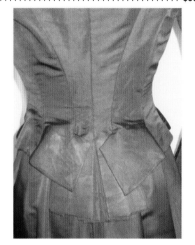

Back Close-up of 1880s Faille Suit

Suit, two-piece, chestnut-colored faille, blouse w/center
front hook & eye closure, center front seams, boning
& brown moiré silk bow detail, back pleating, lined in
printed cambric w/honeycomb design, skirt unlined &
tiered at bottom, excellent condition, missing one hook
closure, some discoloration to lining, slight fraying at
skirt hem, mid-1880s (ILLUS. of back close-up)
. . . . **$800-1,200**

Wool-Lined Buckskin Under-Bodice

Under-bodice, buckskin lined w/bright blue wool, ca.
1880s, one Dr. Jaeger advised wearing woolen
underwear all year for health reasons (ILLUS.)
. . . . **$50-75**

Lovely Ivory Silk 1890s Wedding Dress

Wedding dress, two-piece, ivory silk, 1890s; note - white
& ivory were not traditional for wedding dresses until
the late 19th c. (ILLUS.) **$275-450**

1870s Lavender Silk Wedding Dress

Wedding dress, two-piece, lavender plaid silk w/false
vest & lace trim, ca. 1870s (ILLUS.) **$175-400**

MEN'S

Late Victorian Packaged Man's Shirt

Dress shirt, Manitou brand, white, in original packaging, late 19th c. (ILLUS.) **$50-60**

Late Victorian Man's Sport Jacket

Sport jacket, dark grey wool w/plaid shawl collar, cuffs & pocket trim, cord frog closures, last quarter 19th c. (ILLUS.) **$75-125**

Victorian Man's Casual Wool Jacket

Jacket, casual style in brown wool w/tape trim, ca. 1870-90 (ILLUS.) **$75-150**

CHAPTER 4 - 1900-1920

Long White Cambric Christening Gown, Circa 1900

CHILDREN'S

Christening gown, white cambric, small tucked collar of eyelet w/more tucks & eyelet insets down center, bottom flounce heavily embroidered w/white thread & eyelets, ca. 1900, excellent condition, few climate stains, one small hole near left armhole (ILLUS., above) **$650-900**

Early 20th Century Child's Faux Fur Coat

Coat, faux fur, ca. 1900-10 (ILLUS.) **$75-125**
Coat, spring season, light cotton w/scalloped edging, short sleeves, loop & button closure, decorative embroidering along cape collar & center front, ca. 1910, fair condition (ILLUS. right with two other coats, top next page) **$85-100**

Coat, spring season, medium weight cotton, mini-cape at shoulders, short sleeves, picot trim & embroidery along sleeves & cape collar, center front mother-of-pearl button & hook & eye closure, extensive wear on collar & front, ca. 1910 (ILLUS. center with two other coats, top next page) **$150.00**
Coat, spring season, medium weight cotton, short sleeves, center-front hook & eye closure, decorative crochet edging along cape collar & sleeves, extensive wear to collar & front, ca. 1910 (ILLUS. right with two other coats, top next page) **$100.00**

Girl's Drop-Waist Cotton Dress

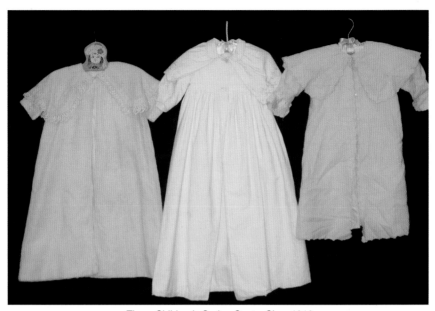

Three Children's Spring Coats, Circa 1910

Dress, grey & white print drop-waist cotton w/cape collar, buttons down the back, ca. 1900 (ILLUS., bottom previous page) **$95-125**

Girl's Two-Piece Dress, Circa 1900

Dress, two-piece, brown wool, bodice in tweed, skirt w/black tape trim, ca. 1900 (ILLUS.). **$100-125**

Girl's Pigeon-Breasted Two-Piece Dress

Dress, two-piece, pigeon-breasted style, aqua satin trimmed w/lace & glass beads, wide sash-style belt, ca. 1900 (ILLUS.) **$150-200**

Boy's Tweed Jacket & Knickers

Jacket & knickers, boy's, wool tweed, ca. 1910-20, the
set (ILLUS.). **$75-100**

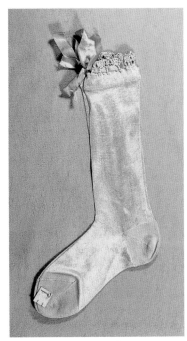

Blue Child's Silk Stockings

Stockings, pale blue silk w/drawstring tops, w/original
store tag, early 20th c., pr. (ILLUS.)
. . . . **$15-20**

Boy's Linen Sailor Suit, Circa 1900

Sailor suit, boy's, yellow-striped linen w/white
embroidered neck insert & belt, scalloped &
embroidered collar, ca. 1900 (ILLUS.) **$95-150**

Early Boy's Striped Two-Piece Swimsuit

Swimsuit, boy's, striped cotton, separate top & pants,
drawstring waist, ca. 1900 (ILLUS.) **$85-150**

LADIES'

Pretty Green Ball Gown, Circa 1900

Ball gown, green silk faille & velvet w/lace sleeves & yoke w/lavender flower appliqués, dark green silk underskirt, ca. 1900 (ILLUS.) **$350-600**

Early 20th Century Batiste & Lace Blouse

Blouse, white cotton batiste w/a boned high neck of bobbin lace & ruffle trim, hook & eye closure, lace insertions down body of garment w/vertical pin tucks,

half waistband center front, long sleeves w/horizontal pin-tucked bands & lace insertion at each flared wrist, lace ruffled trim, small pearl buttons down center back, very good condition, some scattered age yellowing, on rust mark on front, 1900-1908 (ILLUS.) **$250-300**

Early 20th Century White Printed Voile Blouse

Blouse, white cotton voile printed w/small brown circles, features a deeply pointed turnover collar, kimono-style short sleeves, gathered waistline & flared lower section, snaps down center front, excellent condition but snaps added recently, 1910-18 (ILLUS.)
. . . . **$220.00**

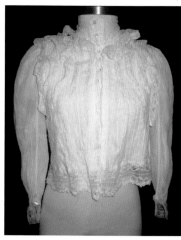

Front of a Cotton Voile Blouse, Circa 1910

Blouse or shirtwaist, white cotton voile, high neckline w/heavily ruffled & laced bodice, continuing to yoked upper back, buttons at center front, tucks at shoulder to bust & at sleeve cuffs trimmed w/lace, two-inch wide strip of lace at hem, back w/self-fabric tie at lower center waist, excellent condition, one small stain on back of one sleeves, yellowing of lace, ca. 1910 (ILLUS.) **$350-450**

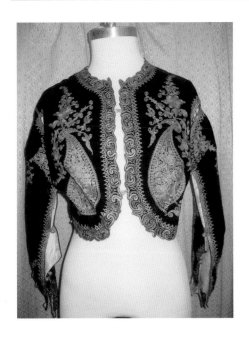

Three Views of an Elaborate Early 20th Century Bolero Jacket

Bolero jacket, black velvet w/elaborate gold embroidery & braiding, scalloped embroidered trim, slit from shoulder down sleeves w/gold ball & loop closures, lined w/glazed white cotton, very good condition, some fraying to braiding & wear to lining, early 20th c., probably from Turkey (ILLUS. of three views)
.... **$850.00**

White Cotton Chemise Slip

Chemise-slip, white cotton, possibly nainsook, decorative stitching & details on straps & bodice, monogrammed, ca. 1900, perfect condition (ILLUS.)
.... **$125.00**

*Three Views of a Rare
Chinese Silk Robe & Dress
Ensemble*

Chinese robe with dress ensemble, originally worn for an audience w/the Emperor of China, the robe of white silk
ground w/curvilinear appliqued yoke on black satin w/gold thread & embroidery, opens at center front, black satin
strip piping down center front, silver filigree ball buttons & loop closures, kimono-type sleeves pieced at upper arm,
bands of embroidery on black satin near embroidered cuff, elaborate embroidery & appliqué throughout, perhaps
representing stages of courtship w/mostly flowers & foliage, lined w/ivory satin; the dress w/an ivory china silk
bodice, V-neck w/small tuck near point of V creating inverted pleat, normal waistline, skirt of damasked ivory silk
in several panels, center front & back panels rectangular w/extensive embroidery on bottom of panel & edged on
sides w/2" bands of blue embroidery on black satin, surround gold & embroidered ribbon, center panel slit to reveal
chartreuse damasked silk lining, side panels of same damasked silk, pleated in series of 1/2"-3/8" accordian folds,
floral embroidery worked into pleats towards bottom of hem, edged w/same black satin border, dress falls 8 inches
below hem of robe, very good condition, one or two msall stains on robe lining & underdress bodice, some loose
threads, ca. 1915, the ensemble (ILLUS. of robe, dress & close-up of the back of robe) **$5,000.00**

Victorian Lady's Detachable Collar with Collar Button & Box

Collar, detachable-type w/embroidered decoration, shown w/a painted porcelain collar button & maroon cloth-covered collar box, all ca. 1900, collar button $15-25, collar box $30-40, collar (ILLUS.) **$15-20**

Lady's Striped Cotton Day Dress

Day dress, lavender & white striped cotton w/lavender cotton trim & embroidery & cutwork sleeves, tiny lavender glass flower-form buttons up the back, ca. 1905-1910 (ILLUS.) **$100-150**

Dress, black silk w/black gaazar overlay, lined w/ black taffeta, high neck w/ecru tulle & lace insert embroidered w/metallic yarn, leg-of-mutton sleeves, high-waisted w/black silk rosette at self-fabric attached sash, embroidered trim across center front, boning at bodice, hook & eye closure at center back, hem edged w/small ruffle of black silk, excellent condition, one small hole in left shoulder, ca. 1905-10 (ILLUS., top next column) **$7,500.00**

Black Silk Dress with Gaazar Overlay

Blue Chiffon Dress Trimmed with Silk

Dress, blue chiffon over grey-printed silk under layer trimmed w/pompons, ca. 1910-12 (ILLUS.) **$125-175**

Dress, cotton batiste day dress w/eyelet & lace inserts, buttons w/swirl design closure down the center front, three-quarter length sleeves, skirt attached to a two inch wide piece of embroidered gauze, bottom portion of skirt banded horizontally w/lace & eyelet inserts, bottom tiers feature bands of net, excellent condition, one tear near buttonholes, ca. 1910 .... **$1,800.00**

Lovely Ivory Net & Lace Dress, Circa 1910

Dress, ivory net & lace, lavishly embroidered, w/silk lining, ca. 1910 (ILLUS.) **$200-300**

Voile Lingerie Dress, Circa 1915

Dress, lingerie-style, cotton voile w/very fine self-striping woven vertically, smocking at shoulders & hipline, tucking at bodice, rectangular neckline w/lace center panel, lace inserts at cuffs & hips, horizontal zig-zag pattern at the back, excellent condition, minimal hemline fraying, ca. 1915 (ILLUS.) **$2,500.00**

Blue Lace-Trimmed Dress, Circa 1910

Dress, light blue cotton broadcloth w/lace around neckline dipping to V in the back, small tucking at waistline, machine-embroidered eyelet inserts, hook & eye closures down center front, good condition, some fabric discoloration inside & down one sleeve, ca. 1910 (ILLUS.) **$500-650**

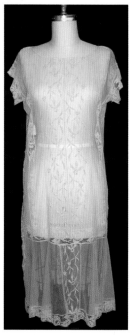

Front of a Lingerie Dress, Circa 1918

Dress, lingerie-style, ivory net w/ecru embroidered center & side panels, crochet lace insertations front & back, also used as trim on cap sleeves & hem, features self-fabric piping at rounded neckline, very good condition, minor tears to net in places, ca. 1918 (ILLUS.)
. . . . **$2,000.00**

Black-Trimmed Pink Silk Dress

Dress, pink silk, tiered skirt & black sequin-trimmed over-bodice & black velvet ribbon trim on skirt & gathered sleeves, ca. 1910-15 (ILLUS.) **$150-200**

Lace-Trimmed Tissue Silk Dress, ca. 1915

Dress, pink tissue silk w/a lace-trimmed large sailor-type collar & sleeves, sash w/silk tassels, ca. 1915 (ILLUS.)
. . . . **$150-200**

Simple Printed Cotton Prairie-style Dress

Dress, prairie-style, tan printed cotton w/ruffle trim, ca. 1900 (ILLUS.) **$125-175**

Wool & Chiffon Dress with Crochet Trim

Dress, tan wool & print chiffon w/Irish crochet trim, ca. 1910-12 (ILLUS.) **$125-225**

Lovely Ecru Mesh & Silk Dress, ca.1909

Dress, two-piece, blouse & skirt of ecru mesh overlay, beige silk lining, embellished w/lace inserts, satin ribbon, satin-covered buttons & crochet trim, blouse closes over the shoulder w/hooks & eyes, sweep-length corselet skirt w/hook & eye closure at center back, fair condition w/wear to silk lining & ribbon trim, some small tears to mesh, ca. 1909 (ILLUS.)
. . . . **$1,500-2,000**

Dress, two-piece, sheer black linen w/a blue carnation print, neck, bodice front, sleeves & hem trimmed in black lace, ca. 1900 (ILLUS.) **$175-275**

Dress, white cotton batiste w/lace inserts on bodice, sleeves & skirt, small ruffles & tucks throughout bodice, leg-of-mutton sleeves w/hook & eye closure at cuffs, high neck, flounced hem w/lace inserts & ruffles, center front buttons & hook & eye closures, center back panel of white embroidered batiste, excellent condition, one or two stress tears near cuffs, ca. 1900
. . . . **$600-750**

White Embroidered Tulle Dress, Circa 1900

Dress, white embroidered tulle in a clover pattern w/lace trim around neckline, tiered ruffled yoke, skirt & sleeves, hook & eye closure down center front, excellent condition, slight fraying, ca. 1900-05 (ILLUS.)
. . . . **$3,000-4,500**

Black Linen Floral Dress with Lace Trim

Heavy Ivory Cotton Lady's Duster

Duster coat, heavyweight ivory cotton w/embroidery trim & large shell buttons, ca. 1900-10 (ILLUS.)
. . . . **$100-150**

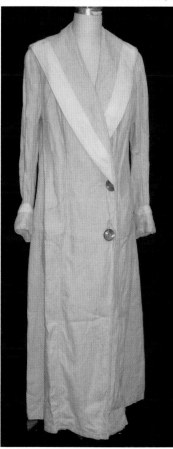

Early Lady's Duster or Motoring Coat

Duster or motoring coat, unbleached linen w/inset of ivory-colored bird's-eye piqué along lapels of shawl collar & detailed on square drape in back, also on back waist detail, princess seams down back, turned-back full cuffs trimmed w/same bird's-eye piqué, two oversized abalone buttons w/plastic inset down center front, fancy cat patch pockets, two low vents in back, excellent condition, one small stain in front near buttons, slight discoloration to piqué trim on sleeves, ca. 1915 (ILLUS.) **$950-1,200**

Late Victorian Black Evening Dress

Evening dress, black silk & lace w/gold-embroidered underbodice, ca. 1900 (ILLUS.) **$175-300**

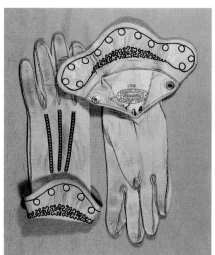

Victorian Lady's Gloves Made in Paris

Gloves, tan leather w/brown embroidery, stamped inside "Paris," ca. 1900, pr. (ILLUS.) **$20-30**

Early 20th Century Lady's Faux Fur Jacket

Jacket, faux fur w/velvet trim & marcasite buttons, ca. 1905 (ILLUS.) **$125-175**

Two Views of a Fancy Satin Cutaway Jacket, Ca. 1910

Jacket, cutaway-style, black satin decorated w/soutache braid & black silk cord overall, V-neckline trimmed w/rick-rack & black braided crescents & loops, slight 'kick-up' at shoulders, long decorated sleeves, closed w/two large black faceted buttons & loops at the front center, unlined, very good condition, very minor fraying to braid, hem needs restitching, ca. 1910 (ILLUS. of two views) **$1,800.00**

Lady's Light Linen Jacket, Circa 1910

Jacket, unlined light linen, knee-length, three oversized carved abalone buttons on either side of center opening, modified dolman sleeves, two slanted pouch pockets at hip level, ca. 1910, perfect condition (ILLUS., previous page) **$500.00**

Melton-Style Lady's Jacket with Cape

Jacket with cape, Melton double-breasted style, tan wool w/tape trim, ca. 1905 (ILLUS.) **$100-150**

Blue Velvet Opera Coat

Opera coat, slate blue velvet w/oversized gathered & rolled collar, ruching & pleating through collar, chest & shoulders, small tucks on collar & cuffs, lined in heavy ivory crepe, labeled "Oppenheim Collins & Co.," fair

condition, lining probably replaced, some fabric wear especially around collar, elbows & sleeves, some hemline fraying, ca. 1914 (ILLUS. of front) . . . **$400.00**

Early Lady's Kimono-Style Robe

Robe, kimono-style, seafoam green patterned silk w/ wide lace collar & hem, cord frog closures, ca. 1905 (ILLUS.) **$175-250**

Lady's Rose-Colored Robe

Robe, rose-colored flower print w/rose satin edging & large square collar, ca. 1910-15 (ILLUS.) . . . **$100-150**

Early 20th Century Shoulder Cape of Black Beaded Net

Shoulder cape, black net, the high collar faced w/black faille, trimmed w/black lace & black jet pasementerie,hook & eye closure at center back, body of garment decorated w/pounded jet forming chevron stripes at center front & back, capelet trimmed w/jet fringe, good condition, early 20th c. (ILLUS.)
. . . . **$300.00**

Lady's Floral Cotton Voile Skirt

Skirt, cotton voile w/green floral print, gored, slightly gathered from waistline w/extra tucks at back for fullness, two double-tiers of lace-edged ruffles at slightly trained hem, center back hook & eye closure, ca. 1903-15, good condition, few tears at flounced hem & waistline (ILLUS.) **$450-650**

Early 20th Century Two-Piece Wool Suit

Suit, tailored two-piece outfit of dark blue wool serge, jacket features high notch, narrow peaked lapels & princess seaming from shoulders to hem, front & back, two welt pockets at lower hips, partially covered by decoratives on-seam strip, embellished w/textured embroidery in a diamond shape, single carved button closure just under lapel at center front, slim-fitting long sleeves w/adjustable two-button cuffs & bound buttonholes, deep back vent on center seam w/same strip & embroidery trim, weighted at hem, lined w/ purple paisley satin brocade; slim-fitting skirt w/two welt pockets at hipline, thick gros-grain ribbon at inside waistline, side snaps added at later date, skirt shortened at later date, unlined, excellent condition, alternations considered undesirable, ca. 1910-1919, the outfit (ILLUS.) **$600.00**

Lady's Two-Piece Reversible Suit

Suit, two-piece, woven w/two different silk fibres so the color changes from green to orange depending on the angle, ca. 1905 (ILLUS., previous page) . . . **$150-200**

Lady's Cotton Swimsuit, Circa 1900

Swimsuit, knee-length blue cotton w/button-on overskirt, ca. 1900 (ILLUS.) **$120-200**

White Batiste Lace-Trimmed Tea Dress

Tea dress, white cotton batiste w/embroidery & lace inserts, pink tucks & lace-draped shoulder overlay, back center panel w/horizontal bands of pin tucks from neckline to hem w/lace insert on either side, button closure down center front, pink-tucked skirt gathered at lace insert & horizontal bands of small tucks at skirt bottom, elbow-length sleeves w/lace trim, excellent condition, small tears in lace trim, ca. 1910 (ILLUS.) **$1,200.00**

Early 20th White Layered Net Tea Dress

Tea dress, white net in a double layer, a slight V-neckline at front & back, decorated w/white soutache braid in a meandering pattern, top layer closes on right side w/hidding snaps covered by crocheted balls from shoulder to hip, bottom net layer closed w/hooks & eyes, bands of cream-colored ruffles attached to first layer of net at bodice, long sleeves tucked inside for drape over ruffled wrist, top layer w/soutache braid at hemline in the meandering pattern, bottom layer tiered w/an additional three layers of net, one w/cream silk ruffled bands at the hemline, excellent condition, metal fittings possibly added later or replaced, early 20th c. (ILLUS.) **$650.00**

White Linen Tennis or Sport Dress, Ca. 1913

Tennis or sport dress, white linen woven w/contrasting pinstripes in relief running vertically down the front & horizontally on the center panel, lower ankle-length, decorative crocheted buttons covering hidden hook & eye closures on the center front panel, scoop neckline, high waistling & slim-fitting skirt, short sleeves, bodice tucked at back, excellent condition, few spots of discoloration, ca. 1913 (ILLUS.) **$800.00**

Front of Ornate Silk Satin Ensemble

Wedding dress ensemble & shoes, two-part dress of heavy ivory silk satin, detachable shirt jacket, ruched high neckline of ivory tulle overlay w/slight ruffled trim & rolled satin cording, hook & eye overlapping closure at left shoulder, finishing in boned attached corset of same ivory satin, heavily pleated sleeves that continue to ruffled cuffs w/same tulle trim & rosette edging, attaches to a long trained overskirt w/hook & eye closure, scalloped detail running on princess seam along length of skirt, finishes in same tulle & ruffled trim as sleeve cuffs, underskirt of simple muslin, lined in cream silk & finished in ruffles, good condition, some discolorations, stress tear at back shoulder, ca. 1903-10, wedding dress ensemble (ILLUS.) **$6,500.00**

MEN'S

Woolen Cadet Uniform from 1902

Cadet uniform, two-piece, dark greyish-blue sturdy woolen fabric, cutaway jacket w/quilted cotton lining on top, braiding & brass buttons, bound buttonholes, substantial appliqué on cuffs, collar & down tapered tails in back, tails lined in black satin, labeled "1-20-1902 - New York Clothing House - 102-104 E. Baltimore St. - Next to Corn. St. Paul - Baltimore - Mr. J. Dukehart - 5th Regt. Co. of B," 1902, good condition, epaulets missing, minor damages; unlined pants w/braiding, button fly & back waist belt, fair condition w/several holes & some staining, the set (ILLUS.) **$200-400**

Early 20th Century Cutaway Coat

Cutaway coat, heavy black wool w/satin lapels, satin-covered buttons & black silk lining, back features same covered buttons & two tapered tails, labeled "Becker & Son - Indianapolis," paper label in front breast pocket reads "Becker & Son - Indianapolis - Mr. Albret Gall - Date Feb. 1909," excellent condition, some wear to buttons, basting at buttonholes remains, possibly an unfinished piece, ca. 1909 (ILLUS.) **$400-500**

Large Man's Cotton Duster, Circa 1910

Duster coat, white cotton, desirable large size, ca. 1900-10 (ILLUS.) **$50-75**

Front, Back & Close-up Views of Man's Formal Dress Suit, Circa 1915

Formal suit with tails, all pieces of black wool broadcloth, vest features neckline w/rounded lapels trimmed w/black satin, two waist stand pockets, four covered buttons down center front, vents at side, back of vest of black satin twill w/back waistbelt, lined w/ivory satin; trousers w/flat front, on-seam pockets at hips, button fly, low-rise & tapered legs, tabs at waist to adjust waistband, two welt pockets in back, waist area lined w/ivory-colored sateen; cutaway Eton-style coat w/black satin-trimmed collar & peaked full satin lapels, angled breast pocket, double row of covered buttons, satin-trimmed sleeve cuff w/single covered button at each sleeve, features deep vent at back w/single inverted pleat, two button detail at back waist, lined w/black satin twill, very good condition, wear to covered buttons on jacket & vest, minor discoloration to lining of vest, small smudge on trouser front, trousers may not be original to suit, ca. 1915, three pieces (ILLUS. of front, back & close-up of each) **$400.00**

Man's Long Johns with Original Box

Long johns, w/original box, ca. 1900 (ILLUS.). . **$75-100**

Man's Circa 1900 Nightshirt

Nightshirt, white cotton w/center front buttons & breast pocket, ca. 1900, excellent condition, small climate stains inside back collar (ILLUS.) **$95-100**

Man's Flannel Nightshirt, Circa 1900

Nightshirt, flannel, ca. 1900 (ILLUS.). **$35-45**

Grouping of Early 20th Century Men's Shirts

Shirts, all of cotton or flannel, some w/monograms, ca. 1900, all excellent condition w/some fading to flannel, each (ILLUS. of group) **$85-150**

Swimsuit, black wool, ca. 1900 (ILLUS.) **$50-75**

Original Boxed Set of Valor Brand
Man's Undershirts

Undershirts, Valor brand, in original cellophane wrappers & box, ca. 1915-20, pr. (ILLUS.) **$50-75**

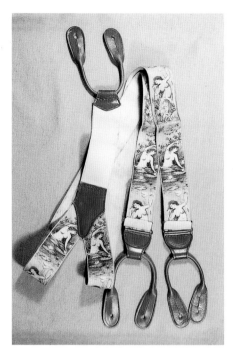

Late Victorian Man's Suspenders
Decorated with Nudes

Suspenders, pink background decorated overall w/blue frolicking water nymphs, ca. 1900 (ILLUS.)
. . . . **$150-200**

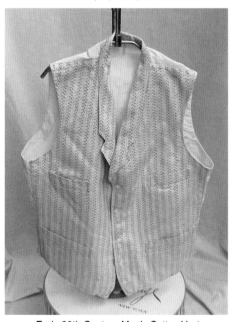

Early 20th Century Man's Cotton Vest

Vest, blue & white woven cotton, ca. 1910-20 (ILLUS.)
. . . . **$35-50**

Man's Swimsuit, Circa 1900

PART III - 1920-1980

CHAPTER 5 - 1920-1930

CHILDREN'S CLOTHING

Girl's Late 1920s Peach Chiffon Dress

1920s Girl's Blue Jumper

Dress, little girl's, peach chiffon backed w/sturdier beige-colored fabric, self-fabric piping around armholes & slight V-neck, peach silk ribbon detail at upper right shoulder & lower waist, snap closure at left shoulder, bodice w/vertical shirring at lower waist continuing to self-fabric scalloped piping, tiered skirt w/alternating layers of scalloped chiffon & handmade lace insertions, late 1920s- early 1930s, very good condition, some staining to front & wear to ribbon details (ILLUS. of close-up) **$450.00**

Jumper, blue cotton, 1920s (ILLUS., top next column)
. . . . **$25-35**

Pinafore & embroidered cap, orange & black rayon, 1920s, the set (ILLUS., bottom next column)
. . . . **$35-45**

1920s Orange & Black Pinafore & Cap

LADIES' CLOTHING

1920s Black Crepe Beaded Blouse

Blouse, black crepe w/red & black beading (ILLUS.)
.... **$50-75**

1920s Embroidered Voile Blouse

Blouse, embroidered cotton voile, lace edging along collar, hem & insert at sleeve cuffs, narrow shoulder yoke continues to tucked fabric on bodice, covered snap closure down center front, fair condition, extensive staining to fabric, tears on collar, few tears on lace inserts, one large tear at shoulder yoke (ILLUS.) **$55.00**

1920s Green Silk Embroidered Blouse

Blouse, green silk satin featuring a rounded neckline & snap closure at both shoulders w/black yarn embroidery along neckline, bottom of kimono-style sleeves & across the chest, decorative tucking at seams of lower waist, snap closure at hem, late 1920s - early 1930s, good condition, some fading (ILLUS.)
.... **$65.00**

Victorian-Style 1920s Wool Blouse

Blouse, Victorian-style, black wool w/collar of embroidered net, embroidery on front bodice, three-quarter length sleeves w/three-inch net-covered band at cuffs, self-fabric covered & embroidered decorative buttons at cuffs also hiding snaps down center front, inside belt at gathered waist w/hook & eye closure, excellent condition (ILLUS.) **$550.00**

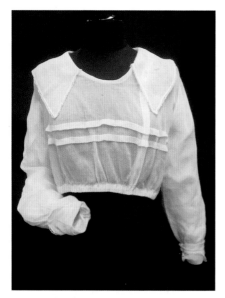

Late 1920s White Cotton Voile Blouse

Blouse, white cotton voile w/modified sailor collar trimmed w/openwork, side snap closure at center left, bands of unpleated ruffle on the bodice front & back, long sleeves tapered to deeply banded cuffs w/slightly turned-backs & edged w/same openwork, gathered waistband, excellent condition, some repairs to waistband, snaps may be replacement, on tiny hole in back, late 1920s - early 1930s (ILLUS.) . . . **$200.00**

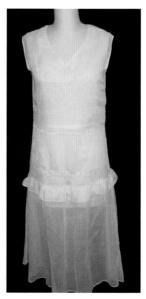

1920s Yellow Organdy Day Dress

Day dress, pale yellow organdy w/yarn embroidered flowers & narrow openwork at yoke, V-neck, single ruffle around skirt, good condition, some fraying at seams (ILLUS.). **$500.00**

1920s Net & Lace Camisole

Camisole, fine white net w/a front insertion of beige lace, ecru embroidery & floral chainstitch embroidery at the center, openwork at elastic hemline, self-fabric straps, center back hook & eye closure, fair condition, one large hole in net at left side, hemline elastic stripped (ILLUS.) **$45-60**

1920s Cutaway Day Jacket

Day jacket, cutaway-style, ivory linen, shap bib-front suggesting a vest, double row of small buttons down center hiding snaps, crocheted lace inserts overall, excellent condition, perhaps originally lined, one very small collar stain (ILLUS.). **$1,200.00**

1920s Black Velvet & Lace Dress

Dress, black cotton velvet w/trimmings of black cord & round & rectangular beads, lace insert in elongated V trimmed w/elaborate passementerie pieces of beads & spoked circles, black foulard triangular panel inserts at each side from hip level to hem, overlaid w/pieces of black lace, tucked at top w/same black cord & bead trim, short sleeves, tulip hem, excellent condition, one tear at bottom of lace inserts (ILLUS.) **$400.00**

1920s Black Rayon Print Dress

Dress, black print rayon w/solid black & ivory rayon trim w/hip ribbon ties (ILLUS.) **$75-100**

1920s Black Satin Long-Sleeved Dress

Dress, black satin, mid-calf length, long sleeves w/black crepe trim at cuffs & hairline-thin beige chiffon edging, extra-wide lapels trimmed w/black crepe that falls in soft folds around the extended neckline, small tucks on satin at shoulderline, deep V-neck w/rhinestone & pearl brooch accent at low waistline w/pleat of crepe at center & horizontal bands of tucks at hem, excellent condition, rhinesonte & pearl brooch accent detached on one side, some fraying to chiffon edging at cuffs (ILLUS.) **$850.00**

1920s Burgundy Velvet Dress with Embroidered Net

Dress, crushed burgundy velvet, embroidered ecru net inserts at neck & on sleeves, white, orange & silver seed pearls, trimmed w/black velvet, low waist yoke w/ smocking at center front & much larger smocked area at center back, good condition, back center zipper added later, one large tear off seam in back (ILLUS. bottom previous page) **$150.00**

1920s Embroidered Drop-Waist Dress

Dress, drop-waist style, white w/embroidered decoration, ca. 1920 (ILLUS.) **$100-150**

Flapper Dress of Black Chiffon & Beads

Dress, flapper-style, black silk chiffon w/clear beading & rhinestones, loosely capped sleeves w/beaded trim & decorative opening at shoulders, beige silk insert at heavily beaded V-neck, both front & back, elaborately pointed hem, each point trimmed in beads, good condition, few missing or loose beads, some staining

to beige silk insert, tear at neckline (ILLUS.)
. . . . **$800-1,200**

Satin Beaded Flapper Dress, Circa 1926

Dress, flapper-style, deep plum-colored satin, keyhole neckline w/white & black beading overall, kimono-style sleeves, drawstring sewn inside dress, encased in narrow cotton sleeve, self-fabric beaded sash, ca. 1926, excellent condition, small tear on shoulder seam (ILLUS.) **$1,200-2,000**

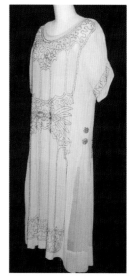

Beaded Flapper Dress

Dress, flapper-style, taupe silk chiffon w/intricate beading, light green side panels, scoop-neck, short kimono-type sleeves, featuring two marcasite buttoned details on each side giving way to a slightly flounced hem of light green chiffon, very good condition, small tear in front near bodice (ILLUS.) **$1,500.00**

Fine 1920s Gold Guipure Lace Dress

Dress, gold guipure lace w/floral motif, sleeveless, mid-calf length, gathered sections at center bottom, both front & back, gold tulle piping at neckline & around armholes, excellent condition, possibly originally had tulle or chiffon lining, few frayed areas at hem (ILLUS.)
. . . . **$1,800.00**

1920s Hand-made Silk Embroidered Dress

Dress, hand-made silk, originally used as a wedding dress, double-layer beige silk chiffon w/black satin sleeves & same chiffon inset w/black satin appliqués & black silk-threaded embroidery, lower portion of skirt & full satin back, black satin swath faced w/beige chiffon sewn at shoulders & meant to wear thrown over right shoulder to fall asymmetrically in front of dress, back waist belt of black satin faced w/chiffon, self-fabric pieces sewn as ribbons & gathered to form flower at left shoulder, hem tiered in front, good condition, some tears to chiffon along shoulder, ca. 1922 (ILLUS.)
. . . . **$2,500.00**

1920s Peach Silk & Lace-Overlay Dress

Dress, strapless underdress of peach silk sewn to ivory netting around armscyes & neckline forming straps, gold & bronze lace overlay covering straps & bodice & falling into points, same lace sewn at points of skirt & extending to a trained hem w/scalloped edges, light blue gros-grain ribbon sewn to V at front waist & continuing to netting at straps & then extending to back neckline w/bow, normal waistline w/tight gauges continuing to soft pleats & full skirt, bottom portion of skirt faced w/blue taffeta, gathered silk satin flowers in light blue & peach sewn to the point of the gros-grain V at front waist & at bottom right hem, good condition, lace torn in some areas, one stain to front, ca. 1929 (ILLUS.) **$450.00**

1920s Chiffon Floral Dress

Dress, thin black chiffon w/large pink flowers, ca. 1920s
(ILLUS.) **$50-75**
Dress & matching slip, slip of light plum-colored silk
w/a camisole top w/gold gros-grain straps & a 10"
w. chiffon insertion at the hemline; the dress of
matching chiffon in three diaphanous layers, round

neckline, shirred shoulders, drop waist w/swath of
fabric at left side crossing across right shoulder to
be pinned at shoulder, handkerchief draped hemline,
good condition, straps of slip broken, stress tears to
shoulder of dress, one small discoloration mark on
lower front, late 1920s (ILLUS., below). **$200.00**

Late 1920s Chiffon Dress & Slip

Front & Back of Black Velvet & Beige Lace 1920s Dressing Robe

Dresssing robe, black silk velvet w/beige lace at neckline, sleeves & trained hem, black silk chiffon tie at inside waist, good condition, some holes in lace along back shoulders, some lace restoration along neckline & train (ILLUS. of front & back, bottom previous page) **$3,000.00**

Lovely 1920s Evening Coat

Evening coat, black satin lined w/black sateen, black lace on deep cuffs & deep hem, lace insert on front upper bodice continuing over shoulders to the back, black braiding trim on lapels, hook & eye closure down the center front, two black silk thread-covered buttons meet just under lapels for decoration, hidden elastic set in self-sleeve at lower waist, excellent condition (ILLUS.) **$2,700.00**

1920s Black Satin Evening Coat

Evening coat, black satin w/fringe trim (ILLUS.) **$100-150**

1920s Kimono-Style Evening Coat

Evening coat, kimono-style, black rayon w/colorful stylized floral embroidery & fringe trim (ILLUS.) **$95-150**

1920s Gold Embroidered Black Net Evening Dress

Evening dress, black net embroidered w/gold, consisting of a slip dress of black pebbled chiffon w/a double-faced bustline & hemline, self-fabric straps, the over-dress of black net embroidered w/gold metallic thread in a meandering design, low surplice neckline

edged w/gold & a drop waistline, skirt features center embroidered panel w/gold stripes flanked by shirred black chiffon inserts, black chiffon slip dress labeled "Chandler & Co., Inc. - 1-6-26 - No. 4023 - Mrs. D.O. Wade," 1926, very good condition, a few stress tears at shoulderline of embroidered over-dress (ILLUS.)
. . . . **$800.00**

Beaded Chiffon 1920s Flapper Dress

Evening dress, flapper-style, white chiffon w/beading & tiered bottom, ca. 1925 (ILLUS.). **$100-150**

Beaded Black Chiffon Flapper Dress

Evening dress, flapper-style, black chiffon w/beading & "car wash" skirt, ca. 1925 (ILLUS.) **$150-200**

Lovely 1920s Ivory Satin Dress Trimmed with Flowers

Evening dress, ivory silk satin, sleeveless, V-neck, low waist, self-fabric piping along neckline, armholes & flounced hems, side closure, three flowers made from ivory taffeta & sewn on a cord & attached to center front, side tucks at waist, multi-tiered flounced & trained hem, good condition, some staining to fabric, one tiny hole near hem, hook & eye closures removed & replaced w/snaps at a later date, ca. 1926 (ILLUS.)
. . . . **$700-800**

Pink Chiffon Beaded Flapper Dress

Evening dress, flapper-style, pink chiffon w/beaded trim (ILLUS.) **$200-300**

Black Velvet & Gold Brocade 1920s Evening Dress

Evening dress, smock-style w/black silk velvet shoulder & neck yoke, gold brocade bodice & long full sleeves tapering to black velvet snap-banded cuffs w/a slit just before the wrist for drape, 4 1/2" w. black velvet insertion at the hip gathered off-center w/enamel & paste Art Deco style buckle w/trailing swath attached to remainder of the velvet skirt, 4" w. gold brocade band under blet, mint condition, mid-1920s (ILLUS.) **$1,000.00**

1920s "Spun Gold" Evening Dress

Evening dress, woven entirely of lustrous silk gold thread giving a spun-gold look, thin gold ribbon straps, one attached to front of bodice by snaps, low waist originally tucked in three horizontal tiers, side hook & eye closure, swath of same fabric purposely frayed at bottom, shirred at top to form fanned ruffles & originally sewn to side waistband, fair condition, some

discoloration & wear to fabric, tucks stripped along first horizontal tier, swath of fabric unattached & torn at bottom, early 1920s (ILLUS.) **$1,350.00**

Early 1920s Black Satin & Lace Gown

Gown, black satin sleeveless floor-length design w/black lace overlay as a chemise tunic, features modified bateau neckline, long full three-quarter-length sleeves w/flared split cuffs, lined w/black tulle connected by pumpkin-colored silk straps, braided black satin 'girdle' at waistline w/black satin rosettes & double-faced ribbons at left side & pumpkin silk & black satin rosettes at right w/long side swaths of black satin faced w/pumpkin silk billowing from the sides down the length of the garment, side snap closure, bodice lined w/glazed cotton, closes w/hooks & eyes, very good condition, some tears to lace at shoulder & skirt, ca. 1922 (ILLUS.) **$900.00**

1920s Art Deco Design Shawl

Shawl, assuit-style, black netting w/hammered silver metal strips woven in an Art Deco geometric design, fair condition, fraying at borders (ILLUS.) **$800.00**

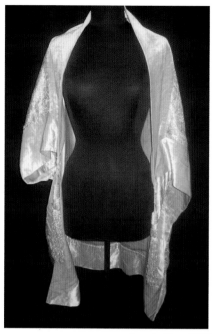
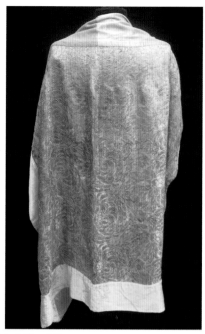

Lovely Circa 1920 Velvet Shawl-Cape

Shawl-cape, apricot-colored panne velvet w/gold brocade center, tucks at neckline, wrapped buttons on two large velvet-topped & gold cord tassels attached to upper corners that attach to small loops at the sides creating armholes, verso all panne velvet w/small gold braid trim, overall 43 x 52", excellent condition, one button missing from tassel, ca. 1920 (ILLUS. of two views, top of page) **$2,800.00**

Skirt, heavy black satin , gored & w/a scalloped hem & purple, pink & gold yarn embroidery, center back snap closure, good condition, small area of wear (ILLUS., previous column) **$300.00**

1920s Lady's Blue Silk Stockings with Original Tag

Stockings, blue silk, patent-dated 1928, w/original tag, pair (ILLUS.) **$20-30**
Summer dress, unbleached ecru net w/lace edging around armholes & hem, lace inserts down the front & back, center panels of ecru net embroidery, good condition, few small tears, one small stain near bottom, ca. 1925 . . . . **$1,500.00**
Sweater, yellow knit w/sailor-style collar & embroidered buttons (ILLUS., top next page) **$35-55**
Swimsuit, black one-piece produced by Jantzen (ILLUS., middle next page) **$50-75**

1920s Embroidered Black Satin Skirt

1920s Yellow Knit Lady's Sweater

1920s Jantzen Lady's Swimsuit

Lovely Peach Taffeta & Black Chiffon Tea Dress

Tea dress, peach taffeta w/a gathered bodice & a black chiffon overlay begininng at the shoulders, decorated w/sequins & beading, white tulle sleeves, light satin throat piece, decorated skirt, excellent condition (ILLUS.) **$1,250.00**

1920s Ivory Crepe & Lace Wedding Dress

Wedding dress, ivory crepe w/Battenburg lace trim (ILLUS.) **$175-200**

Pretty Black Chiffon Wrap

Wrap, black silk chiffon w/tiny bold & silver beads in a chevron design down the back, very good condition, minor holes, some hairline runs in the chiffon (ILLUS.) **$500.00**

MEN'S CLOTHING

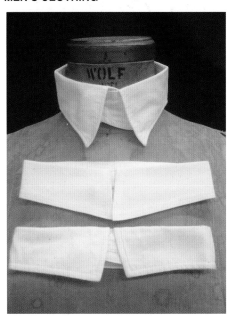

Group of 1920s Detachable Collars

Wrappings for Collars

Collar wrappings, for group of collars, each reads "Kant-Krease - A Flexible Collar For All Seasons...," excellent condition, late 1920s - early 1930s, each (ILLUS. of two)............................ **$See collars**

Collars, detachable, cotton, different styles & widths, labeled "Kant-Krease - Made by Tooke Bros. Limited," excellent condition, late 1920s - early 1930s, each (ILLUS. of three, and of wraps)............. **$25-35**

Drawers, ankle-length white cotton w/buttoned waist yoke w/side tabs & adjustable tie belt in back, full legs reinforced from inside w/additional panel of fabric, tapering to cuffed adjustable bottoms w/wrapped buttons, open fly, labeled "Louis Thal - Riga - Kalku iola 12," very good condition, tiny holes here & there, ca. 1920 (ILLUS. top next column)......... **$150.00**

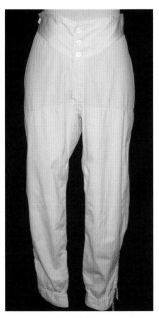

1920s White Cotton Drawers

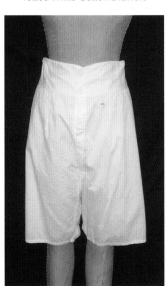

Man's White Cotton Lawn Drawers

Drawers, white cotton lawn, knee-length w/vertical woven stripes on body of garment & horizontal stripes on 4" w. waistband, embroidered buttons & loops on waistband, back waist belt w/decorative embroidered buttons, narrow tabs at top of waistband, open fly, tiny monogram on left side, labeled "Osvald Robert Budapest - Nagymezo-utca 23," excellent condition, ca. 1920 (ILLUS.)....................... **$85.00**

1920s Tweed & Check Lounging Jacket

Lounging jacket, brown tweed faced w/small brown & beige hound's-tooth check on shawl collar-lapels & used as trim on patch pockets & turn-back cuffs, two roses of brown braid frong closures at center front, lined w/hound's-tooth fabric, illegible label, excellent condition, light wear to some seams (ILLUS.)
. . . . **$185.00**

1920s Man's Tweed Lounging Jacket

Lounging jacket, brown tweed faced w/small brown & beige hound's-tooth check on shawl collar/lapels & used as trim on patch pockets & turn-back cuffs, two rows of brown braid frog closures center front, lined w/ hound's-tooth fabric, illegible label, excellent condition, light wear to some seams (ILLUS.). **$275.00**

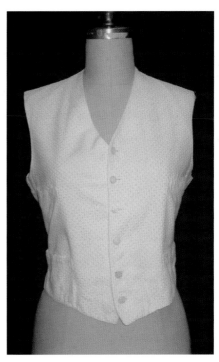

1920s Summer Weight Cotton Vest

Vest, summer weight, front of textured white cotton printed w/tiny gold dots creating an overall diamond design, two rows of angle-set stand pockets at center front, back of whtie nainsook, back waist belt, pearlized celluloid studs down center front, ca. 1920, excellent condition, one small rust stain at waist belt (ILLUS.) **$95.00**

CHAPTER 6: CLOTHING - 1930-1940

CHILDREN'S CLOTHING

Coverall, boy's, light brown cotton w/elastic waistband, large patch pockets in the legs, center front snap closure, very good condition, some discoloration to fabric w/some brittle spots (ILLUS. center with two other 1930s boys' outfits) **$175.00**

1930s Little Girl's Cotton Lawn Dress

Dress, pink cotton lawn w/patterns of white paisleys & pink & yellow flowers, green leaves & stems, V-neck, ruffled round collar, puffed sleeves, ruffled front yoke, gathered skirt, ruffled flounce at hemline, self-fabric tie belt, fair condition, some stress tears to fabric along back shoulder, staining in places (ILLUS.) **$55.00**

Two 1930s White Girls' Dresses

Dress, white cotton voile w/three tiers of lace ruffles around wide crew neckline & three around edge of short sleeves, wide satin ribbon sash w/lace ruffles

continuing to bottom of skirt, excellent condition, satin ribbon sash probably replaced, ca. 1930 (ILLUS. right with white lawn dress). **$250.00**

1930s Girl's Dress in a Cotton Print

Dress, white cotton w/tiny floral print & a large collar, 1930s (ILLUS.) **$25-40**

Dress, white lawn w/scalloped bertha collar, lace edging at tight crew neckline & sleeves, white embroidery & openwork, high waist & gently gathered skirt w/openwork & embroidery towards bottom portion of skirt, snaps down center back, good condition, some fraying at hem, few small tears in sleeve lace trim, ca. 1935 (ILLUS. left with white voile dress). **$250.00**

1930s Youth Varsity Jacket

Three 1930s Boys' Outfits

Jacket, youth-sized, varsity-type, primarily of heathered gray wool w/cream-colored leather shoulder & back yoke & pocket edging, wool knit collar, cuffs & waist, lined w/striped rayon twill, center front zipper closure, some wear & cracking to leather in covered areas, good condition (ILLUS.) **$175.00**

Outfit, boy's, one-piece crisp brown cotton w/white cotton trim, self-belt w/button closure, center front buttons, excellent condition (ILLUS. right with two other 1930s boys' outfits, top of page) **$275.00**

Suit, boy's, two-piece, beige linen, jacket w/white scalloped collar & cuffs, matching pants button to shirt, excellent condition (ILLUS. left with two other boy's outfits, top of page). **$250-300**

1930s Sonja Henie Sweater & Original Box

Sweater, white knitted Sonja Henie model in original box, 1930s (ILLUS.) **$45-75**

LADIES' CLOTHING

1930s Navy Blue Wool Swimsuit

Bathing suit, navy blue wool woven in a fine herringbone pattern, red wool cord running through slits at the neckline & continuing around the neck, crossing in the back, scoop back, skirted suit w/attached trunks of the same blue wool, labeled "Jantzen - Kenwood Woolens, Inc. Chicago - Reg. U.S. Pat. Off. - Size 38," excellent condition, very little pilling two small satins on back (ILLUS. with souvenir pillow cover) **$250.00**

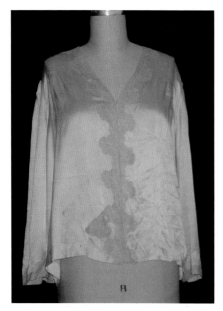

1930s Silk Bed Jacket

Bed jacket, peach colored silk satin w/draped sleeves & lace trim around neckline & cuffs, single hook & eye closure at center front, good condition, some repair work to back (ILLUS.) **$90-125**

1930s Middy-Style Canvas Duck Blouse

Blouse, middy-style, off-white canvas duck, hip-length w/dark blue sailor collar w/traditional striping, long sleeves w/tapered buttoned cuffs edged in same blue trim, also used for edging at hem, center front zipper added later, scarf tie added, excellent condition, original scarf tie missing (ILLUS.) **$125.00**

Elegant 1930s Formal Peach Cape

Cape, formal-style, soft peach-colored fabric w/slight nap, faced w/light pink satin, features a hood w/puckered edge, cream-colored silk cord braiding down the center front, hook & loop closures, slightly trained hem, one patch pocket, rounded & shirred at top edge on inside lining, excellent condition (ILLUS.) **$800.00**

1930s Banded Cape Collar

Cape collar, rayon crepe, in shades of wine, grey & ivory, patterned w/graduated fish scales, mint condition (ILLUS.) **$125.00**

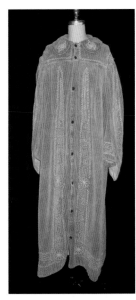

1930s Pink Cotton Velvet Cloak

Cloak, pink cotton velvet, robe styling w/Peter Pan collar & white soutache braid throughout in a meandering designs & geometric forms, long sleeves w/hanging sleeves draped over, faced w/white satin, very good condition, some fading, some discoloration to lining (ILLUS.) **$250.00**

1930s Black Velvet Day Dress

Day dress, black velvet w/silver thread trim & finely gauged tulle around the slightly V-neckline, shirring at shoulderline, heavily shirred bodice w/rounded yoke, low yoked waistline, long bishop sleeves banded at wrists, side zipper closure, excellent condition, probably some fabric-covered buttons missing at bodice, repair work under one arm (ILLUS.). . **$250.00**

Pretty Peach Rayon Day Dress, Ca. 1930

Day dress, lustrous peach rayon, rounded narrow shawl collar continuing to bodice as ties, slightly dipped in front to form slight V, enameled Art Deco design buckle at end of tie, long sleeves w/snaps at cuffs, darts at shoulders & lower bustline to waist yoke, front inverted pleat, labeled "Size 40," ca. 1930, excellent condition (ILLUS.) **$600-700**

1930s Printed Rayon Day Dress

Day dress, printed rayon in colors of pink, orange, red & grey depicting a floral splash-like design, round neckline w/self-piping, small puffed sleeves w/narrow banded cuffs, front bodice ends in U-shape w/a bias-cut flounce at the skirt, the back of the bodice ends w/handkerchief points, again w/a bias-cut flounce as skirt, envelope panels at the sides, front hemline 4" shorter than in back, side snap closure, excellent condition, front hemline unfinished (ILLUS.) **$400-450**

Dress, bias-cut on flesh-colored silk crepe w/painted dark blue flowers & details, attached self-belt, weighted cowl-neck, scalloped stitching on skirt, side-snap closure, good condition, small tears at armscyes & a few in the skirt (ILLUS.) **$650-800**

Late 1930s High-Necked Crepe Dress

1930s Dress with Geometric Print

Dress, a black, red & white small geometric Art Deco print w/matching wrap sash tie & lace trim, ca. 1930 (ILLUS.) **$30-45**

Dress, black crepe, high-necked stand-up collar, bodice shirred & slit in front, raglan sleeves w/deep armholes & tapering to wrists, narrow-width lustrous black ribbon embellishment on sleeves & overall back of skirt & extending to front side panels, self-fabric belt w/fabric-covered buckle, hook & eye closure at neck front, button & loop closure at neck back & snap closure at left side, excellent condition (ILLUS.) **$650.00**

1930s Painted Silk Crepe Dress

1930s Black Rayon Crepe Dress

Dress, black rayon crepe w/tucks at shoulderline & in
sunburst pattern at back of neck, surplice neckline w/
contrasting trim of light pink lustrous fabric continuing
to waist yoke, embellished w/small rounded self-
fabric-covered buttons & loose flaps of black rayon
& contrasting pink fabric, long sleeves w/snaps at
tapered cuffs, decorative stitching at elbow & five
small covered buttons along w/fabric flap decorations
running down wrist, asymmetrical waist yoke of
contrasting black fabric w/excess as sash tying at left
hip & continuing to slightly flared skirt, good condition,
pink contrasting trim possibly added later, one tear off
seam at back, ca. 1930 (ILLUS.) **$300.00**

1930s Floor Length Black Crepe Dress

Tea Length 1930s Black Velvet Dress

Dress, black velvet tea-length design, panel at bodice
wraps around waist forming a surplice neckline &
finishes w/self-belt & self-fabric-covered buckle to
close at side, skirt in three panels at front, raglan
sleeves tapered to wrist w/three snap closure at wrist,
good condition, one seam open at lower skirt & under
one arm (ILLUS.) **$450.00**

Dress, floor-length, flat black crepe, sleeveless
w/rounded shallow V-neck, front & back yoke at
bodice forming V to center front waist, five small fabric-
covered decorative buttons at break, final yoke from
lower waist to hem, two rows of five same buttons
diagonally set at back shoulder line, fair condition, two
back buttons missing, large tear off seam in lower skirt
(ILLUS., top next column) **$200.00**

1930s Rayon Crepe Floral Print Dress

Dress. rayon crepe w/an overall print design of flowers
& birds mostly in blues, greys, yellows & greens w/
wine-colored accents, swath of fabric from shoulders
gathered to waist & attached by self-fabric-covered
button, side-draped peplum continuing to waist &
attached w/snaps, center pleats at lower skirt, side
zipper & center front hidden zipper at neckline, labeled
"A Stylebrooke Original," excellent condition, some
discoloration to fabric on button, ca. 1937-47 (ILLUS.)
. . . . **$200-300**

1930s Pink Lace & Satin Dressing Gown

Dressing gown, pink lace neckline w/a high neck & pink satin trim, wrapped button & loop closures, lace short sleeves & lower skirt, pink satin insertion comprising

bustline torso & upper skirt, very good condition, fabric on buttons fraying (ILLUS.). **$125.00**

Dressing gown & jacket (robe de chambre), very fine peach cut-velvet on a chiffon ground, bias-cut w/surplice neckline, bodice w/hemstitch detailing, long floor-length bias-cut skirt, 1 1/2" w. straps high across the back w/buttons & loop closure down the center back, loose-fitting jacket w/scalloped flowing & pleated bell sleeves, excellent condition, the set (ILLUS. of two views, bottom of page) **$2,500.00**

Two Late 1930s Black Satin Evening Dresses

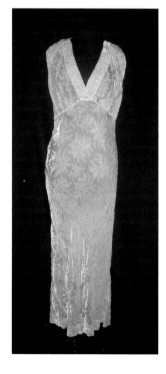

Two Views of a Lovely 1930s Cut-Velvet Dressing Gown & Jacket

Evening dress, black satin w/a rounded short slit neckline, slight shoulder padding, modified cape-type flounce in front, gather & run through self-fabric sleeve at center, normal waistline w/loose tucks at hips to form "pockets," center mid-back zipper closure, late 1930s - early 1940s, excellent condition (ILLUS. right with other black satin evening dress, previous page)
. . . . **$400.00**

Evening dress, black satin w/cross-over surplice-type neckline ending in tucks at rounded raised waistline, center panel from waist yoke wraps to one side & buttons w/self-fabric-covered button & to other sewn in place at alternate side creating a cross-over effect seen from the back & a dramamtic drape at lower center front, kimono cap sleeves, side zipper closure, late 1930s - early 1940s, excellent condition (ILLUS. left with other black satin evening dress) **$475.00**

1930s Lace Evening Dress & Jacket

1930s Black Crepe Ribbon-Trimmed Evening Dress

1930s Evening Dress in Black Chiffon & Peach Silk

Evening dress, floor-length black crepe w/a V-neck & bias-cut bodice w/shirring at shoulderline & tucks below bust creating fullness around bustline, padded shoulders & puffed tapered short sleeves, front & back trimmed w/rows of black & gold brocade ribbon, right side zipper closure, late 1930s - early 1940s, excellent condition, slight stripping of stitches (ILLUS.)
. . . . **$600.00**

Evening dress, ivory lace, w/matching jacket, the set (ILLUS., top next column) **$45-65**

Evening dress, the underdress of peach silk w/a black chiffon overlay featuring a deep V-neckline front & back w/black lace insertions at center, the overlay tightly pleated at lower skirt, silk rosettes at the shoulder & at the waist, accompanying narrow black velvet belt w/paste buckles, underdress w/snap closure, overlay closes w/hooks & eyes, underdress in fair condition w/staining & tears overall, the overlay in good condition w/minimal stress tears (ILLUS.)
. . . . **$800.00**

Black Satin & Crepe Evening Gown

Evening gown, black satin-backed crepe, scoop neck w/low back, black tulle overdress, black lace trim along V-shaped neckline & edge of center front zipper, at cuffs & same lace insertions at tiers of skirt, slim-fitting sleeves w/tucks at elbows & lace-wrapped buttons at wrist, good condition, lace separated from edge of zipper on one side, late 1930s - early 1940s (ILLUS.) **$650-850**

Evening gown, black velvet, sweetheart neckline, soft gathers under bustline, high waist w/yoke, self-fabric tie on either side of waist, slightly trained floor-length skirt, puff sleeves w/gold thread embroidery & small gold disk appliqué, keyhole back w/two self-fabric covered buttons w/loop closure high at back of neck, side zipper closure, good condition, some repair to seam at waist, alteration work at shoulder (ILLUS. of full-length & upper portion, bottom of page) . . **$800.00**

1930s Fine Tulle & Lace Evening Gown

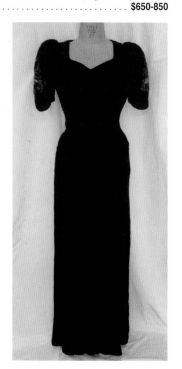

1930s Black Velvet Evening Gown & Close-up of the Sleeve

Evening gown, bodice of micro-pleated pink chiffon & fine black tulle overlay w/a black lace insertion suggesting a cape collar & sleeves, tight rounded neckline w/self-fabric piping, fitted waist continuing to floor-length tiered skirt, black tulle peplum w/lace insertion at hipline continuing to back as a drape, wrapped buttons & loop closure at back of neck, side zipper, lower skirt lined w/black satin, excellent condition, one or two minor tears, a very small size gown (ILLUS., previous page) **$700.00**

Organdy & Tulle 1930s Evening Gown

1930s Yellow Chiffon Evening Gown

Evening gown, bodice of pink organdy embroidered w/white flowers & stems, sweetheart neckline, self-fabric rosette at waistline, black rayon triangular waist w/black tulle overlay tightly gathered at waistline & falling into long skirt, pink satin ribbon at rosette, side zipper closure, good condition, some tears in tulle skirt & near zipper closure, some discoloration around neckline, ca. 1935 (ILLUS.) **$300.00**

Evening gown, butter yellow chiffon overlay, sleeveless, tucked at shoulders & bustline, V-neck, diamond-shaped waist yoke, gathered side & back peplum over a gathered gored skirt w/a slightly trained hem, side zipper closure w/hooks & snaps to cover it, attached slip of bright yellow sewn at waist yoke & w/the same butter yellow chiffon spaghetti straps, excellent condition, one mark left by a pinhole at the neck (ILLUS., top next column) **$1,000.00**

Elegant 1930s Crepe & Chiffon Evening Gown

Evening gown, coral silk crepe w/orange chiffon overlay, slight V-neck, neck yoke w/horizontal tucks forming draped bustline, low wrap back w/same fabric straps gathered at shoulder, rhinestones studded overall, heavily studded self-fabric belt, high waistline continuing into long draped skirt w/two tucks on lower skirt portion simulating godets, good condition, some small tears in chiffon overlay, some spots of discoloration & tearing at seams (ILLUS.) . . **$1,800.00**

1930s Electric Blue Evening Gown

Evening gown, electric blue satin w/V-neckline, puffed & gathered sleeves w/self-ties, gathered bustline & full skirt, green velvet ribbon trim, excellent condition (ILLUS.) **$400.00**

Elegant 1930s Blue Velvet Evening Gown

Evening gown, ink blue silk velvet, long sleeves softly gathered at shoulders & cuffs, gathers under bustline, vertical smocking at back shoulders to create a drape effect horizontially across upper back, two rhinestone button closure at neck, self-fabric belt w/rhinestone buckle, good condition, one small tear under bustline & on one side seam, some discoloration along hem (ILLUS.) **$800-1,200**

Front & Back Views of Elaborate Beaded 1930s Evening Gown

Evening gown, heavily beaded, sequined & embroidered tulle using metallic threads, organdy-lined bodice, sweatheart neckline, gathered tulle of finer gauge creating straps w/long swags of looped nylon horsehair creating a tier effect on skirt & trimming hem, center back zipper w/same lighter tulle gathered at waistline for long, full train, good condition, some discoloration to bodice lining, few loose metallic beads (ILLUS. of front & back) **$3,500-5,000**

Lovely 1930s Black Lace Evening Gown

Elegant 1930s Velvet on Chiffon Gown

Evening gown, lace of black net w/flat designs of pineapples & foliage, V-neck w/center shirring & full bustline, 2" w. lace-covered straps faced w/black lustrous faille & ruffled lace trim, full skirt w/slightly trained hem faced w/nylon horsehair for stiff support, scoop back w/center zipper, excellent condition, one very minor lace tear (ILLUS.) **$1,200.00**

Evening gown, magenta-colored cut-velvet on chiffon, modified bateau neckline, shirring at shoulder, softly draped bodice, high princess waistline w/same fabric belt w/covered slide buckle, dolman cape sleeves, floor-length w/slightly trained hem, slit back w/single wrapped button at neckline, excellent condition (ILLUS.) **$650-800**

Front & Back Views of 1930s Gown & Capelet Ensemble

Evening gown & capelet, both of gold-colored organza, sleeveless gown w/scoop neckline, yoke under gently gathered bustline, flamenco-style ruffles that continue to the back, deep V-back w/self-covered button & loop closure, high-set cascading back ruffles, capelet w/two tiers of ruffles & snap closure around the neck, stain towards botton of skirt, some tears around ruffles, the emsemble (ILLUS. of front & back)............................. **$1,200.00**

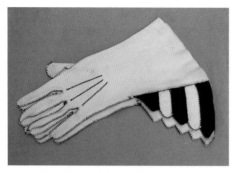

1930s Black & White Suede Gloves

Gloves, black & white suede w/Art Deco style banded trim, pair (ILLUS.) **$20-30**

1930s Striped Gown & Jacket Outfit

Gown & jacket, taffeta gown w/stripes of red, wine, cream, green, black & (changeable) taupe w/shirred & gathered bustline, horizontal stripes on the bodice front & back & continuing after the high waist to chevron stripes, black velvet-covered spahgetti straps & side-snap closure; hooded jacket made of black velvet w/same taffeta trim along lapels & on inside of the hood, features short sleeves & high princess waist continuing to back, gentle tucks at waistline create drape at bust & upper back, center front zipper closure, excellent condition, ca. 1935 (ILLUS.)
. . . . **$900-1,200**

Two Views of a Black Chenille Gown & Matching Cardigan

Gown & matching cardigan, pieced of black chenille yarn, the dress w/a high neck, cap sleeves, the bodice slightly wider than fitted waist, skrit flares slightly at hemline, faceted jet buttons w/shank & loops down center back, shrug cardigan w/jet buttons & loops down center front, accompanying belt w/jet buckle in the form of a medallion w/a butterfly, excellent condition, jet medallion on belt buckle broken (ILLUS. of two views). **$800.00**

1930s Kimono Robe

Kimono robe, rayon crepe w/a green ground decorated w/purple liles & white flowers, floor-lenght, unlined, possibly an export worn as a dressing gown, 57" l., good condition, small stains & teares on back (ILLUS.)
. . . . **$350.00**

1930s Lady's Leather Leggings

Leggings, full grain light brown leather w/zipper & three buckle closure at calf, stirrup straps snap on one side & buckle on the other, lined w/brown felt, 19" l., good condition, some wear to leather (ILLUS.) **$150.00**

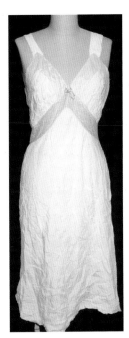

1930s Blue Rayon & Lace Nightgown

Nightgown, light blue rayon w/lace trim, princess waist, rayon straps & small pink bow detail, excellent condition (ILLUS.). **$85.00**

1930s Pink Satin Nightgown

Nightgown, pink silk satin w/a gathered bodice w/lace ruffled trim, gathered satin straps, lace insertions at princess waist, slightly gathered skirt w/lace insertion at the hem, excellent condition (ILLUS.). **$350.00**

1930s Seafoam Silk Satin Nightgown

Nightgown, seafoam silk satin, bodice features
surplice neckline w/embroidered scalloped edging,
embroidered butterflies & openwork along bustline
continuing to scalloped straps w/shirred detail, high
princess waistline w/embroidery & self-fabric belt to
tie around waist, bias-cut skirt w/scalloped hemline &
center split, excellent condition (ILLUS.) **$450.00**

1930s Polka Dot Party Dress

Party dress, navy blue & white polka dotted rayon
crepe, lower calf length, purple organdy gathered
around neckline stopping to points mid-center & same
organdy to interline crepe sleeves & formed into a
rosette at the neck, caped shoulder continues to flap
covering bodice & draping past sewn waistline, tucks

at lower skirt side center to simulate godets, self-fabric
belt w/fabric-covered slide bucklet, excellent condition
(ILLUS.) **$375-600**

Peach Lace & Blue Chiffon Party Dress

Party dress, peach lace sleeveless bodice lined w/peach
chiffon w/chiffon piping, slight V-neck w/blue chiffon
bow detail at center continuing to the blue chiffon
tiered skirt w/tucked bands at the hipline, self-bows at
center & handkerchief hems, snaps at left shoulder,
good condition, peach chiffon lining in pieces, some
bading, small holes in skirt, ca. 1930 (ILLUS.)
.... **$200.00**

1930s Pink Chiffon Party Dress

Party dress, pink flowered chiffon, "Over the Garden Wall" label, ca. 1930 (ILLUS.). **$50-75**

Embroidered Silk 1930s Party Dress

Party dress, very thin coral-colored silk w/yellow silk embroidered collar & deep smocked waistline, bias-cut skirt w/outside seams & chain-stitch embroidery throughout, puff smocked sleeves w/drapey finish, good condition, a few stains, some restoration to one sleeve (ILLUS.). **$200-450**

1930s Peignoir Set in Chiffon

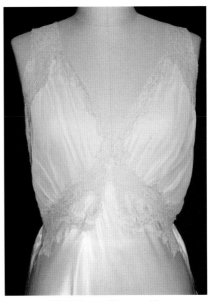

1930 Peignoir Close-up View

Peignoir set, robe of light pink chiffon w/beige lace insertions at shoulders & in a meandering pattern at waistline & used as edging at snap sleeve cuffs & hemline, tucks at bustline & along back waist, hidden snap closure under bust; the gown w/tucked chiffon bodice front, satin back also w/lace insertions along neckline, hem, straps & in meandering pattern at waist, satin skirt w/self-fabric belt to tie around waist, godets at hemline for increased sweep, excellent condition, the set (ILLUS.) **$495.00**

Back of Lovely Chiffon & Velvet Shawl

Shawl, green silk chiffon & cut-velvet, edged w/black beaded & crocheted tassels, perfect condition (ILLUS. of the back). **$1,200.00**

Front & Back Views of a 1930s Blue Rayon Shoulder Wrap

Shoulder wrap, midriff-style, robin's-egg blue rayon twill w/overlay of ecru lace, embroidered tulle & lace edging, armscyes & neckline edged in pink velvet w/bow details, good condition but overall fabric fading (ILLUS. of front & back) **$100-150**

1930s Black Net Lace Shrug

Shrug, black net lace w/black sequins machine-stitched & hand-sewn in a meandering & floral design, short sleeves w/black lace gusset, hems made from rolled net, three-snap closure down center front, good condition, some minor tearing to net & lace (ILLUS.) **$2,500.00**

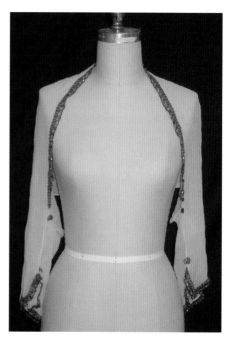

1930s Crepe Georgette Shrug

Shrug, ivory crepe georgettte trimmed w/textured gold braiding & swags of looped gold thread & tiny colorful beads, clusters of small gold disks at the arm openings, excellent condition (ILLUS.) **$450.00**

1930s Lady's Wool Ski Suit

Ski suit, both pieces of navy blue wool, cropped 'bell-boy' jacket w/low pointed turn-back lapels, right lapel buttons high at left side for warmth, long sleeves w/ adjustable button & tab cuffs, two rows of blue buttons down center front plus one extra button at lower left side right tab to secure waist, two zippered pockets at center front, lined w/light grey serge fabric; pants feature side button closures at both sides, diagonally-set welt pockets w/buttoned flaps, inside waist belt, tapered stirrup legs & knit cuffs, pants lined w/same grey serge, jacket labeled "Piperno Alcordo - Roma," excellent condition, some slight stretching at knit pant cuffs (ILLUS.) **$800.00**

1930s Black Velvet Stole with Gold Stars

Stole, black velvet faced w/gold satin & painted w/gold constellations in starbursts & dots, edges trimmed w/small black velvet balls, 16" w., 67" l., very good condition, two balls missing, few tiny dots of wear (ILLUS.) **$395.00**

1930s Tweed Knit Lady's Sweater

Sweater, tweed knit w/brown braid trim (ILLUS.)
. . . . **$30-55**

1930s Lady's Black Swim Coverup

Swim coverup, black w/white piping, long-waisted, ca. 1930 (ILLUS.) **$40-50**

1930s Beige & Black Chiffon Tea Dress

Tea dress, bodice of beige silk chiffon w/self-fabric rolled edging at neckline & armholes, front overlay of additional chiffon layer, lace-edged & shirred at sides, crosses at front & closes in back w/crystal button & loop & snap closure, skirt of black lustrous stiff fabric w/black chiffon overlay, waist yoke forming low V extending to godet & lower portion of skirt, both front & back, side snap closure, excellent condition (ILLUS.) **$1,500-1,800**

1930s Floral Tea Dress

Tea dress, fine rayon w/floral print on a blue ground, bertha collar w/two painted wooden buttons hiding snap closure at square neckline, self-fabric tie belt, excellent condition (ILLUS.) **$200-300**

1930s Lace & Velvet Tea Dress

Tea dress, bodice of beige lace, w/back lace continuing to front & draping over shoulder for cape-like effect, rounded waistline & bias-cut crushed velvet skirt w/dropped yoke, self-fabric belt closes w/rhinestone clasp, side snap closure, excellent condition, rhinestone clasp perhaps replaced (ILLUS.) **$1,100.00**

1930s Peach Organdy Tea Dress

Tea dress, one-piece peach organdy w/white accent, soft feminine silhouette w/sloping bertha collar circling to back, modified kimono-style sleeves extending to elbow, blousoned bodice, side seams shirred at waist over white organdy slip-top attached to slightly gathered ankle-length skirt, peach organdy collar, sleeve & skirt fashioned w/horizontal bands of white organdy laced together w/tiny hemstitch, peach organdy appliqués in ring design on the skirt & sleeves w/gros-grain ribbon bows & embroidered silk rosettes,

tiny snaps at center back closure, excellent condition
(ILLUS.) **$500.00**

Floral Silk Overlay Tea Gown

Tea dress, underslip of crepe georgette in dusty rose
w/ivory silk straps, slightly scooped neck, darts at
waistline, hemmed to knee-length w/deep flounce
consistering of three layers, the first of magenta
chiffon w/handkerchief hem, followed by two layers of
mauve-colored tulle, hook & eye side closure, a china
silk overlay w/a pale lavender ground w/large purple
flowers & black stems & skirt ending in a handkerchief
hem & joined w/a final flounce of dusty rose tulle, hook
& eye slide closure, fair condition, probably homemade
w/some sloopy work, stress tears along overlay straps
& side seams, some dark stains on front (ILLUS.)
. . . . **$350.00**

1930s Floral Chiffon Tea Dress

Tea dress, very sheer black silk chiffon w/floral print,
V-neck, shirring at shoulder line to form soft drape
at bustline, high princess waist, full short sleeves
narrowing at cuff, self-fabric belt attached w/snaps,
self-covered button & loop closure down center front
& side zipper closure, good condition, hole in belt &
signs of repair, some fraying at cuffs, possibly missing
underdress (ILLUS.) **$400.00**

1930s White Embroidered Net Tea Gown

Tea gown, fine white net w/white embroidery on the
short puffed cape sleeves & on the lower skirt near the
hemline, a ruffled wide scoop neckline w/a V at back,
shirred shoulders, gathered bust, skirt of ten-gored
panels, very good condition, minor holes, matching
slip missing (ILLUS.). **$700.00**

1930s Mail-Order Wedding Dress & Veil

Wedding dress & veil, lace, mail-order type in original box, the ensemble, ca. 1930 (ILLUS., previous page) **$75-125**

1930s Wedding Ensemble

Wedding ensemble, purple velvet wedding dress w/ matching jacket & hat & a honeymoon negligée in pink w/lace trim, together w/photo of the bride & groom, 1936, the ensemble (ILLUS.) **$150-175**

Wedding gown, bias-cut gown of ivory cut velvet, featuring leg o' mutton sleeves w/tucks on padded shoulders & above elbow for fullness & tapering to adjustable slim-fitting cuffs, high neckline w/self-strap continuing to back of neck, shirred bodice at center front creating a drape at bust, long slim-fitting skirt w/extremely long train extending 44" from back of the skirt, wrapped ball buttons w/loops down center back, good condition, one large area of gown discolored, small burn holes at hem, few stress tears at shoulders, ca. 1935 (ILLUS. of two views, bottom of page) **$850.00**

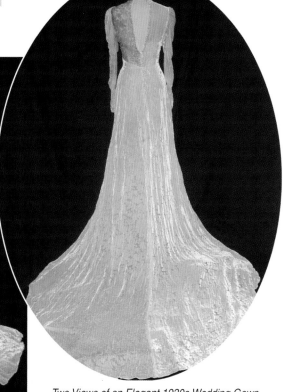

Two Views of an Elegant 1930s Wedding Gown with Long Train

MEN'S CLOTHING

Fine 1930s Man's Leather Car Coat

Car coat, mahogany brown leather, possibly horsehide, double stitching on collar, yoke front & back, pockets & trim, leather-covered buttons, leather belt w/metal buckle, lined w/brown rayon twill, two large rectangular inside pockets, good condition, some desirable softening & wear to leather, one inside pocket restored (ILLUS.) **$350.00**

1930s Man's Brown Wool Robe

Robe, brown wool in a herringbone weave w/elongated shawl collar/lapels, trimmed w/brown & white braiding also used on the sleeves & as trim on the patch pockets, one on left chest & two on hip, two tab loops at back waist held the missing belt, small leather strip over chest pocket marked w/original owner's name, excellent condition (ILLUS.) **$475.00**

Brocaded Late 1930s Dicky Vest

Dicky vest, the front brocaded overall in shades of bronze & gold w/gunmetal-grey ground, high neck faced w/black satin, back waist belt of black satin, remainder lined w/black cotton faille, vest closes w/slight overlap & hidden snaps, excellent condition, back belt w/added insert, late 1930s - early 1940s (ILLUS.) **$95.00**

1930s Wool Pinstripe Two-Piece Suit

Suit, two-piece, navy blue wool w/beige pinstripes, jacket w/padded shoulders, single button notched lapel, chest level stand pocket, hip level welt pockets, two buttons center front; trousers w/high waist, pleats from waistband to tapered cuff, measuring 19 inches around, button fly, welt pockets at hips & back, late 1930s, excellent condition (ILLUS.) **$350.00**

CHAPTER 7: CLOTHING - 1940-1950

CHILDREN'S CLOTHING

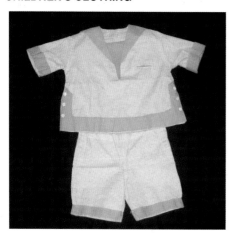

Ivory Cotton Sailor Suit, Circa 1940

Sailor suit, ivory-colored cotton printed w/tiny black squares, blue chambray trim & mother-of-pearl buttons, excellent condition, ca. 1940 (ILLUS.)
.... **$65.00**

LADIES' CLOTHING

Late 1940s Bathing Suit

Bathing suit, rubberized nylon w/tucked & gathered busltine continuing to extensively elasticized shirring down the front, elastic smocking completely covering the back & sides, single self-fabric strap around the neck, elastic around leg openings, labeled "Jantzen - Made in USA," excellent condition, never worn, late 1940s (ILLUS.) **$250.00**

Blouse, beige silk w/short kimono-style sleeves, scalloped beading across shoulders, late 1940s, excellent condition (ILLUS. right with blue rayon blouse) **$75.00**

Two 1940s Rayon Blouses

Blouse, blue rayon w/short kimono-style sleeves w/ appliqué & sequins across the neck & shoulders, w/a collar, center back buttons, excellent condition, late 1940s (ILLUS. left with beige blouse)....... **$175.00**

Light Purple Rayon Crepe 1940s Blouse

Blouse, light purple rayon crepe w/V-neckline decorated w/gold & silver sequins depicting leaves & foliage, also on the short sleeves, tucked bands along the lower portion of the blouse front & back, side zipper closure, excellent condition (ILLUS.) **$125-150**

1940s Blue Satin Bernetti Blouse

Blouse, slate blue satin w/braiding, beads & light grey yarn embroidery along modified roll collar, neckline, hem, cuffs & back vents, center front zipper, gusseted sleeves, labeled "An Original Bernetti - New York," good condition, some wear to fabric in back (ILLUS., previous page) **$600.00**

1940s Black Rayon Crepe Blouse-Jacket

Blouse-jacket, black rayon crepe featuring a keyhole neckline, short sleeves w/gold & silver sequins in designs of leaves & stems on the front & back, shaped mother-of-pearl buttons down the center front, back w/a low peplum, excellent condition (ILLUS.) **$150-200**

1940s Gabardine Coat

Coat, brown wool gabardine featuring a large spread bertha-type collar ending in deep points at front & draping into gentle point at back, brown velvet trim throughout collar set off w/lighter brown braiding & copper-colored beads, the front constructed from four gored panels, double-breasted w/self-fabric-covered

buttons down center front, long sleeves puffed at padded shoulders & tapering to turn-back cuffs, two slit stand pockets at center front seams, upper back constructed from one panel w/slight tucks at self-fabric buttoned waistband for fullness & continuing to three paneled & gored skirt w/deep inverted pleat at center, lined w/copper-colored satin, marked w/a union label, excellent condition, very minor discoloration in lining (ILLUS.) **$450.00**

1940s Black Wool & Golden Mink Coat

Coat, lightweight black wool w/golden mink fur collar & cuffs, swing shape featuring raglan sleeves w/pleated padded shoulders, single rhinestone-studed button closure at center top, stand sash pockets at hip, lined w/black acetate, very good condition, some wear to fabric (ILLUS.). **$200.00**

1940s Magenta Rayon Crepe Day Dress

Day dress, magenta rayon crepe, slight V-neckline trimmed w/beige lace, tucks on upper & lower bodice emanating from horizontal tabs embroidered w/flowers, padded shoulders w/elbow-length sleeves, banded embroidered cuffs, skirt full towards bottom w/ dark blue crepe bands, back waist belt, left side snap closure, carved black buttons down front center, w/the first three functional, excellent condition (ILLUS.) **$425-475**

Dress, black crepe w/modified bateau neckline that is slightly lower in back, embellished w/beads, pearls & faceted rhinestones, long kimono sleeves, stiff acetate-like sash attached at waistline, tucked at sides, fastens w/hook & eye closure at back w/two pieces finishing into a train, center back zipper, excellent condition (ILLUS. right with other black crepe dress) **$300.00**

Two 1940s Black Crepe Dresses

Dress, black crepe w/slight V-neckline & self-fabric embellishment of tightly box-pleated strips sewn around neckline & down center front panel, ending in V at lower waist, tucks at either side of center panels & at bottom giving way to a fuller skirt, self-fabric belt closes in back w/hook & eye & bowl detail, long tight sleeves tapered to cuff & zippered, center back zipper closure, excellent condition (ILLUS. left with other black crepe dress) **$275.00**

1940s Black Crepe Dress with Trim

Dress, black rayon crepe w/a V-neckline, gathered short sleeves trimmed w/elaborate slate blue appliqué & orange & turquoise cabochon stones & gold braid, excellent condition (ILLUS.) **$475.00**

1940s Black Crepe Dress with Rhinestone Ornaments

Dress, black rayon crepe w/a wide scoop neckline, cap sleeves, self-piping at bodice & neckline, natural waistline w/threaded loops for a belt, gored skirt w/a pleated panel at the front center, rhinestone ornaments on tabs at the bodice & sleeves, side zipper closure, very good condition, belt missing, one area of discoloration near waistline (ILLUS.) **$175.00**

1940s Palm Tree Print Rayon Dress

Dress, black rayon w/aqua & grey palm tree print across bodice & down skirt, high neck, center back zipper & side zipper closure, box pleats from waistline giving skirt fullness, long kimono sleeves, twisted thread belt loops at waist, slight shoulder pads, excellent condition, belt missing (ILLUS., previous page)
. . . . **$375.00**

1940s Fuchsia Crepe Dress

Dress, fuchsia crepe, drop-waist style w/large bow trim (ILLUS.) **$35-55**

1940s Black Dress with Sequined Trim

Dress, black w/long bands of sequined trim on the bodice (ILLUS.) **$30-60**

1940s Green-trimmed Brown Crepe Dress

Dress, brown crepe w/green embroidery (ILLUS.)
. . . . **$35-50**

1940s Flowered Print Dress with Sash

Dress, green flowered fabric w/lavender hip sash (ILLUS.) **$45-65**

1940s Print Dress with Peplum

Dress, green & purple print w/peplum flounce & sequined bodice, from the estate of a woman who was "Miss Milwaukee" in the 1930s (ILLUS.). **$75-100**

Nave Blue Rayon Dress with White Appliqués

Dress, navy blue rayon twill, small shawl collar, decorative self-fabric-covered ball buttons down center front to waistband, inverted pleats from shoulderline to waist, elaborate white gros-grain ribbon appliqué on chest pocket & alternating hip pocket, shoulder pads, openwork trim on sleeves, side zipper, white gros-grain ribbon at waistline added much later, excellent condition, very slight yellowing to white ribbon (ILLUS.) **$600.00**

1940s Navy & Paisley Print Dress

Dress, navy blue & pink paisley print fabric w/button trim (ILLUS.) **$35-50**

Late 1940s Navy & Lime Green Dress

Dress, navy blue w/lime green accents & rhinestone buttons, late 1940s (ILLUS.). **$35-55**

1940s White Dress with Red Braid Trim

Dress, white w/short puffed sleeves & red braid trim on the bodice (ILLUS.). **$40-60**

1940s Rayon Dress & Jacket Ensemble

Dress & jacket ensemble, the cap-sleeved dress of rayon crepe w/a mottled print in shades of grey, black & beige, V-neckline w/collar, high princess waistline w/6" w. insertion of draped black rayon crepe, shirred at the sides & continuing to a gored long skirt w/side zipper closure; the cropped bolero jacket of black rayon crepe w/slight shoulder pandding, pointed collar & double row of white plastic buttons at front center opening, three-quarter length sleeves w/turn-back cuffs faced w/the same mottled print fabric as the dress, excellent condition, an extremely small size (ILLUS.) **$225.00**

Pretty 1940s Rayon Dressing Gown

Dressing gown, wine-colored rayon, floor-length w/chartreuse & heart-patterned inset along placket continuing down center front of garment & pleated, short full sleeves gathered at shoulders & tucked at bustline along sides of placket to form soft drapes, chartreuse fabric-covered buttons at center front to waistline, zipper down center front, self-fabric tie in back at waistline, labeled "Styled by Saybury - Reg. U.S. PAT OFF.," excellent condition (ILLUS.) **$150.00**

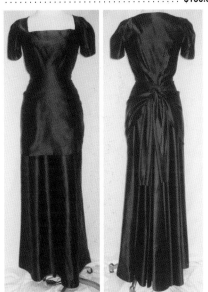

Two views of a Lovely 1940s Black Satin Evening Dress

Evening dress, black satin w/a square-cut neckline & short sleeves slightly puffed at the shoulders, natural waistline dipping lower in back, wide swath of fabric attached at the front waistline wrapping around to the back & ties to form a generous knot, long bias-cut skirt w/a wide sweep at the bottom, godet at back of skirt just under the center point of the waistline for increased fullness, slightly traimed hemline, side zipper closure, excellent condition, small seam opening at shoulder (ILLUS.) **$500.00**

1940s Evening Dress with Beading

Evening dress, floor-length, black rayon w/gold, silver & rhinestone beading around the keyhole neckline & sleeves, tucks originating from upper waistline to bust, back w/decorative cut-out & decorative self-fabric-covered buttons down center back, side zipper, labeled "John Wanamaker," excellent condition, some beads missing around neck, late 1940s (ILLUS.) **$300-450**

1940s Blue Crepe Evening Dress with Taffeta Flourish

Evening dress, navy blue rayon crepe w/a V-neck, three-quarter length sleeves, asymmetrical tucking on the bodice & again on the center left of the skirt, large blue taffeta flourish & swaths on the left side, back center zipper closure, excellent condition (ILLUS.) . . **$700.00**

Lovely 1940s Evening Dress

Evening dress, rose-colored rayon crepe, shirred padded shoulders, V-neckline w/elaborate beading & sequin work just under the neckline, self-fabric bow detail w/beaded ends, slim-fitting long sleeves w/ adjustable snap cuffs & curvilinear edges, hidden snap closure at center front, natural waistline continuing to a narrow box-pleated straight skirt slit at hemline center left, attached self-fabric belt at waist, tucked back waistline, excellent condition, one little abrasion near one elbow (ILLUS.) **$1,200.00**

1940s Brown Girdle

Girdle, brown rubberized fabric w/quilted satin panel & satin-covered boning, heavy side zipper w/inside hooks & eyes, garters w/rubber stoppers & metal

hardware, excellent condition, some wear to rubber
stoppers on garters (ILLUS.) **$95.00**

Leopard Fur Muff for 1940s Jacket & Muff Set

Jacket & muff set, the short boxy jacket covered w/
leopard fur front & back, w/a Kelly green tweed Peter
Pan collar & long sleeves, cuffs trimmed w/green braid
& lined w/green satin, the muff covered completely w/
pieced leopard fur, brown satin interior, side zippered
compartment & brown braid handle, jacket labeled
"Styled by A. Rehkamp" & w/personal monogram,
good condition, fading to inside lining of jacket, fair
amount of tearing of pelt on jacket front, 2 pcs. (ILLUS.
of both) **$400.00**

Mink stole, cape-style, dark brown, elbow-length at
sides w/long ends in front, lined w/brown satin w/same
brown satin ribbons around shoulder area to secure
cape to neck, 72" long end to end, 18" wide at center
tapering to 8" w. at ends, late 1940s - early 1950s,
fair condition, lining repaired, extensive discoloration
to lining in places, some wear to fur at edges (ILLUS.
right with golden brown mink stole) **$95.00**

Late 1940s Loungewear Outfit

Hostess outfit-loungewear, acetate w/maroon ground &
multi-colored stripes, jacket w/rounded collar w/loose
ends that fashion into a tie at the neck & into separate
points at back, self-covered buttons down center front,
turn-back flared cuffs, normal waist & peplum, one
side seam pocket, trousers w/high waist, side zipper
& tapered legs, labeled "Fashioned By Flobert - Lot
- Size 46 - Acetate," excellent condition, late 1940s
(ILLUS.) **$350.00**

Two Vintage Mink Stoles

Mink stole, narrow stole of golden brown mink, lined
w/brown satin w/silver brocaded flowers, inside patch
pockets at edges, labeled "Mt. Pleasant Furriers
- Since 1914 - Schenectady, N.Y.," 58" l., 23" wide at
center, tapering to 11" w. ends, good condition, some
discoloration to label, late 1940s - early 1950s (ILLUS.
left with brown cape stole) **$250.00**

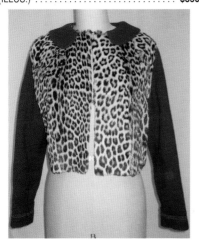

1940s Leopard Jacket from Jacket & Muff Set

Townley - Bonwit Teller," excellent condition, ca. 1947 (ILLUS., below) **$475.00**

Labeled 1940s Playsuit & Bolero Jacket

Various Views of 1940s Nightgown & Bed Jacket Set

Nightgown & bed jacket set, both pieces of fabric w/a light blue background printed w/clusters of flowers & lace-like bows, nightgown bodice of rayon crepe, sleeveless, V-neck front & back w/lace trim at neckline & around armholes, gently gathered at bustline, skirt of rayon acetate, floor-length w/self-fabric belt attached at sides; the bed jacket of same rayon acetate, Peter Pan lace-trimmed collar & puffed short sleeves w/two patch pockets at either hip, trimmed w/purple velvet bow, purple velvet ribbon at neckline for closure, good condition, fabric of jacket faded to lighter color, the set (ILLUS.) **$175-225**

Playsuit & bolero jacket, two-piece, red, blue & green plaid cotton madras, elasticized neck & legs, shirred at sides w/side zipper closure, jacket w/puffed elasticized sleeves & back hem, brass hook & ring closure down center front, labeled "Claire McCardell Clothes by

Late 1940s Mexican Skirt Painted with Flowers & Maidens

Skirt, black cotton painted w/green, blue, gold & copper metallic paint depicting a design of a wide band of latticework, flowers & leaves repeating above a band of figures of Mexican ladies carrying baskets of flowers on their heads, their three-dimensional skirts w/petticoats, the skirt features a 2" w. self-waistband that ties at either side of the waist, excellent condition, one small white spot in waistband, Mexico, late 1940s - early 1950s (ILLUS.). **$500.00**

1940s Wool Skirt Suit

Skirt suit, both pieces of lightweight wool, blue ground w/black vertical stripes & shadowed horizontal stripe creating a tiny plaid pattern, jacket features rounded collar w/pointed ends, shoulder pads, boxy cut in front, two sets of stand pockets, upstanding front part faced w/black velvet, brass buttons down center front, kimono-type long sleeves w/underarm gussets, turn-back cuffs, center back inverted pleat, tucks along back waistline, creating slight pulled-in effect at back waist, self-fabric belt loops at sides, jacket lined w/black rayon crepe; skirt w/slight pleats at one-inch-wide waistband, two small decorative flaps at side suggsting flap pockets, side zipper & single hook closures, jacket labeled "Saks Fifth Avenue," excellent condition, belt missing, the suit (ILLUS.) **$400.00**

1940s Skirt Suit in Black & Turquoise Crepe

Skirt suit, two-piece, the jacket/blouse of black rayon crepe w/slight padding at shoulders, tucks from shoulders to yoke w/small pointed lapels faced w/

turquoise crepe, turquoise also used as a decorative detail on the upper bodice alongside turquoise embroidery in a meandering pattern, turquoise crepe vestee panel attached w/snaps to the center front, three-quarter length sleeves, dropped waistline & peplum w/same turquoise decoration & embroidery; A-line skirt of black rayon crepe w/a narrow self-fabric belt, side zipper & single hook closure, jacked labeled "Martha Manning Original," excellent condition, buckle on belt missing, hemline shortened (ILLUS.)
.... **$150.00**

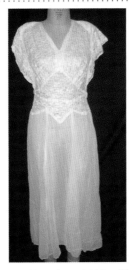

Late 1940s Lace & Nylon Slip

Slip, bodice of machine-made lace, V-neck, cap sleeves & gathers under bustline continuing to waistline, skirt of nylon tricot, side zipper, good condition, small shoulder pads possibly added later, two small holes near back zipper, some staining, ca. 1947 (ILLUS.)
.... **$85.00**

1940s Haftel Navy Blue Wool Suit

Skirt suit, two-piece navy blue wool, the jacket featuring a round Peter Pan collar, long slim-fitting kimono-style sleeves w/underarm gussets, turned-back cuffs faced w/blue satin, padded shoulders, two rows of self-fabric-covered buttons down center front, bound buttonholes, princess seams from shoulder to hem, nipped-in at waist creating slight drape at bust, bottom six-inch portion of jacket padded to create fullness at hips, lined throughout w/navy blue crepe; the skirt gored in contrasting navy satin (as used on cuffs) sewn to form a lattice pattern, side zipper & single hook closure, unlined, jacket labeled "Louis Haftel - Lincoln Road Miami Beach," excellent condition (ILLUS., previous page) **$450.00**

Skirt suit with beaded jacket, both jacket & skirt of navy blue worsted wool, jacket features shawl collar & meandering pattern of iridescent beading overall, attached capelet & down front center inset, four self-fabric-covered buttons, bound buttonholes, lined in blue rayon crepe, skirt of same fabric w/side zipper & button closure, unlined, darts from waistband down center & back, back slit, labeled "B. Altman & Co. - Fifth Avenue - New York," perfect condition, the outfit (ILLUS.) **$650-800**

MEN'S CLOTHING

Two Late 1940s Bathing Trunks

Bathing trunks, each wool, ribbed & w/a tab pocket, one in all-red & the other in blue w/a belt of webbing & goldtone metal slide buckle, late 1940s - early 1950s, mint condition, each (ILLUS. of two). **$125.00**

1940s Lady's Suit with Beaded Jacket

USAAF-Issue 1944 Eisenhower Jacket

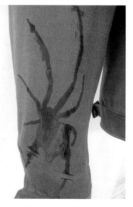

Close-up of Spider on Eisenhower Jacket

"Eisenhower" jacket, USAAF-issue, olive drab virgin wool gabardine w/epaulets, large chest patch pockets, banded waistline w/adjustable tabs at sides, full sleeves w/three-inch bands at buttoned cuffs, center front button closure w/covered placket, lined w/tan serge fabric, labeld "381," one sleeve later painted w/a large spider, good condition, some tearing to lining near neck, 1944 (ILLUS.) **$95.00**

1940s Motorcycle Jacket

Motorcycle jacket, black leather, probably cowhide, oversized snap lapels, angle-set zippered pockets, adjustable zippered sleeves, leather waist belt w/ grommets & metal buckle, epaulets w/snaps, lined in quilted rayon, front zipper closure, labeled "Kit Karson R - The Ideal Garment," excellent condition w/desirable leather aging (ILLUS.) **$300.00**

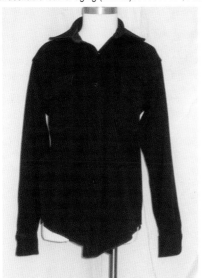

1940s Blue Wool Navy Shirt

Navy shirt, navy blue melton wool, anchor-embossed plastic buttons down center front & on patch pockets & cuffed sleeves, neck, placket & cuffs lined w/blue serge, labeled "C.P.O. Navy Shirt - A Melton Product," good condition, some discoloration & wear (ILLUS.)
. . . . **$95.00**

1940s Man's Cashmere Overcoat

Overcoat, 100% black cashmere, small collar & notched lapel, single-breasted w/large carved horn buttons down center front, diagonally-set off-seam welt pockets w/flaps faced w/gold satin, pockets chamois-lined, long full sleeves set-in at shoulder in front, raglan at back w/turn-back cuffs, faced w/gold satin, vent at center back hem, coat lined w/gold satin, one inside welt pocket at chest level edged w/gold satin, labeled "100% Imported Cashmere," good condition, one button missing, one small tear along seam at back vent, some wear to inside lining (ILLUS.) **$325.00**

1940s Man's Blend Shirt & Linen Pants

Shirt, orlon & woold blend w/contrasting tweed trim on
collar & chest patch pockets, button & loop closure
under neck w/buttons down center front, adjustable
buttoned cuffs, back shoulder yoke w/side box pleats,
labeled "Fox Men's Shop - Sherman Oaks, Calif.
- 65% Orlon-Wool 35% - Washable Trim," excellent
condition, one button broken at center front (ILLUS.
with linen trousers, previous page) **$85.00**

Late 1940s Three-tone Gabardine Sport Jacket

1940s Burgundy Wool Smoking Jacket

Smoking jacket, burgundy boiled wool w/contrasting
purple shawl collar & cuffs, w/accompanying purple
belt, excellent condition (ILLUS.) **$150.00**

Sports jacket, gabardine in three tones, beige for the
shoulder yoke, collar & lapels, light grey across the
chest & dark grey for the lower garment, single-
breasted & loose-bodied featuring three buttons
down the center front, large patch pockets at either
hip, upside-down stayed godet at back from shoulder
line to waist in beige gabardine w/decorative button
detail at the points, lined w/light blue lustrous twilled
fabric, labeled "Eton Hall Sportswear - Tailored on Fifth
Avenue," excellent condition, late 1940s - early 1950s
(ILLUS.) **$500.00**

Trousers, linen in sturdy tight weave, full-cut legs, pleats
from waist to cuffs, small slit pocket at waistband,
back welt pockets, 1" w. belt loops, button fly, excellent
condition (ILLUS. with orlon/wool blend shirt)
. . . . **$145.00**

CHAPTER 8: CLOTHING - 1950-1960

CHILDREN'S CLOTHING

1950s Plaid Cowgirl Outfit

Boy's Shorts Set with Separate Sweater

Shorts, shirt & sweater, boy's, blue & yellow seersucker shorts & matching shirt w/a hand-knit blue sweater, ca. 1950, sweater $20-25; shorts set (ILLUS.).... **$15-25**

Cowgirl outfit, vest & skirt of dark blue cotton plaid w/white suede fringe & appliqué, suede patch pockets on skirt, labeled "Trego's Westerner - Woodward, Oklahoma," good condition, some wear to suede fringe & appliqués (ILLUS.).................... **$95.00**

Girl's 1950s Pink Pinafore

Pinafore, pink w/blue ric-rac trim, 1950s (ILLUS.)
.... **$25-35**

1950s Checked Wool Suit & Shirt

Suit, two-piece, white & brown checked wool, jacket features welt pockets w/center button closure, lined w/light brown linen, cropped pants w/side button closure, back welt pockets, lined w/striped calico fabric, accompanying shirt of white cotton, labeled "A. Starr Best Chicago," excellent condition, includes long-sleeves white shirt, the outfit (ILLUS.) **$225.00**

Youth-Sized 1950s Western Shirt

Western shirt, girl's youth-sized, black rayon w/smooth weave, decorated w/white & silver embroidery of stars & horseshoes on the front, pearl snap center front closure & cuffs, angle-set slit pockets at chest, back yoke, labeled "H Bar C Ranchwear Washable - Exclusive Design," fair condition, fading to fabric (ILLUS.) **$150.00**

LADIES' CLOTHING

Late 1950s Candy-Striped Bathing Suit Ensemble

Bathing suit ensemble, all pieces of nylon, the bra-top w/a shaped bustline pieced in chevron stripes w/contrasting red & white striped trim, halter neck tie, center back closure; the short bolero jacket w/a spread collar & lapels, short cuffed sleeves w/a slight puff at shoulders, patch pockets at waist, worn open; the short flared skirt-style bottoms of 14 gored panels pieced in chevron stripes, 2" w. waistband, center back zipper & single button closure, trunks underneath of white nylon tricot, bottoms labeled "I. Magnin & Co.," excellent condition, trunks stained, late 1950s, the set (ILLUS.) **$350.00**

Two Views of a 1950s Bathing Suit & Skirt Ensemble

Bathing suit & skirt ensemble, glazed cotton multi-colored bathing suit & skirt in shades of deep purple, red, green & orange, the print depicting stylized feathers or leaves, the bathing suit features a boned corset top w/sweetheart & tucked neckline & convertible straps, high waistline & short skirt, center back zipper closure on dress, corset closes w/hooks & eyes, lined w/black rubberized fabric, accompanying skirt w/oversized patch pocket at center left, single cuttons & size zipper closure, good condition, attached bloomers/panties missing on suit (ILLUS. of suit alone & with the skirt) **$175.00**

1950s Red Nylon Bed Jacket

Bed jacket, double-ply red tricot nylon, Peter Pan collar w/red satin piping & wide satin ribbon w/flower embroidery detail, single-button & loop closure, labeled "Vanity Fair - Tricot All Nylon - Size Small," perfect condition (ILLUS.). **$20-30**

A Red and a White 1950s Marabou Feather Bed Jacket

Bed jacket, red marabou feathers, sewn in strips to an acetate shell, excellent condition (ILLUS. right with white marabou bed jacket) **$350.00**
Bed jacket, white marabou feathers, sewn in strips to an acetate shell, excellent condition (ILLUS. right with red marabou bed jacket). **$350.00**

A 1950s Black Bullet-style Bra & 1960s Black Cotton Lace Bloomers

Bra, bullet-style, satin-covered wire cups w/black tulle, rubberized fabric & elastic back, fastens w/hooks & eyes, labeled "Lilees by Lily of France - 32-33 - Bonwit Teller - New York, Boston," very good condition, some wear & fading on back strap (ILLUS. with 1960s black cotton lace bloomers) **$55.00**

Elaborate 1950s Silk Cape

Cape, stiff ivory silk faille faced w/faille in seafoam color, features a boned roll collar, trimmed w/meandering strands of braiding, beading, rhinestones & shells, front piece meets under neck & remainder cascades down sides in gentle curves continuing to very wide gored flare to floor, inverted pleat at center back, good condition, some discoloration, one small burn mark & hole at front (ILLUS.) **$1,800.00**

1950s Capri Pants & Blouse Outfit

Capri pants & blouse outfit, blouse of fine cotton w/floral print, labeled "Fabric by Liberty of London - 100% Cotton - Lady Hathaway - The Bermuda," excellent condition, $45-50; capri pants of peach glazed cotton, ankle vents, center back zipper, labeled "Best Mode of Miami," excllent condition, pants (ILLUS. of outift, previous page) **$65.00**

Group of Three 1950s Decorated Cardigan Sweaters

Cardigan sweater, cream wool blend decorated w/white & green beads & oversized white beads depicting grape clusters, white satin piping around neckline, cuffs & center, hook & eye closures, labeled "Windsor - 70% Lambswool 20% Angora 10% Nylon - Hand Decorated in Hong Kong B.C.C. - Size 40," excellent condition, some discoloration to label & around neck lining (ILLUS. left with two other decorated cardigan sweaters) **$275-300**

Cardigan sweater, green wool w/white beading depicting flowers, leaves & other details, green crocheted buttons, lined in green rayon, labeled "Alexanders - 100% Pure Wool - Fully Fashioned - Made in British Hong Kong - RN 14677 - Size 18," good condition, few loose beads (ILLUS. bottom right with two other beaded cardigan sweaters) **$150.00**

Cardigan sweater, ivory cashmere knit w/gold & silver beads, heavily beaded over shoulders, beaded center w/hanging clusters, white crepe lining, labeled "Size 36," perfect condition (ILLUS. bottom right with two other decorated cardigan sweaters) **$200-250**

Cardigan sweater, light blue wool blend knit completely covered w/iridescent clear sequins, hook & eye closure down center, light blue silk lining, labled "Oidar & Co. - 17, Cameron Rd. - Kowloon - Hong Kong - Size 40," good condition, discoloration to lining at armscyes & neck, separation of lining & body around neck (ILLUS. top right with two other decorated cardigan sweaters) **$150-175**

Grouping of Three 1950s Beaded Cardigan Sweaters

Cardigan sweater, pink acrylic knit w/black & metal beads depicting flowers & swirls, heavily beaded trim on cuffs, neckline & center, perfect condition (ILLUS. left with two other beaded cardigan sweaters) **$125.00**

Cardigan sweater, red wool knit w/white beaded flowers, stems & details, pearlized round red buttons, lined in red china silk, good condition, some beads missing & loose, two buttons missing (ILLUS. center with two other beaded cardigan sweaters) **$150.00**

1950s Hattie Carnegie Silk Taffeta Cocktail Dress

Cocktail dress, black silk taffeta w/horizontal ribbs, strapless bodice w/strategic folds of fabric over the bustline, attached net corset inside & boned at every seam w/hook & eye closure, self-fabric buttons down center front, full skirt tucked at high waistline & falling to lower knee, labeled "Hattie Carnegie," excellent condition (ILLUS.) **$2,800.00**

Heavily Shirred 1950s Black Taffeta Cocktail Dress

Cocktail dress, black taffeta heavily shirred throughout the fitted bodice, waist & hips, lined w/black tulle, a wide scoop neckline w/a narrow self-fabric bow at the center, cap sleeves, an 18" l. flounced tier beginning at upper thigh & continuing through the length of the dress w/same narrow self-fabric bow detail & faced w/black tulle for fullness, center back zipper closure, labeled "Suzy Perette New York," mid-1950s - early 1960s, excellent condition (ILLUS.) **$800.00**

1950s Black Taffeta Cocktail Dress

Cocktail dress, heavy black taffeta w/black ribbon crochet along the neck yoke & at tiered full skirt interspersed w/black velvet insertions, features modified cap sleeves & a fitted waist, center back zipper, excellent condition (ILLUS.) **$600.00**

Lovely Beaded 1950s Cocktail Dress

Cocktail dress, light tan strapless style w/beige organdy overlay, heavily beaded w/tiny white & pink square beads & loose beaded swags, features beaded high round neckline, long sleeves, illusion decolletage w/long pink beaded swag attached at center back neckline covering center back zipper, excellent condition (ILLUS.). **$500.00**

Two Views of a 1950s Cocktail Dress with Bustle

Cocktail dress, pink nylon taffeta w/bronze-colored lace overlay, wide scoop neck, cap sleeve, drop waist to a V, gently gathered skirt lined w/stiff tulle peticoat between overlay & underskirt, nylon taffeta sash of deeper pink & stiffer fabric starts under bust darts & wraps around to back cascading into two gathered layers of bustled taffeta, chevron tiered & attached at bottom hem to tulle petticoat in back, center back internal zipper & hook & eye closure, sash closes in back w/snaps, good condition, broken zipper (ILLUS. of front & side) **$600-750**

Lovely 1950s Christian Dior Satin Cocktail Dress

1950s Ivory Linen Day Dress

Cocktail dress, salmon-colored duchess satin, the bodice w/horizontal accordian pleating & a halter neck w/a self-fabric strap around the neck, a 5 1/2" w. waistband above the 33" l. sunburst pleated skirt, self-fabric-covered buttons down the center back stopping 18" from the hemline & revealing an inverted pleat running the length of the skirt, labeled "Christian Dior Original - Made in U.S.A. - Christian Dior - New York Inc.," excellent condition, four buttons missing, later strapless bra sewn into the bodice (ILLUS.) **$3,500.00**

Day dress, ivory linen w/slight V-neck, rounded modified shawl collar & sailor tie, drop-shoulder & slightly puffed sleeves w/bound cuffs, natural waistline continues to a box-pleated skirt, side zipper closure, labeled "Narcissa New York," excellent condition but zipper recent addition (ILLUS.) **$175.00**

Two 1950s Crinoline Underskirts

1950s Dress with Whimsical Color Print

Crinoline underskirts, both w/nylon tricot waists w/tiers of stiff nylon tulle, a pink one w/nylon tricot ruffles at bottom, a blue one w/blue lace trim, both excellent condition, each (ILLUS. of two). **$65-95**

Dress, black cotton printed in yellow, orange & brown w/whimsical dogs & their handlers, wide scoop neck & cap sleeves faced w/bright yellow cotton, high waistline & full skirt, side zipper closure, labeled "Cover Girl of Miami," good condition, some fading & discoloration (ILLUS.) **$85.00**

1950s Mohair Dress with Satin Neck Sash

Dress, black mohair shaped body w/extended & brushed nap, inverted high V-neckline, the back w/a lower inverted V, center back enclosed zipper, the under-blouse of heavy black charmeuse w/a wide attached self-fabric neck sash, dolman-style three-quarter length sleeves gusseted under the arms, excellent condition, sleeves reconstructed, hemmed shortened (ILLUS.) **$375.00**

A 1950s and 1960s Casual Dress

Dress, blue plaid cotton w/crochet lace trim around the collar, plastic buttons w/rhinestone in center down the front, self-fabric covered belt w/covered buckle, short sleeves, full embroidered skirt lightly gathered at waistline, labeled "Cut - 2975 - RN 13787 - 100% Cotton - Lot 716M - Size 12 - Fashioned for Mae-Moon and a Mission Valley Fabric - Wash and Wear - All Combed Cotton," perfect condition, never worn (ILLUS. left with 1960s sleeveless linen flower-print dress) **$65.00**

1950s Floral Asian-Influenced Dress

Dress, colorful floral print, straight-lined Asian-influenced style (ILLUS.) **$35-50**

1950s Navy Blue Dress with White Trim

Dress, navy blue w/white neckline embroidery & cord belt (ILLUS.) **$45-65**

1950s Embroiderd Black Cotton Dress

Dress, shirtwaist-style, crisp black cotton blend fabric, short sleeves, cream-colored flower embroidery on the front & back bodice, natural waistline continuing to a box-pleated full skirt, black beveled square plastic buttons down center front, excellent condition (ILLUS.)
.... **$350.00**

1950s Pink Shirtwaist Dress

Dress, shirtwaist-style, pink w/black buttons & tie (ILLUS.) **$35-55**

1950s Embroidered Cotton Shirtwaist Dress

Dress, shirtwaist-style, crisp white cotton blend fabric, short sleeves w/blue floral embroidery on the front bodice & back neckline surrounding an openwork lattice design, natural waistline continuing toa box-pleated full skirt, round abablone shell buttons down front center, excellent condition (ILLUS.) **$150.00**

1950s Printed Shirtwaist Dress

Dress, shirtwaist-style, stiff cotton printed w/tavern signs, oversized wooden buttons down center front, center back zipper, elbow-length sleeves w/elastic gather & self-fabric cord tie, pleated full skirt w/self-fabric-faced belt w/wood buckle, excellent condition, some repair to waistline seam (ILLUS.) **$40.00**

1950s Shirtwaist Dress with Necktie

Dress, shirtwaist-style w/necktie, charcoal gray rayon faille w/mustard yellow colored thread woven alternately throughout, kimono three-quarter length sleeves, turned-back cuffs, mustard yellow corduroy tie run through the neckline, wrapped buttons down center front, bound buttonholes, tucks at waistline giving way to fuller skirt, self-fabric belt w/buckle, labeled "An Irene Dare Casual," excellent condition (ILLUS.) **$350.00**

1950s Dress & Jacket Outfit in Two Views

Dress & jacket, both of lustrous fabric, perhaps a rayon blend, purple ground w/bright green & turquoise brocaded chrysanthemums & black leaves, sleeveless dress w/modified sweetheart neckline, bodice seamed for close fit, high waistline continuing to box-pleated straight skirt, slit at left side hem, center back zipper, dress lined w/black organdy; cropped jacket w/stand collar, elbow-length kimono-style sleeves w/underarm gussets, center front zipper closure w/self-fabric rose on tab, jacket lined w/black china silk, good condition, wear visible to fabric, fading at jacket shoulders, one small bodice stain, the set (ILLUS.) **$85.00**

Floral Print Dresses from the 1950s & 1960

Dress, very light green chintz ground printed overall w/large flowers & leaves in shades of purple, blue & dark green, wide scoop neckline, band of same fabric pieces at bodice, full skirt interlined w/nylon net, center back zipper, excellent condition (ILLUS. right with 1960s white nylon tricot with flower embroidered dress) **$95.00**

Gold Duchesse Satin Dress & Jacket Ensemble

Dress & jacket ensemble, both pieces of gold duchess atin, the sleeveless dress w/a scoop neckline, hook & eye closure at left shoulder & molded bustline w/diagonally set darts continuing to the high waistline distinguished by self-fabric piping, a gored A-line skirt w/side zipper, bodice lined w/gold organza & skirt lined w/gold linen, the cropped boxy jacket w/a rounded neckline & bracelet-length sleeves, self-fabric-covered oversized buttons & bound buttonholes, 4" w. band of brown mink fur along the hem, lined w/gold silk, labeled "Saks Fifth Avenue" & a union label, late 1950s -early 1960s, excellent condition, the set (ILLUS.) **$575.00**

Fine 1950s Balenciaga Dress & Wrap

Dress & shoulder wrap, designer-made, both pieces of warp-printed silk in greens varying from emerald to chartreuse w/red & pink flowers, top of dress wraps around waist to form a V-neck & attaches to side-zippered skirt w/snaps, elbow-length sleeved blouse gusseted under the arms, lined w/black silk chiffon, skirt of two overlapping panels gently gathered at waist, wraps w/self-fabric belt lined in nylon horsehair, shoulder wrap w/two self-buttons, labeled "Balenciaga - 10, Avenue George V - Paris," perfect condition (ILLUS.) **$5,000.00**

Dressing robe, cape-style, ivory cotton chenille, two shades of green trim, green palm trees w/brown trunks, tassel & cord tie at neck in same shades of green as trim, excellent condition, some fading to tassel & cord trim (ILLUS. right with red chenille robe) **$250.00**

Two 1950s Chenille Dressing Robes

Dressing robe, red cotton chenille in horizontal stripes across the body & sleeves, band of tulip pattern on sleeve cuffs & lower portion of robe, one patch pocket at centered hip & same corded tassel belt, good condition, some fading, belt shows some wear (ILLUS. left with cape robe) **$125-150**

1950s Ivory Satin Evening Coat

Evening coat, swing-style, ivory satin w/half-length sleeves w/black beaded cuffs (ILLUS.) **$45-65**

1950s Strapless Pink Chiffon Evening Gown

Evening gown, strapless, pink acetate lining w/blush pink colored chiffon overlay, features an asymmetrical bodice mostly beaded in loops & flowers w/tiny silver beads, pink prong-set rhinestones & pearls, the left breast covered w/horizontal tucks of chiffon w/attached gathered swath of fabric in a slightly lighter shade draping down the front & trailing on the floor, bodice finishes w/a V-waist asymmetrically set towards the right w/a full chiffon skirt gathered at the waistline, lined w/crisp pink acetate, left side zipper closure, labeled "Gothé New York," excelllent condition, one or two minor pulls in chiffon, some spotting to lining at hem (ILLUS.) **$1,500.00**

Lace-trimmed 1950s Formal

Formal dress, brown acetate, scoop neck w/overlay of soft brown tulle, swath of rhinestone-studded beige lace sewn just under actual neckline & draping slightly over shoulders, tucks of same tulle create surplice effect at neck, same lace used on normal waistling, gathered full skirt, side zipper closure, late 1950s, good condition, some discoloration to tulle (ILLUS.) **$200-400**

Two 1950s Formals in Excellent Condition

Formal dress, floor-length yellow acetate w/yellow lace overlay on boned bodice continuing to split peplum in front, full peplum in back, stiff yellow tulle covering remainder of skirt & same tulle gathered as trim on neckline & peplum bottom, side zipper closure, accompanying shrug of same lace, trimmed w/same gathered tulle, excellent condition (ILLUS. right with lavender & blue 1950s formal) **$275-400**

1950s Ivory Duchesse Satin Formal

Formal dress, heavy ivory duchesse satin, short bodice heavily beaded & sequined in a floral design, boned at every seam, lavender duchesse satin gathered to form wide straps & fashioned along w/same ivory satin to create a cummerbund-type sash, high waistline & full skirt, tucked at waist at intervals for fullness, center back zipper w/inside ties, gathered tulle underskirt, fair condition, some tearing & fraying of satin especially at bodice, staining at various points, late 1950s (ILLUS.) **$350-500**

Formal dress, lavender acetate strapless dress faced across modified boned bodice w/light blue nylon tricot, silver loop trimming & rhinestones, high waist w/silvery blue acetate fashioned into cummerbund sash & shirred in center & on either side, skirt features stiff light blue tulle overlay w/ruffled tiers of light blue nylon to hem, purposely frayed at edges, same light blue nylon tightly gathered to form ruffles around neckline, side zipper closure, labeled "AFL-CIO - In'l Ladies Garment Workers Union," excellent condition, few tiny spots under sashs (ILLUS. left with yellow 1950s formal, to the left of this column) **$400.00**

Lovely 1950s Duchess Satin Formal with Shrug

Formal with shrug, duchess satin w/sweetheart strapless neckline & sequins & beading overall, self-fabric beaded belt, bodice boned at every seam, grosgrain inner waist belt, side zipper closure, hem faced w/stiff tulle, fair condition, some discoloration, tearing in parts & some beads & sequins missing, the outfit (ILLUS., previous page) **$1,800.00**

1950s Satin & Velvet Hostess Gown

Hostess gown, black velvet bodice draped in back, blue satin quilted yoke & collar, dolman sleeves, full skirt of same quilted satin, velvet-wrapped buttons down center front of bodice, zipper closure down center front, labeled "Styled by Dorian," excellent condition (ILLUS.) **$525.00**

1950s Imitation Persian Lamb Coat with Rabbit Fur Collar

Jacket, black woolen fiber curled, tufted & sewn to fabric backing to imitate Persian lamb, rounded neckline w/ dark rabbit fur collar, single hidden snap closure under collar, three-quarter length sleeves, side slit pockets at either hip, lined w/black rayon twill, good condition, some wear to neckline (ILLUS.) **$195.00**

1950s Embroidered Mexican Jacket

Jacket, blue wool felt w/multi-colored yarn embroidery depicting Mexican life, made in Mexico, good condition, some wear to fabric, discoloration in parts (ILLUS.) **$120.00**

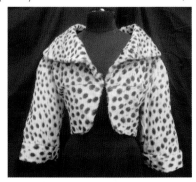

1950s Cheetah Fur Bolero Jacket

Jacket, bolero-style, cheetah fur, large collar, three-quarter-length wide sleeves & turned-back cuffs, single wrapped hook & eye closure at center front, lined in black satin, excellent condition (ILLUS. of front) **$2,200.00**

1950s Wool Jacket & 1970s Wool Poncho

Jacket, mustard yellow boiled wool w/black & white rayon yarn embroidery, unlined, labeled "Marnel - 100% Lana - Hecho en Mexico," excellent condition (ILLUS. right with 1970s wool poncho, previous page)
.... **$125.00**

1950s Black Jacket with Mink Collar

Jacket, narrow stips of black ridged ribbon crocheted & sewn in a swirl pattern, golden mink fur shawl collar w/set-in three-quarter length sleeves, single hook & eye closure just under collar, lined w/black crepe, scalloped edge hem, excellent condition (ILLUS.)
.... **$325.00**

Late 1950s Cotton Seersucker Jumpsuit

Jumpsuit/playsuit/romper, cotton blend seersucker fabric, white ground w/blue & green floral medallions, square neckline, sleeveless, twisted thread loops for accompanying belt at natural elasticized waistline continuing to the A-line skirt w/front & back inverted pleats revealing the split legs, center back zipper, labeled "Jean Roberts by Decatur Garment Co.," excellent condition, belt missing, late 1950s - early 1960s (ILLUS.) **$45.00**

Everyday Japanese Silk Kimono

Kimono, everyday-type, rinzu silk (woven in a geometric pattern) w/a bright floral design, inside w/bright red silk lining at the top & magenta silk below, scalloped red silk ribbon trim along the inside hem, 49" w. across shoulders, 56" l., Japan, mid-20th c., excellent condition (ILLUS.)..................... **$600.00**

Formal Japanese Kimono

Kimono, formal style apparently handstitched, of black silk crepe w/a painted design of flowers, cranes & a landscape, gold metallic threads 'couched' onto small carriages depicted on the bottom half, design continues into the inside of the gown, also five white circular crests, two on front, two on short sleeves & one in the back center, red silk lining, mid-20th c., 51 1/2" w. at shoulders, 58" l., excellent condition, some stitching on inside a bit loose (ILLUS.) **$400.00**

Reproduction of 1930s Party Dress

Party dress, reproduction of 1930s era dress possibly made in the 1950s, cream-colored satin, lined in similar white fabric, blue & cream-colored corded trim & self-fabric flowers w/rolled blue rosette appliqué overall, wide modified keyhole neckline, short sleeves w/slight flare, princess seams front & back, trained hem, center back zipper, excellent condition, one small pull to fabric in back (ILLUS.) **$295.00**

Two Views of a Short Japanese Kimono

Kimono, short loose knee-length garment of dark grey silk crepe w/grey & orange leaf & sprig design done in 'weft-ikat' technique, the interior w/a pictorial lining of birds & flowers, peach silk lining on sides & inside sleeves, Japan, mid-20th c., 38" w. across shoulders, 37" l., excellent condition, small spotting on inside lining (ILLUS. of front & back) **$275.00**

1950s Black Lace Peignoir Set

1950s Black Fur Muff

Muff, black long-haired fur, perhaps black-dyed fox, black satin lining & black silk cord handle, excellent condition, some stress visible to edge of muff opening (ILLUS.) **$150.00**

Peignoir set, black lace, the gown of black nylon tricot, black lace over beige tulle at bustline & deeply flounced gathered hem, black satin piping at empire waist, thin black ribbon drawstring, black satin leaf-shaped appliqués over bust & at points just under bustline, rhinestone trim; the robe of same black lace over double-ply beige tulle, deep V-neckline front & back, very full puffed & elasticized sleeves, black ribbon tie closure at empire waist, same black satin appliqués & rhinestone details, back lace sewn to top seam & then let loose to simulate watteau train, labeled "Lucie Ann Lingerie - Beverly Hills," excellent condition, late 1950s, the set (ILLUS.) **$600.00**

Peignoir set, red gown of double-ply nylon tricot, sleeveless w/slight cowl neck & rose appliqués, the red robe of single-ply nylon tricot w/puffed double-ply short sleeves w/elastic & ruffled trim, collar w/tucks, rose appliqués & red satin ribbon tie & single snap closure, labeled "100% Nylon - Exclusive of Trim - RN 19800 - Size Medium," good condition, discoloration to red ribbon, the set (ILLUS. left with blue peignoir set) **$95.00**

1950s White Nylon Tricot Peignoir Set

1950s Giselle Peignoir Set

Peignoir set, both pieces of white nylon tricot, the robe w/a lace-covered Peter Pan collar & raglan puffed sleeves; the gown w/a gathered bodice, princess waist & full skirt w/lace appliqué, excellent condition, 2 pcs. (ILLUS.) **$175.00**

Peignoir set, gown of very pale blue double-ply nylon tricot, sleeveless w/gathered & smocked yoke, lace trim & floral appliqués, robe of same double-ply nylon tricot, gathered & smocked yoke & shoulders w/lace trim & small floral appliqués, puffed short sleeves w/elastic & lace trim, single button & loop closure & self-fabric tie closure, labeled "Gotham - Gold Stripe - All Nylon - Exclusive of Decoration - RN 14447 - Size S," perfect condition, the set (ILLUS. right with red peignoir set) **$95.00**

Peignoir set, robe & gown of cream-colored nylon chiffon, both feature satin appliqué, gown w/satin straps, labeled "Giselle - Hecho en Cuba," good condition, some fraying to edges of inside seams, one very small hole in back of gown, the set (ILLUS.) **$400-500**

1950s-Style Flannel Poodle Skirt

Two 1950s Nylon Peignoir Sets

Poodle skirt, 1950s-style but created later, grey flannel circle skirt w/a felt & yarn poodle appliqué, complete w/wiggle eye, center back zipper closure, excellent condition (ILLUS.)...................... **$150.00**

Robe, ivory two-ply nylon w/ivory lace-covered puff sleeves & lace band around neckline, three lace-covered button & loop closures at neck, labeled "Vanity Fair - Made in U.S.A. - Nylon - Size 34," perfect condition by possibly missing matching nightgown (ILLUS. right with rose nylon robe, bottom this page)
.... **$55.00**

Labeled 1950s Schiaparelli Robe

Robe, pale pink nylon w/gathered neckline & loosely gathered sleeves, pink velvet ribbon & lace-trimmed yoke, ribbon belt, snap closure on bodice, hook & eye closure at waist, labeled "Schiaparelli - New York," perfect condition (ILLUS.)............... **$150.00**

Mint Green Satin Robe

Two 1950s Delicate Nylon Robes

Robe, mint green satin of rayon & silk blend, featuring a square neckline w/lace insertion & at high waistline, tucked bodice & long skirt, elbow-length sleeves slightly puffed at shoulders tapering to ruffled cuffs, tiny pearlized buttons at center front waist, labeled "By Iris - 38 - 'Bemberg' Rayon and Silk," ca. 1950, good condition, some fading to fabric along left sleeve & other places, accompanying gown missing (ILLUS.)
.... **$150.00**

Robe, quilted rose nylon, shaped double-ply red tricot nylon, shaped 'New Look' silhouette w/wasp waist & full skirt, princess seaming, center zipper & satin bow, Peter Pan collar, slit pockets at hips, labeled "Evelyn Pearson - Lounging Apparel - Size 10," excellent condition (ILLUS. left with ivory nylon robe) . . . **$75.00**

1950s Beige Net Shell with Sequins & Beading

Shell, beige net w/iridescent beige sequins, pink beads & pearl beads overall, lined w/beige acetate, center back zipper, fair condition, one large tear to net at one shoulder, some discoloration to lining (ILLUS.)
.... **$25.00**

1950s Shorts & Blouse Outfit

Shorts & blouse outfit, blouse of nylon seersucker w/pearlized buttons down center front, excellent condition, $45-50; cotton seersucker shorts w/"Hubba Hubba" print of dancing couples, button side closure, good condition, some discoloration to fabric at waist, shorts (ILLUS. of outfit) **$125-150**

1950s Knitted & Beaded Shell

Shell, black knitted wool & acrylic blend, sleeveless, decorated overall w/black beaded loops & swags & dangling strands of black faceted beads, center back zipper closure, excellent condition (ILLUS.)
.... **$150.00**

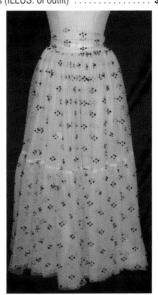

1950s Yellow Dotted-Swiss Wrap Skirt

Skirt, wrap-type, bright yellow dotted-Swiss veiling w/flocked dots in four colors - magenta, blue, green & black, lined in same bright yellow tulle, self-fabric flocked tie w/exaggerated flounced hem backed in unflocked dotted-Swiss, perfect condition (ILLUS.)
.... **$800.00**

1950s Quilted Skirt & Blouse Outfit

1950s Zuckerman Wool Skirt Suit

Skirt & blouse outfit, polyester crepe blouse w/ openwork at neck, short sleeves & center back buttons, excellent condition, $48; cotton skirt w/colorful patchwork print, additionally hand-quilted, side zipper & single button closure, excellent condition, skirt (ILLUS. of the outfit) **$70.00**

Skirt suit, both pieces of red wool in a boucle weave, cropped jacket w/stand-up collar w/extended ties to know or bow as a flourish, set-in long sleeves, front w/long slimming seams, double-breasted w/staped 'pebbled' pink buttons, lined w/red china silk; the pencil skirt w/a narrow waistband & side zipper closure, lined w/red china silk, jacket labeled "Ben Zuckerman New York" & a union label, excellent condition, the set (ILLUS.) **$500.00**

Late 1950s Dior Wool Skirt Suit

Skirt suit, both pieces of grey wool, the short slim-fitting jacked w/a small collar & lapel, oversized buttons & bound buttonholes down the center front, decorative flaps high on the waist suggesting pockets, long sleeves, back buttoned waistbelt & side vents, lined w/grey silk; the straight skirt w/tiny tucks under 1" w. waistband, center back zipper & hook closure, lined w/grey silk, jacket labeled "Christian Dior-New York - Marsal Park Avenue," good condition, some wear to lining, two tiny wear holes on front, late 1950s - early 1960s, the set (ILLUS.). **$475.00**

1950s Rose Pink Woolen Skirt Suit

Skirt suit, two-piece, dusty rose woolen material w/a slight nap, coat w/a modified shawl collar w/rhinestone & white & grey beading, covered buttons down the center front, padded shoulders & kimono-style bracelet-length sleeves tapering to beaded cuffs, slight padding at the hips & curved patch pockets;

the mid calf-length pencil skirt w/a deep slit on the left side, jacked lined w/pink crepe, labeled "Fred A Block Original Fabric - Made in France by Lesure - #117039," early 1950s, fair condition, missing one button, small stains on both pieces (ILLUS.)
. . . . **$275.00**

1950s Skirt & Sweater Ensemble

Skirt & sweater ensemble, red orlon sweater w/ scattered flower & leaf-shaped sequins & beads, center front buttons, labeled "Hi Bulk Orlon - Dupont Acrylic Fiber," good condition, minor pilling of yarn, $85; black taffeta skirt w/three-dimensional roses & black velvet leaf appliqué, side zipper closure & two carved buttons at top, excellent condition, skirt (ILLUS. of the ensemble). **$200.00**

1950s Two-Tone Full Slip

Slip, full-type, two-tone, a bodice of beige nylon satin w/chiffon tucks across neckline & lace edging, slight V-waist yoke, brown satin skirt w/tucked chiffon flounce & black lace trim, labeled "Barbizon - Camifair - Lyon - Satin - Sylfaire," excellent condtion (ILLUS.) . **$45-60**

1950s Lady's Sports Shorts by MacGregor

Sport shorts, thick royal blue fabric w/satin finish, sailor pant styling w/button closures at either side, black football-shapped toggles at waist, labeled "MacGregor Goldsmith - Cincinnati Ohio U.S.A. - Size 30," good condition, some fabric wear, one toggle missing & replaced w/brass button (ILLUS.). **$55.00**

Labeled 1950s Embroidered Sun Dress

Sun dress, composed of eight panels of white bark cloth ground w/light blue flower embroidery w/green stems & leaves, flower appliquéd straps over ivory muslin, tight bodice & full skirt, center back zipper, labeled "Tina Leser Original," excellent condition (ILLUS.)
. . . . **$500.00**

1950s Convertible Printed Silk Sun Dress

Sun dress, convertible, printed china silk in shades of cream, orange, yellow & plum depicting Aztec designs in horizontal bands, boned bodice lined w/cream-colored faille & featuring shirring over the bustline & convertible straps, attached by hooks & eyes at the front that, when removed, fall down back of the dress & bodice becomes strapless, center back zipper, high waistline w/a gathered full skirt, very good condition, some small tears to straps, some areas repaired (ILLUS.) **$600.00**

1950s Red Cotton Plaid Sun Dress

Sun dress, red cotton plaid, wide shoulder straps (ILLUS.) **$30-50**

1950s Black Long-sleeved Sweater

Sweater, black long-sleeve style w/beaded trim (ILLUS.) **$35-65**

1950s Sleeveless Sequined Sweater

Sweater, sleeveless, overall silvered sequins decorated w/scattered embroidered flowers, made in Hong Kong (ILLUS.) **$40-60**

Black Catalina Brand Swimsuit

Two Views of an Ornate Japanese Wedding Kimono

Swimsuit, black skirt-style, Catalina brand w/'flying fish' label, ca. 1950 (ILLUS., previous page) **$45-55**

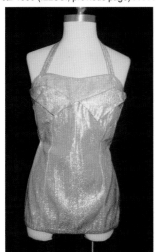

1950s Silver Lamé Swimsuit

Swimsuit, silver lamé, stiff nylon knit w/silver thread, bone-lined bodice, adjustable halter neck fastened w/buttons, center back zipper, apron front w/attached bathing tucks of same fabric, excellent condition (ILLUS.) **$275.00**

Wedding kimono, silk satin worn as an outer wrap for the ceremony, embroidered peony floral designs in white, lilac & various shades of pink starting at the back & continuing over the garment, additional adornment using the 'shusu' technique using metallic yars placed side by side to resemble brocade, the lining & hem padding in red silk, Japan, mid-20th c., 51" w. at shoulders, overall 67" l., good condition,

small stains on lining & collar, small tears in lining (ILLUS. of two views, top of page) **$1,200.00**

Western pants, 1960s lightweight grey & black-striped gabardine, high-waisted, full legs tapering at cuffs, pearl snaps at slit pockets on front & at back flap pockets, single button & zipper fly, lining at waistband, labeled "H Bar C Ranchwear," excellent condition (ILLUS. with 1950s red garbardine Western shirt) **$200-250**

Embroidered 1950s Lady's Western Shirt

Western shirt, beige garbardine w/contrasting front & back yoke & cuffs in dark brown & contrasting piping in white, snap center front placket & cuffs, angle-set slit pockets at chest, chain-stitched embroidery of steer heads & cacti on the front & back, darts at waist ensure close fit, labeled "Connie Sportswear - Denver," excellent condition (ILLUS.) **$400.00**

MEN'S CLOTHING

Fancy 1950s Lady's Western Shirt

Western shirt, green rayon gabardine w/traditional front & back yoke & contrasting yellow piping, snap center front placket & cuffs, elaborate sequin appliqués depicting peacocks & flowers in shades of fuchsia, yellow, green & blue, darts at front & back ensure close fit, very good condition, some fraying at hem, some fabric fading (ILLUS.) **$600-650**

1950s Men's Plaid Flannel Bathrobe

Bathrobe, red & black flannel in a tartan plaid design, shawl collar & turn-back cuffs, w/a matching belt, labeled "Luxurobe," excellent condition (ILLUS.)
. . . . **$55.00**

Lady' Western Outift with 1950s Shirt & 1960s Pants

Western shirt, red rayon gabardine w/black front & back yoke & cuffs, contrasting beige piping, leather applique & chainstitch embroidery, yokes w/angle-set slit pockets & trimmed w/beige fringe, pearl snap center front closures & cuffs, labeled "H Bar C Randwear - Washable - 14," good condition, wear visitble to fringe & appliques (ILLUS. with 1960s grey striped pants)
. . . . **$500.00**

Two Views of a Late 1950s Green Bowling Shirt

Bowling shirt, Kelly-green cotton w/convertible collar, short sleeves, two patch breast pockets w/"Al" embroidered over the left one, center front buttons, shoulder yoke at back w/pleats at sides & a large

round center white applique w/black flocked letters &
a race car marked "Concourse 41 - MCRC," labeled
"The Lanor Bowling Shirt - Made in Canada," excellent
condition, some wear to flocked letters, late 1950s
(ILLUS. of two views) **$150.00**

Hawaiian Shirts from the 1950s, 1960s & 1970s

Very Elaborate Black Velvet & Gold Braid Coat

Coat, below knee-length, of black velvet elaborately
decorated overall w/gold soutache braid in varying
widths in meandering & swirl design, red velvet stand-
up band collar trimmed w/gold braid, 3" w. red velvet
waistband, brushed gold flat buttons down the center
front w/hidden buttonholes, lined w/brown & beige
striped calico fabric, neck & shoulder area reinforced
w/blue & white striped canvas duck, possible part
of a guard's uniform, excellent condition, some
discoloration to red velvet & lining, some buttons
missing, mid-20th c. (ILLUS.) **$2,200.00**

Hawaiian shirt, lustrous cotton w/bold geometric & leaf
orange print, center button front closure, excellent
condition (ILLUS. bottom front with two other Hawaiian
shirts) **$85.00**

Jacket, souvenir-type, rayon satin w/a yellow satin
collar, sleeves, waistband & pocket flaps, the body of
blue satin w/breast patch pockets, blue cuffs w/satin-
covered buttons, center front buttons behind the
placket, embroidery down the sleeves, at hip level &
on the back, the back w/a large head of a tiger below
"Japan," fair condition, considerable wear to sleeves
w/fabric shredding & holes, early 1950s (ILLUS. of
front & back, bottom of page) **$850.00**

Front & Back Views of a 1950s Japanese Souvenir Jacket

1950s Man's Long-sleeved Pink Shirt

Shirt, long-sleeved, deep pink w/embroidered stylized sprig band, ca. 1950 (ILLUS.). **$35-55**

1950s Smock-style Cotton Shirt

Shirt, smock-style, cotton, gray ground w/yellow floral & graphic print, yoke buttons to body of shirt at neckline, one patch chest pocket, tucks at back yoke, excellent condition w/slight fading (ILLUS.). **$65-85**

1950s Wide-Striped Shirt

Shirt, textured cotton, in shades of blue alternating w/ wide stripes of brown weave & black & grey pinstripes, convertible collar, left breast patch pocket, long

sleeves w/adjustable buttoned cuffs, shoulder yoke, plastic buttons down center front, straight hem. side vents, labeled "Saks Fifth Avenue A - S," & fabric care label, excellent condition (ILLUS.) **$120.00**

1950s Red Silk Sports Jacket

Sports jacket, woven red silk w/slubs of black silk yarn, narrow collar & lapels, patch pocket at chest & large patch pockets at either hip, three filigreed goldtone metal buttons down the center front w/two smaller decorative buttons at the sleeve cuffs, center back vent, partially lined w/striped foulard, labeled "Sunshine Fashion Clothes - Burdine's Store For Men - All Pure Silk - Needled by Hand," excellent condition, mid-1950s (ILLUS.). **$95.00**

Late 1950s Charcoal Grey Wool Suit

Suit, two-piece, charcoal grey 100% virgin wool, jacket w/normal width lapels, patch pocket at right chest & large patch pockets at each hip, two-button closure, four decorative buttons at cuffs, lined w/very high quality thick textured black satin, three slip pockets inside lining; trousers w/narrow waistband & belt loops,

pleats from waist to tapered hem, no cuffs, angle-zippered fly, top lined w/same thick black satin, inside buttons at waist front & back for suspenders, jacket labeled "Forstmann - 100% Virgin Wool," late 1950s - early 1960s, excellent condition, the set (ILLUS.)
. . . . **$390.00**

1950s Blue Gabardine Two-Piece Suit

Suit, two-piece, light blue gabardine w/subtle slubs of red & darker blue, the jacket w/a narrow collar & lapels, single patch breast pocket, two oversized patch pockets at hips, single-breasted w/two-button closure at center front, decorative buttons on cuffs, unlined; the trousers feature narrow belt loops, no waistband w/pleats running the length of the leg, on-seam slit pockets at hips, back welt pockets, tapered legs w/cuffs at hem, zippered fly, jacket labeled "M-H Clothes of Distinction," very good condition, some age darkening to seams & around pockets & jacket cuffs (ILLUS.) **$500.00**

Suit, two-piece, thin brown textured fabric, jacket features narrow lapels & three button closure, single center back vent, stand pocket at right chest, two flap pockets at hips, acetate-lined only at sleeves & front, back unlined & slightly transparent; pants lined only at waistband, pockets, fly & crotch, pleats from waist to hem, no cuffs, two welt seam pockets at hips, to welt buttoned pockets at back, single hook closure & zippered fly, narrow belt loops, jacket labeled "Styled For Carriage Trader - Palm Beach - Browning King & Co., Inc.," & fabric care label, good condition, perhaps some fading, the set (ILLUS.) **$150.00**

1950s Alpine-Style Wool Sweater

Sweater, alpine-style, mostly beige wool w/a blue & red snowflake design across the shoulders & down the sleeves, black knit placket w/pewter clip closures, excellent condition (ILLUS.) **$95.00**

A 1950s and 1970s Varsity Jacket

Varsity jacket, green boilded wool w/cream-colored leather sleeves & pocket edging, acryllic knit collar, cuffs & waist, lined w/green lustrous fabric, center front snap closure, labeled "Timberline by Bill Bros. - Milwaukee - Size 44," good condition, some discoloration to sleeves, tearing to lining (ILLUS. left with 1970s varsity jacket) **$150.00**

1950s Man's Brown Two-Piece Suit

CHAPTER 9: CLOTHING - 1960-1970

CHILDREN'S CLOTHING

1960s Girl's Blue Tulip-Printed Dress

Dress, little girl's, acetate & nylon w/a blue ground w/red & white tulip print, contrasting fabric of red w/white polka dots used as an insertation at the waistline, self-fabric belt & tiered sleeves, slight V-neck, center back zipper, labeled "Junior Petites PBJ" & a fabric care label, excellent condition (ILLUS.) **$22.00**

Teenage Girl's Plaid Pajama Set

Pajama set, teenage girl's outfit, a camisole top & bloomers, both of nylon tricot printed w/pink & white plaid design, camisole features a gathered bustline w/three-inch wide waistband & spaghetti straps, bloomers w/elasticized legs & self-ruffled trim, labeled "Carter's- Nylon Tricot - 11 - Junior Figure," excellent condition, perhaps some faint fading to fabric, ca. 1960 (ILLUS.) **$35.00**

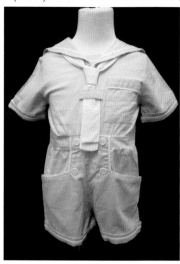

1960s Little Boy's Sailor Suit

Sailor suit, light blue cotton, white tie, white piping, elasticized waist & button center back, excellent condition (ILLUS.). **$65.00**

1960s Child's Norwegian Sweater

Sweater, Norwegian-made, knit of wool yarns, white ground w/navy blue collar & placket, yoke & hem depicting reindeer, snowflakes & geometric shapes, carved pewter buttons down center front, labeled "Made in Norway," excellent condition w/slight yellowing to white wool (ILLUS.). **$175.00**

LADIES' CLOTHING

Labeled 1960s Bathing Suit

Bathing suit, cotton faille w/black "lace" overlay, convertible self-fabric straps button in back, built-in bra, lined & seamed without boning, extensive shirring at back sides w/center back zipper, elasticized attached panties under trunks, self-fabric rolled tie at back, labeled "Rose Marie Reid," excellent condition (ILLUS.) **$110.00**

Bathing suit (maillot) & skirt ensemble, both pieces of cotton printed w/abstract rendering of fish scales in three shades of green w/black outlining & including the facsimile signature of Emilio Pucci in places, swimsuit bodice fitted w/boning & a generous amount of elasticized ruching on each side, side zipper &

neckline w/thin self-strap tie around neck, center bow, ending in a box-pleated mini-skirt w/attached elasticized modified trunks underneath, long, full skirt w/seams running circularly around the underside for larger skirt protrusion, double wrap w/center bow & box pleats, size 12, labeled "Emilio Pucci - Florence Italy - Made in Italy - 100% pure cotton," excellent condition, never worn, ca. 1960, the ensemble (ILLUS. of ensemble & swimsuit). **$2,000.00**

Bloomers, black cotton lace w/black lace ruffled bands overall, elastic waist & legs, labeled "Fashions by Ludmilla - Geo. Debs of Calif. - SM," excellent condition (ILLUS. in two views with 1950s bullet-style black bra) **$28.00**

1960s Paisley Pattern Blouse

Blouse, rayon w/multi-colored paisleys, carved plastic buttons down center front, notch collar, labeled "Made by Janie in California," excellent condition (ILLUS.) **$65.00**

Two Views of a Designer Bathing Suit - Skirt Ensemble by Emilio Pucci

1960s Nylon Brunch Coat

Brunch coat, ivory nylon acetate w/black lace overlay, satin piping around neckline, empire waisted in front w/peach-colored satin ribbon through gathered lace sleeve, plastic & rhinestone buttons down center front, labeled "Ohrbach's Leisure Shop - Lot 17 - Small," good condition, some staining to lining around neckline (ILLUS.) **$85.00**

1960s Long Black Wool Jersey Coat

Coat, floor-length, black wool jersey w/a high band 'Nehru'collar, slim fit, long fitted sleeves, large white plastic buttons down the front on the left, lined w/black acetate, labeled "Bonwit Teller - Lew Prince of Aldrich. - Size 10," & fabric care label, excellent condition, buttons replaced (ILLUS.)............... **$125.00**

Two 1960s Faux Fur Coats

Coat, faux fur cape-style of acrylic flat pile, green knit lining, two slash openings for arms at waist, three hidden snap closures at neck, labeled "Mr. Blackwell Design- Dry Clean Only," excellent condition (ILLUS. left with other faux fur coat) **$400.00**

Coat, faux leopard fur in acrylic pile, oversized buttons down center front, long sleeves lined in black satin, labeled "Styled by Russel Taylor - Clean by Fur Method," excellent condition (ILLUS. right with other faux fur coat) **$200.00**

Fine Pauline Trigere Coat & Dress Ensemble

Coat & dress ensemble, both pieces of brocaded fabric w/a black ground decorated overall w/gold spheres; the dress features a wide scoop neck, long sleeves tapering to snap cuffs, tucks high on bustline achieving a smock-style effect continuing to the full bodice & skirt w/an 18" l. straight-cut bottom tier, center back zipper, lined w/sheet black organdy, accompanying belt of same fabric w/fabric-covered buckle & hidden hook closure faced w/black cotton faille; the swing-style coat w/a 2 3/4" w. stand-up collar structured underneath

w/wire for support & overlap hidden hooks & eyes
& single oversized wrapped button closure, raglan
bracelet-length sleeves, a 2" w. padded band at upper
thigh level continuing to 18" l. straight-cut bottom tier,
lined w/black knit jersey, labeled "Pauline Trigere,"
excellent condition, the set (ILLUS.) $1,200.00

Bill Blass Designer Coat & Purse

Coat & purse/muff combination, coat of ivory duck
w/multi-colored paisleys & patterns in mainly shades
of red w/some yellows, greens, blues & black trim,
empire waist seam, concealed large snap center front
closure, two slash pockets; pouch-style purse faced
w/same fabric, reverse in black w/ottoman rib in two
shades of grey, same on top of purse for trim & to
serve as sleeve to hold mauve corded drawstring,
inside lined in slate blue rayon weave, one zippered
compartment, muff section on sides of purse faced
w/maroon-colored satin, labeled "Bill Blass for Bond
Street," late 1960s, both pieces excellent condition,
the set (ILLUS.) $1,200.00

Cocktail Dress with "Petaled" Skirt

Cocktail dress, beige silk, twilled w/satin finish, sleeveless
w/sweetheart neckline at front, lower V-neckline at
back, fitted bodice, seamed but not bonded, natural
waistline, pannier skirt w/applied "petal" shapes beaded
& trimmed w/gold twilled satin emanating from waistline
in graduating lengths, shortest in front continuing to
longest at back, finished by overlapping at center back,
held in place by hidden snaps, straight skirt underneath
w/slit at center back hem, center back hidden zipper,
labeled "Distinctive Apparel Park Shop- 33 Lincoln
Road, Bklyn. N.Y.," good condition, some discoloration
to fabric, some beads missing (ILLUS.). $650.00

1960s Black Chiffon Cocktail Dress

Cocktail dress, bodice of ivory faille w/black chiffon
overlay decorated w/small black square paillettes,
bateau neckline, gusseted armscyes, high waistline
w/self-fabric piping, skirt of black semi-lustrous fabric
w/fine black slubs, lined w/black acetate, center back
zipper, labeled "An Original Junior Vogue New York," &
unioin label, excellent condition (ILLUS.) $275.00

Blue Chiffon Cocktail Dress, Ca. 1960

Cocktail dress, dusty blue sleeveless design w/minutely tucked chiffon bodice, self-fabric piping at rounded neckline & armscyes, 4" w. mauve satin insertion at high waistline w/side bow finish & trailing endsd, purple acetate full skirt w/tucked chiffon overlay, bodice lined w/fine blue net, center back zipper, labeled "R & K Originals," excellent condition, some fading to satin insertion & bow, ca. 1960 (ILLUS., previous page) **$275.00**

1960s Royal Blue Satin Cocktail Dress

Cocktail dress, royal blue satin sleeveless design w/4" w. self-fabric garduated straps creating a severe V-neckline in front, blending into a scoop neckline & yoke in back, the front continuing to an Empire waist w/a large self-fabric bow at the center, bell-shaped skirt w/small tucks at waistline front & back, hidden zipper at center back, lined w/mauve-colored acetate, labeled "B. Altman & Co. - Fifth Avenue New York," good condition, moderated discoloration to armscyes (ILLUS.) **$300.00**

1960s Blue Brocade Cocktail Dress

Cocktail dress, sleeveless blue brocade, ca. 1960 (ILLUS.) **$35-55**

1960s Burgundy Cocktail Dress

Cocktail dress, sleeveless burgundy dress w/bateau neckline, velvet-covered bustline lined w/satin, 6" w. chiffon-covered waist horizontally tucked & continuing to a barrel-shaped skirt also chiffon-covered & sewn in swags creating three thiers w/brown velvet bows & gathered rolled hemline, side zipper closure, skirt lined w/acetate w/nylon net overlay, excellent condition, bows need freshening up (ILLUS.) **$650.00**

1960s Paisley Print Day Dress

Day dress, silk w/a multi-colored paisley-style print in shades of teal blue, pink, cream & lavender, mini-Chinese collar that falls into a V opening at center front, small self-fabric sleeves, skirt falls at natural waist & is gathered for fullness, zipper closure at right side, self-fabric loops on waist for belt, labeled "Linda Howard, Portland Square, New York, London W.I," fair condition, small stain on bodice, some stitching loose on sleeves, small holes (ILLUS.) **$60.00**

1960s Apricot 'Baby Doll' Dress

Dress, 'baby-doll' style, apricot acetate sleeveless dress w/apricot-colored chiffon overlay, the bodice featuring strips of embroidered chiffon around the square neckline & empire waistline, bishop sleeves made from sturdier organdy w/insertions of the same embroidered chiffon running vertically, band of the same lace over acetate just above the elbows, lower length of sleeves faced w/stiff tulle for fullness & tapering to elastic cuffs, skirt of dress tucked under the waistband for fullness, center back zipper w/a white gros-grain ribbon bow, mid- to late 1960s, good condition, minor tears to chiffon (ILLUS.). **$175.00**

Fine 1960s Emilio Pucci Black Dress

Dress, black semi-sheer jersey w/a high rounded neckline & bracelet-length sleeves, slim fit dress falls to lower knee, center back zipper, accompanying belt

of self-fabric rolled cord w/end tassels of charcoal grey glass beads, labeled "Emilio Pucci - 8 - Florence-Italy - Made in Italy - Made in Italy Especially for Saks Fifth Avenue" & a fabric care label, ca. 1968, excellent condition (ILLUS.). **$400.00**

1960s Anne Fogarty Black Jersey Dress

Dress, black woolen jersey, V-neckline, kimono-style slim-fitting long sleeves w/self-fabric-covered ball & loop closures down the bottom length of the sleeves, gored sides for extra fullness & swing, center back zipper, labeled "Anne Fogarty" & fabric care label, very good condition, minimal pilling to fabric (ILLUS.)
. . . . **$400.00**

Late 1960s Jeweled Dress

Dress, bodice of black polyester knit, mock-turtle neck w/slight gathers under stand-up collar to form soft drapes, sleeveless, center back zipper, the full skirt of piled fabric in oranges, fuschias, blues & black, cabochon-cut "stones" on wide waistband, skirt lined in black acetate, perfect condition, late 1960s (ILLUS., previous page) **$175.00**

Asymmetrical Trigere Black Crepe Dress

Dress, bodice of black woolen crepe, high neck & long sleeves tapering to zippered cuffs, shoulder pads, asymmetrical seam at center right, asymmetrical bottom tier of black taffeta w/asymmetrically set center swath & wide scalloped hem, center back zipper, labeled "Pauline Trigere," mid- to late 1960s, good condition, some snags to crepe & spotting to taffeta tier (ILLUS.) **$600.00**

Oscar de La Renta Bohemian-style Dress

Dress, Bohemian-style, heavy black cotton in reverse brocade forming an overall design of chevron stripes, features a V-neckline w/a scant 2" w. embroidered trim in shades of blue, orange & yellow, the trim continuing

on the waist belt, closes w/hooks & eyes, the gathered skirt w/a natural waistline w/the same embroidered trim down the sides & along the hemline, hidden zipper center back, lined w/black acetate, labeled "Oscar de La Renta boutique," excellent condition, late 1960s - early 1970s (ILLUS.). **$450.00**

1960s Floral Brocade Dress

Dress, brocade fabric w/a black background decorated w/stylized blue & grey flowers, bateau neckline, three-quarter-length sleeves, self-box at raised waistline w/a deep inverted pleat continuing to the hemline at center front, center back zipper closure, excellent condition (ILLUS.) **$125.00**

1960s Brown Tweed Dress

Dress, brown tweed fabric, wide tucked neckline w/roll-over collar, modified raglan short sleeves, natural waistline & two decorative buttoned flaps suggesting pockets, straight skirt, center back zipper w/kick-pleat at hemline, excellent condition (ILLUS.) **$65.00**

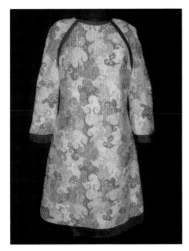

1960s Ribbed Dress with Metallic Threads

Dress, fabric w/raised ribs, woven w/metallic threads in places, fanciful swirl design in shades of pink, purple, greens, blue & yellow, raglan sleeves w/flared cuffs, purple shantung silk trim on neckline, cuffs, hem & used to delineate raglan seams on both front & back, center back zipper, lined w/light green rayon, late 1960s - early 1970s, excellent condition, lining shows signs of wear (ILLUS.) **$45.00**

1960s Courreges Striped Dress

Dress, fine silky cotton w/navy blue & white stripes, square neckline trimmed w/contrasting white trim, short sleeves slightly gathered at shoulders, trimmed w/same contrasting fabric, also used on stand pockets at lower center front, asymmetrical left side closure w/blue & white plastic buttons, labeled "Courreges Paris - Made in France" & fabric care label, late 1960s - early 1970s, excellent condition, one orange mark on front near buttons (ILLUS.) **$85.00**

Designer Peasant Dress by Geoffrey Beene

Dress, gypsy- or peasant-style, silk w/an orange ground w/stylized flowers in shades of yellow, green, pink & black, low scoop neckline & unlined bodice, five pairs of orange grommets & self-fabric cording to lace-up, empire waistline, gently gathered long skirt lined in ivory-colored organza & ending in a doubled flounced tier, fitted armhole & sleeve also ending in a double flounced cuff, low scoop back, center back zipper w/hook & eye closure, labeled by Geoffrey Beene, late 1960s, perfect condition (ILLUS.) **$1,500-1,800**

1960s Geoffrey Beene Black Crepe Dress

Dress, heavy black crepe w/a high rounded neckline extending to a bib-like swatch over the bodice, buttoned to the waistline w/large black plastic buttons attached to self-fabric vinyl-backed belt, bracelet-length sleeves zippered at turn-back cuffs w/ decorative buttons, high waistline w/a full skirt slightly tucked at waistline, side slit pockets, center back zipper, lined w/black organza, inner gros-grain waist belt w/hook & eye closure, labeled "Geoffrey Beene - Saks Fifth Avenue," excellent condition (ILLUS. previous page) **$800.00**

Dress, light green lace w/a large round lace collar falling over a green satin stand collar at neck, oversized green satin bow attached high at neckline, long slim-fitting sleeves w/lace flounce at cuff & snap closure, self-fabric-covered buttons & loop closure down center back, lined w/nude-colored nylon tricot, unlined sleeves, mid- to late 1960s, excellent condition (ILLUS.) **$225.00**

1960s Navy Blue Dress

Late 1960s Emilio Pucci Dress with a Bold Design

Dress, jersey fabric in shades of brown & beige w/blue & chartreuse accents in a bold stylized leaf & vine design & the facsimile signature "Emilio" in places, slim-fitting long sleeves, self-padded rolled neckline & belt, slit fit to lower knee of skirt, center back zipper, Emilio Pucci, excellent condition, 1968 (ILLUS.). **$750.00**

Dress, navy blue w/ivory piqué contrasting facing at collar, self-fabric bow high on neckline, three large blue decorative buttons, gusseted short sleeves & peplum at front waist, lined w/violet acetate, straight skirt & center back zipper, early 1960s, excellent condition (ILLUS.). **$150-175**

Pretty 1960s Green Lace Dress

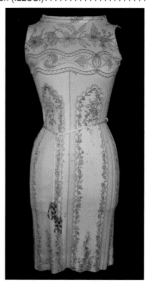

1960s Emilio Pucci Dress

Dress, pastel jersey in shades of seafoam, lavender & beige in a stylized floral print w/facsimile "Emilio" signature in places, features a double row of fabric-covered padded rolls around the bateau neckline, dress falls slimly to lower knee w/darts from the lower bustline to lower waist for slim fit, accompanying belt of self-fabric rolled cord w/end tassels of gold filigree & purple & clear crystal beads, labeled "Emilio Pucci - 8 - Florence-Italy - Made in Italy" & fabric care label, ca. 1968, excellent condition, slight discoloration to armscyes (ILLUS. previous page) **$750.00**

Leslie Fay Floral Knit Dress

Dress, polyester knit, white ground w/pink, purple & yellow flowers & green leaves, cowl neck & sleeveless, swath of fabric shirred & attached at waist forming a sash w/attached goldtone brooch & large white cabochon stone, skirt slightly tucked from waistband, center back zipper, labeled "Leslie Fay for Lord and Taylor - A Leslie Far Original,"& fabric care label, excellent condition (ILLUS.) **$30.00**

1965 Red Wool Tricosa-Designed Dress

Dress, pure wool in tomato red w/a high rounded neckline, long slim-fitting sleeves, a high waistline distinguished by a center panel runing the length of the garment & attached w/rows of stitching & two decorative cabochon buttons at either side, princess seams at back, center back invisible zipper, labeled "Paris Tricosa Made in France" & a fabric care label, mid-1965, excellent condition (ILLUS.). **$200.00**

1960s Hattie Carnegie Silk Dress

Dress, shantung silk w/a beige ground w/red, pink & yellow flowers & green leaves, wide scoop neck w/a tucked bustline, elbow-length sleeves, rounded waistline & straight skirt, center back zipper, labeled "Hattie Carnegie Blue Room," excellent condition, some alteration work (ILLUS.) **$500.00**

Cardin Burgandy Shift Dress

Dress, shift-style, burgandy knit, possibly a wool blend, sleeveless, stitching around neckline, armholes & sides, circular patch pocket high on chest, on-seam slit pockets at either hip, zipper closure at center back, lined w/burgundy satin, labeled "Pierre CARDIN - Paris New York," & fabric care label, excellent condition (ILLUS.) **$600.00**

1960s Lilly Pulitzer Shift Dress

Dress, shift-style, green cotton velveteen, sleeveless, black soutache braid & tassels around neckline & bottom, center back zipper closure, lined w/light green cotton, labeled "The Lilly - Size 12" & fabric care label, by Lilly Pulitzer, mid-1960s, excellent condition, some discoloration to label (ILLUS.). **$175.00**

1960s Pepsi-Cola Shift Dress

Dress, shift-style, yellow cotton sleeveless design w/Pepsi-Cola slogans & a large bottle printed design, round neckline, darts at bustline, center back zipper, labeled "Regatta by Mill Fabrics Corporation - Penney's - 18," mint condition w/original tags (ILLUS.) **$350.00**

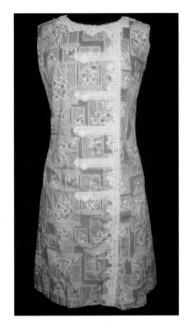

1960s Labeled Shift Dress

Dress, shift-type, probably a cotton blend, a print depicting scenes through a window, light blue ground w/white & green flowers & grass, sleeveless w/white embroidery appliqué around rounded neckline & down faux placket & faux buttonholes, large white textured decorative buttons center front, center back zipper closure, labeled "Shifts Internationale of Miami - 16," good condition, some discoloration around neckline (ILLUS.) **$45.00**

Pauline Trigere Diaphanous Silk Chiffon Dress

Dress, silk chiffon in multiple layers, the hot pink bodice w/a deep V-neckline & long flowing light pink & green sleeves w/self-piping at the edges, natural waistline w/flowing long skirt in multiple chiffon layers shading from light pink to light green, center back zipper closure, tiny overstitching at hemline to produce a rippled edge, accompanying sash scarf of same chiffon in graduating colors of bright green & hot pink & similar tones, labeled "Trigere," Pauline Trigere, excellent condition, minor discoloration to front of skirt, one small mark at back, late 1960s - early 1970s (ILLUS. previous page)................ **$1,150.00**

Dress, sleeveless linen dress & bolero w/brown & yellow flower print, self-fabric whip-stitching through bound fabric grommets around neckline & armscyes, center back zipper, darts at bustline & tucks at lower bustline through waist, string belt loops at each side & self-fabric covered belt & buckle, lined in white acetate, bolero w/single button closure at neck, kimono sleeves, same fabric inset around placket & continuing around entire waistline, good condition, few stains around bustline, jacket lining stained around armscyes (ILLUS. right with labeled blue plaid 1950s dress) **$85-100**

Colorful 1960s Dress by Pauline Trigere

Dress, textured puckered silk w/an overall bold print of curvilinear lines in shades of lime green, shocking pink, gold, white & black, bodice features a high round neckline, dolman sleeves, high 4" w. waistband, skirt slightly tucked under waistband for extra fullness, center back hidden zipper, lined w/white China silk, labeled "Pauline Trigere - Bonwit Teller" & a fabric care label, excellent condition, late 1960s - early 1970s (ILLUS.) **$550.00**

1960s Geoffrey Beene Shift Dress

Dress, two-piece shift-style, the overdress of printed silk organza faced w/black silk chiffon in a stylized floral print in shades of light brown, tan & black cut from two panels w/a seam running down the shouler, features a high rounded neckline w/self-piping, slim-fitting tapering long sleeves w/ostrich feathers at the snap cuffs, V-neckline at the back w/self-piping & self strings to tie a bow at the neck; the overdress falls to the knee w/ostrich feathers along the hemline, the underdress of black silk crepe de china cut line a slip w/printed silk taffeta at lower knee falling 8" long than overdress, rolled hem, lined w/black silk crepe de china, labeled "Geoffrey Beene," excellent condition, mid-1960s (ILLUS.) **$1,500.00**

Late 1960s Wild Floral Print Dress

Dress, very thin jersey material in a wild & colorful floral print, bateau neckline, three-quarters length slim-fitting sleeves, skirt falls to lower knee, self-fabric cord tie belt, labeled "42," late 1960s, excellent condition (ILLUS.) **$350.00**

Dress, white nylon tricot w/blue flower & vine embroidery overall, darts at bust, natural waist, skirt slightly tucked at waist seam, lined w/white nylon, purple satin trim around neckline & cap sleeves, back center zipper, excellent condition, some discoloration to lining fabric at neck (ILLUS. left with 1950s floral chintz dress)
.... **$110.00**

1960s Yves Saint Laurent Brocade Dress

Dress, 'wrinkled' cream-colored cotton brocade w/a meandering lime green design, cream-colored braided trim w/white multi-faceted beads suggesting flowers along the round neckline & at the high waistline, long sleeves w/adjustable zippered cuffs & a band of the same trim, floor-length skirt of six gored panels, center back zipper w/single hook & eye closure at the neckline, dress lined w/white cotton, labeled "Yves Satin Laurent in a Stoffel Fabric," excellent condition, late 1960s (ILLUS.)..................... **$600.00**

Geoffrey Beene 1960s Linen Dress

Dress, yellow linen, sleeveless, slit neckline w/decorative buttons & seaming on lined bodice & slightly gathered skirt, center back zipper, self-fabric tie belt, labeled "Geoffrey Beene," 1967, excellent condition (ILLUS.)
.... **$600-800**

Oscar de la Renta Dress & Jacket Ensemble

Dress & jacket ensemble, both pieces of wool blend, bright orange, dress w/V-neck, sleeveless, darts running from just under bustline to waistline, skirt very slightly gathered at waistline, lined w/orange acetate, center back zipper; jacket straight-cut w/wide lapels, double-breasted w/large black plastic buttons & two buttons at cuffs, reaching to top of hips, lined w/same orange acetate, accompanying belt of black leather w/embossed snakeskin design, wrapped round buckle, lined w/tan hide, jacket labeled "Oscar de la Renta," excellent condition, some softening to leather belt, tan lining shows wear, ca. 1969, the ensemble (ILLUS.)
.... **$895.00**

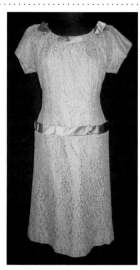

1960s Beige Lace Evening Dress

Evening dress, beige lace, boat neckline w/putty-colored satin ribbon running through slit, two grey rhinestone brooches at the neckline & one at waistband, center back zipper, cap sleeves, labeled "Grace Taylor Original," good condition (ILLUS. previous page)
. . . . **$75.00**

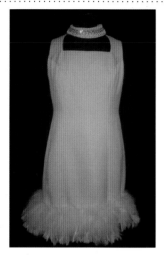

1960s Pink Satin Evening Dress with Feather Trim

Evening dress, bright pink satin, sleeveless w/scoop neck 7 high neck strap decorated w/silver & clear beads, darts at the bustline, fitted through the waist, copious amounts of pink marabou feathers at hemline, open back w/bow at center, buttons donw center back, lined w/pink acetate, excellent condition (ILLUS.)
. . . . **$120.00**

1960s Brocade Evening Dress & Stole

Evening dress & matching stole, thick textured brocade fabric w/a cream ground & slightly whiter raised pattern of oversized curvilinear shapes, the strapless dress w/a shallow 4" w. bustline w/built-in boned corset at bodice, severe empire waist continuing to a box-pleated skirt, an abruptly graduatetd hemine at the front 18" shorter than at the back, lined w/ivory

duchesse satin, insert center back zipper w/hidden snaps closure, accompanying stole measures 14" w. & 54" l., excellent condition (ILLUS.) **$1,850.00**

Lovely 1960s Caramel Silk Evening Gown

Evening gown, caramel-colored satin, surplice bodice boned inside w/an insert panel, embellished w/ rhinestones, peaerls & silver beads, a sweetheart neckline, self-fabric double cord spaghetti straps, high waistline w/tucking & swatch of same fabric hanging loosely at left side, straight floor-length skirt lined w/ peach acetate, center back zipper, labeled "Styled by Prima - New York," good condition, some spotting to fabric, some seams need reinforcing (ILLUS.)
. . . . **$800.00**

Mr. Blackwell Designer Evening Gown

*Mr. Blackwell Designer Evening Gown &
Cape Ensemble*

Evening gown & cape ensemble, gown of black silk velvet, sweetheart neckline, boned bodice, black silk ribbon straps w/slight trained floor-length hem; cape of black silk taffeta, sleeveless, gathered at shoulders, back yoke, self-fabric neck sash, both pieces labeled "Mr. Blackwell Custom," excellent condition, straps originally rhinestone on ribbon but replaced w/black silk, ca. 1960, the ensemble (ILLUS. of gown & gown with cape, gown on previous page) **$1,800.00**

Fine 1960s Bill Blass Organza & Organdy Gown

Gown, bodice of silk organza, green ground w/small yellow, orange & pink floral print, deep scoop neckline, long sheer sleeves w/banded cuffs & self-fabric-covered buttons & bound buttonholes, same buttons down center front of bodice, high waistline & full skirt made of organdy w/contrasting floral print on a beige ground, skirt lined w/beige organdy, hidden snaps down center front, inside gros-grain waist belt, accompanying sash of green organdy fabric, labeled "Bill Blass," excellent condition (ILLUS.). **$650.00**

1960s Labeled Support Girdle

Girdle, support-type, black nylon & spandex w/boning at front & back seams, center front zipper & hook & eye closure, four garters, labeled "Smoothie Controleur - U.S. Patent Number 179.326 - The Strouse Adler Co. - Style 1521 - Size 29" & fabric care label, excellent condition (ILLUS.). **$25-30**

1960s Bonnie Cashin Yarn & Leather Jacket

Jacket, boxy form of olive-colored boucle yarn w/olive green leather collar & elbow patches & leather trim on placket, patch pockets & sleeves, flat goldtone metal buttons down center front & functional buttons on pockets, lined w/olive wool knit, labeled "Sills and Co.

A Bonnie Cashin Design," excellent condition (ILLUS.)
.... **$375-400**

1960s Bonnie Cashin Leather Jacket

Jacket, smock-style, tan leather featuring a Peter Pan collar, tucks at shoulderline, long sleeves w/buttoned cuffs, self-fabric piping at rounded hem w/piped rounded side slits, lined w/tan crepe, labeled "A Bonnie Casin Design - Sills & Co.," good condition, some age-related wear (ILLUS.).......... **$400.00**

1960s Yves Saint Laurent Jacket & Dress Ensemble

Jacket & dress ensemble, the short fitted jacket of heavy ivory brocade w/a shawl collar & single wrapped button at center front, darts at bustline, lined w/champagne-colored crepe satin; sleeveless dress w/a bodice of the same crepe satin, darped neckline & darts at bustline, attached skirt of some ivory brocade, tucks at waistline holding in fullness, peg skirt w/vent at back center hemline, center back zipper closure, accompanying self-fabric covered skinny belt w/covered slide bucklet, dress lined w/beige acetate, jacket labeled "Yves Saint Laurent," excellent

condition, minor discoloration to dress lining (ILLUS.)
.... **$750-800**

1960s Linen Jacket & Dress Ensemble

Jacket & dress ensemble, the sleeveless dress of black linen w/a V-neckline edged w/green linen piping & a band of white linen w/black polka dots, double darts at bustline, high waistline w/pleats continuing to straight skirt, bodice lined w/black acetates, side zipper closures; a black linen jacekt w/slight padding at shoulders, stand-up collar of same white linen w/black dots, green linen piping, kimono-type bracelet-length sleeves tapering at cuffs trimmed w/same green piping & polka dot dotted fabric, front nipped-in at waist w/vertical seaming, back features an elaborate pleated panel & back waistbelt, self-fabric-covered buttons down center front & as trim on cuffs & waistbelt, lined w/green crepe satin, excellent condition (ILLUS.)
.... **$200-225**

1960s Suede & Tweed Jacket & Skirt Ensemble

Jacket & skirt ensemble, the loose-bodied jacket of light brown suede w/a stand-up collar & open placket faced w/light brown & white flat tweed fabric, kimono-style short sleeves w/turn-back cuffs also faced w/same tweed, two patch hand-warmer pockets at center front trimmed w/tweed, lined w/beige crepe; the pencil skirt of same tweed falls to mid-calf w/1 1/2" w. suede waistband, tweed-wrapped button & tab closure, center back seam edges w/same suede, kick slit near hem w/suede detail, jacket labeled "Created by Royal Suedes of New York," late 1960s, excellent condition, some age wear to suede, the set (ILLUS. previous page). **$200.00**

1960s Daisy Pattern Jumpsuit

Jumpsuit, medium weight white canvas w/black & yellow daisy print, bellbottom flares, detachable bra top attached w/button closure, adjustable shoulder straps, zipper back, excellent condition (ILLUS.) **$150.00**

Late 1960s Christian Dior Midi Dress

Midi dress, gold brocade w/red & pink flowers in a stylized design, scoop neck, long sleeves, high waist, skirt gored in four panels, wrapped buttons & loops down skirt at left side, center back zipper, lined w/beige rayon, labeled "Christian Dior for Saks Fifth Avenue - Paris New York - Size 10," & a union label, excellent condition, late 1960s - early 1970s (ILLUS.) **$400-500**

Lace-Trimmed Pumpkin Orange 1960s Mini Skirt

Mini dress, heavy pumpkin-colored polyester crepe w/a high rounded neckline w/a double lace ruffle, self-fabric cord tying into a bow at the back of the neck, long full sleeves w/double lace ruffle cuffs, another self-fabric cord tying to bow, box pleats at center front & center back, center back zipper, labeled "denise are here!," excellent condition (ILLUS.) **$275.00**

1960s Faux Leopard Mini-Dress

Mini-dress, faux leopard of acrylic pile w/real mink fur cuffs, lined w/yellow acetate, back center zipper, good condition, neck at point of V repaired (ILLUS.)
. . . . **$350.00**

1960s Golden Brown Mink Jacket

Mink jacket, golden brown w/a loose boxy cut, no fasteners, meant to be worn open, shawl collar, bracelet-length full sleeves w/turn-back cuffs, slit pockets center front, jacket lined w/taupe-colored satin fabric w/brocaded irises, labeled "Furs by Jimmy Destro - Miami Beach, Fla.," excellent condition (ILLUS.) **$550.00**

1960s Betsey Johnson Mini-dress

Mini-dress, pink cotton w/small bow & ribbon print, shirred & elastic long sleeves, princess seaming front & back, white buttons down center front, labeled "DESIGNED by Betsey Johnson for Paraphernalia," excellent condition, mid-1960s (ILLUS.) . . . **$400-500**

Unusual 1960s Floral Print Paper Dress

Paper dress, made of a specially treated washable fire-resistant paper product, a sleeveless knee-length shift w/a wild floral print in shades of yellow, green, turquoise & pink w/a ruffled flounce at the hem, labeled "42," attached tags read "Reemay - Du Pont's Reg. Trad.," mint condition, never worn (ILLUS.)
. . . . **$200.00**

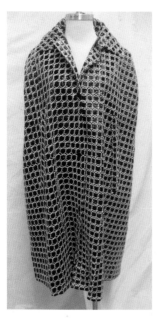

1960s Op Art Rain Cape

Rain cape, Op-Art 'wet-look' style of black vinyl w/raised white joined circles overall, a spread collar, black plastic-covered snaps down center front & center front arm openings, labeled "Made in Japan," excellent condition (ILLUS.). **$600.00**

Labeled Pucci 1960s Velveteen Skirt

Skirt, velveteen in mostly pink, magenta w/peach, olive green, brown & black, printed w/geometric shapes in spider web design, fabric printed w/Emilio signature, lined w/light pink acetate, pointed hem, center front & center back, labeled "Emilio Pucci - Florence Italy - 100% Pure Cotton - Made in Italy - Size 10," ca. 1968, excellent condition (ILLUS.) **$900.00**

1960s Black Crepe Adjustable Hem Skirt

Skirt, straight style w/adjustable hemline, black crepe w/small pleats at waistband & removable zippered 9-inch portion at bottom for shorter hemline, skirt lined w/black acetate, back vent at hem, side zipper & hook & eye closure, labeled "Lorrie Deb of San Francisco - Size 7," excellent condition (ILLUS.) **$225.00**

1960s Nylon Skirt Set

Skirt set, two-piece, black & white checked nylon, top w/red plastic buttons down center front, peplum & self-fabric covered belt, skirt w/side zipper & single button closure, in the style of the 1940s, excellent condition, the set (ILLUS.). **$120.00**

1960s Pink Pique Knit Wool Skirt Suit

Skirt suit, both pieces of pink woolen fabric in a mini waffle pique weave, the cropped double-breasted jacket w/rounded wid lapels & collar, large pink rounded buttons & bound buttonholes down front center, long slim-fitting sleeves w/six working buttons down the cuffs, princess seaming, lined w/pink acetate; the sleeveless dress w/rounded neckline w/a lower scoop in back, natural waistline & straight skirt, on-seam slit pockets, side zipper & hook & eye closure, tiny hooks & eyes on left shoulder, lined w/pink acetate, jacket labeled "Norell - Saks Fifth Avenue," mid- to late 1960s or early 1970s, excellent condition, minor soiling, lining replaced (ILLUS.) **$850.00**

1960s Green Gabardine Skirt Suit

Skirt suit, bright green wool gabardine, the double-breasted jacket w/cheetah fur collar & cuffs, vertically set stand pockets, green plastic buttons w/gold intaglio

& bond buttonholes, an A-line skirt, excellent condition, the set (ILLUS.). **$675.00**

1960s Labeled Skirt Suit

Skirt suit, two-piece, brown & white bark cloth, possibly a cotton & wool blend, jacket in boxy shape w/brown piqué piping around collar & down curvilinear placket, three-quarter-length kimono-sleeves w/gussets, self-fabric-covered oversized buttons down center front, princess seaming both front & back, lined in brown satin, skirt w/tucks at waistband, center back zipper & single button closure, lined w/same brown satin, jacket labeled "Lily Simon - Montreal," excellent condition (ILLUS.) **$150.00**

1960s Balmain Labeled Skirt Suit

Skirt suit, two-piece, green & red wool nubbly tweed, boxy jacket w/cross-over button closure center left, long straight sleeves, oversized buttons & bound buttonholes, single hidden snap closure at top button w/self-fabric knot detail, lined w/dark green china silk, straight skirt w/tucks at waistline, lined w/same china silk, labeled "Florilege - Balmain - Original Paris - 14," excellent condition, the set (ILLUS., previous page)
. . . . **$350.00**

1960s Fleece Skirt Suit from Ensemble

Skirt suit with cape, all pieces of woolen fleece, the loose-bodied jacket of cream-colored fleece faced w/ lavender fleece, worn open, featuring a high neck, long sleeves, side opening patch pockets, hemline, cuffs & placket edged w/contrasting knit braid; the wrap-skirt in lavender fleece faced w/cream, two-button closure at waistline, edged w/same knit braid, the cape (not shown) in lavender fleece faced w/cream, long swath attached at neck to wrap around neck when closed, buttons down center front, edged w/knit braid, late 1960s - early 1970s, excellent condition (ILLUS.)
. . . . **$500.00**

Wildly Patterned Silk Stole

Stole, double-faced silk decorated w/a print done in pen-and-ink style featuing shocking pink stylized horses, well-dressed riders w/shocking pink hats, large paisleys, flower & swirls in black & white, front face dotted w/silver sequins & tiny clear beads, probably 1960s, 19" w., 36" l., excellent condition (ILLUS.)
. . . . **$350.00**

Colorful 1960s Two-Piece Swimsuit

Swimsuit, two-piece, bold floral design in shades of pinks, reds & gold crepe-like fabric, top w/adjustable buttoned straps, elastic band in back & hook closure, trunks feature back center zipper, good condition, some fraying to fabric (ILLUS.) **$55.00**

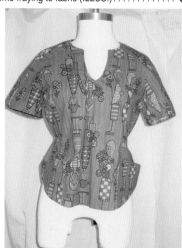

Colorful 1960s Tunic Top

Tunic top, cotton bark cloth in blue w/colorful stylized human figures, short style w/raglan short sleeves, two patch pockets along bottom edge, excellent condition (ILLUS.) **$38.00**

Late 1960s Red Wool Tunic Vest

Tunic vest, bright red wool w/a round neckline & all
edges trimmed w/dark blue vinyl, also used as stripes
on the garment at front & back, w/accompanying belt,
left shoulder closure w/brass toggles, labeled "Sabrina
Knits Ltd. Exclusive Imports - 100% Wool - 14," very
good condition, vinyl edging separated from garments
in one area, minor tiny spotting at lower front, late
1960s (ILLUS.) **$350.00**

Unusual Metallic Disk Tunic Vest

Tunic vest, composed of metallic plastic disks attached
by plastic "staples," two disk strips across bustline,
ankle-length, attributed to Paco Rabanne, excellent
condition (ILLUS.) **$4,000.00**

Colorful Carpet Vest

Vest, carpet-like material of hooked rayon & cotton yarns,
in an ethnic patchwork design, lined w/beige acetates,
w/fabric care label, 25" l. shoulder to hem, late 1960s
- early 1970s, excellent condition (ILLUS.).... **$45.00**

MEN'S CLOTHING

Group of Three 1960s Bathing Trunks

Bathing trunks, each of acrylic knit, in various colorful
abstract patterns, mint condition, each (ILLUS. of
three) **$95.00**

1960s Red & Black Cabana Set with a Polynesian Design

Cabana set, both pieces of cotton w/a red ground printed w/black figures & designs in a Polynesian motif, top features patch pockets at the hips & center front buttons, the trunks lined w/white cotton, elastic waistband w/single button closure, excellent condition (ILLUS.) **$85.00**

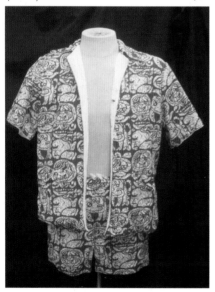

1960s Red & White Cabana Set

Cabana set, both pieces of red & white Polynesian-style print, faced w/white terry cloth, top features side vents & buttons down the center front, trunks w/ elastic waist & drawstring closure, labeled "Jordan Marsh Florida - The Man's Store," very good condition, some matting to terry cloth, minor stains (ILLUS.) **$65.00**

1960s Cabana Set with a Nautical Theme

Cabana set, both pieces w/a nautical theme, the blue ground w/red, white & yellow anchors, ropes & steering wheels, faced w/white terry cloth, the top w/side vents & center front buttons, the trunks w/an elastic waist w/drawstring closure, labeled "Mr. Cabana - M," very good condition, some matting to terry cloth (ILLUS.) **$65.00**

Hawaiian shirt, blue bark cloth w/large flower print, center front cutton closure, excellent condition (ILLUS. top right with 1950s & 1970s Hawaiian shirts) **$50.00**

Two 1960s Men's Plaid Jackets

Jacket, blue, yellow, white & brown plaid patchwork madras-style in a cotton blend, deep back vent, white satin lining, two flap pockets, two inside slit pockets & two-button front closure, excellent condition (ILLUS. right with other 1960s plaid jacket) **$125.00**

Jacket, red, yellow & ivory plaid in an open weave, possibly silk-cotton blend, beige satin monogrammed lining, two flap pockets, single chest slit pocket, two inside slit pockets w/plaid fabric edging, back vent, single button closure center front, labeled "Mark Chrisman - Pompano Beach - Boca Raton - Naples, Florida - Dry Clean Only," excellent condition (ILLUS. left with other 1960s jacket) **$125.00**

1960s Printed Acetate Jacket

Jacket, thick shiny acetate w/a busy print depicting trees, leaves, cartouches, symbols & shapes in shades of brown, lavender, beige, brick red & dark green, body lined w/gold acetate, sleeves lined w/much thinner cream-colored satin, single horn button at cuffs, two horn buttons down center front, hip-level welt pockets, one w/flap, back vent at center lower back, two inside welt pockets in lining, labeled "DAKS - Simpson London Tailored," & fabric care label, late 1960s, excellent condition, the set (ILLUS.) **$225.00**

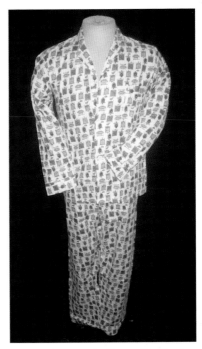

1960s Pajamas with Tavern Sign Design

Pajamas, embossed cotton printed w/small tavern signs, traditional pajama styling, center front buttons on top, elastic waistband & snap fly on bottoms, labeled "Towncrafat - Penney's," mint condition (ILLUS.)
. . . . **$35.00**

Shirt, gray iridescent silk, small vertical tucks down center front, chest patch monogrammed pocket, cuffed shirt sleeves, center front button closure, tucks at back near shoulder yoke, straight hem, labeled "Custon Care by Alfred of New York - Imported Pure Silk," excellent condition (ILLUS. right with other 1960s shirt)
. . . . **$65.00**

1960s Men's Gold Pajamas

Pajamas, crisp cotton, light green ground w/overall gold paisley pattern, top w/V-neck & short sleeves, button center front closure, pants w/elastic waistband & snap fly, labeled "Weldon - Elastic Waistband - All Cotton - C-Large - Short Sleeve - Long Leg," excellent condition, never worn (ILLUS.) **$120-150**

Two 1960s Men's Shirts

Shirt, green & yellow "Shirt-Jac" (combined shirt & jacket), cotton blend, spread collar, chest patch pocket, center front button closure, excellent condition (ILLUS. left with other 1960s shirt) **$42.00**

1960s Hieroglyphic Print Shirt

Shirt, rayon w/red ground printed w/colorful hieroglyphic & cartouche design, band 'mandarin' collar, black piping detail, modified raglan sleeves, chest patch pocket, black plastic buttons, labeled "Made Expressly for Lerner Shops," good condition, minor fraying at collar seam (ILLUS.). **$75.00**

Early 1960s Labeled Rayon Shirt Jac

Shirt Jac, black rayon w/insertions of white, red & grey stripes down the center front, spread collar, long sleeves w/banded buttoned cuffs, 2" w. self-fabric waistband, white plastic buttons down center front, labeled "Clubman - L - Shirt Jac," early 1960s, mint condition (ILLUS.). **$150.00**

Men's Trouser, Shirt & Hat Outfit

Trouser, shirt & hat outfit, Guayabera shirt of blue polyester blend w/two sets of vertical pleats & embroidery on center front, three sets of pleats at back, four patch pockets w/decorative button details on yoke, sleeves, hem & pockets, center front button closure, labeled "Romani Collection - Size M" & fabric care label, late 1960s - early 1970s, $85; hat of ivory-colored woven straw, three-inch high creased crown, two-inch brim w/gros-grain olive green ribbon & flat bow finish, velveteen sweat brow band, 1950s, excellent condition, $55; linen trousers in sturdy tight weave, full-cut legs, pleats from waist to cuffs, small slit pocket at waistband, back welt pockets, one-inch wide belt loops, button fly, 1940s, excellent condition, pants (ILLUS. of outfit) **$145.00**

CHAPTER 10: CLOTHING - 1970-1980

CHILDREN'S CLOTHING

1970s Colorful Child's Sweater Vest

Sweater vest, wool & acrylic yarns knitted in bands of bright orange, green, yellow & white, crocket knit collar & arm holes, pearl knit body, excellent condition (ILLUS.) **$28.00**

LADIES' CLOTHING

1970s Bathing Suit with Lace Overlay

Bathing suit, rubberized fabric w/black lace overlay, low scoop back, built-in bra, elastic gathered straps & piping at neckline, elasticized shirring throughout entire back & sides, skirt front w/attached panties, labeled "De Weese Design - Swim and Sun Fashions

- Los Angeles California - Size 12-34 - Sta-Cup Bra," excellent condition (ILLUS.) **$110.00**

1970s Hungarian Embroidered Blouse

Blouse, finely textured unbleached gauze featuring floral yarn embroidery at the center front & smocking & overstitching around the neckline, short puff sleeves & waist, light blue cord drawstring at V-neckline, labeled "Hand Embroidery Made in Hungary - Karavan N.Y.," excellent condition, tiny pinhole at front, slight age yellowing over left shoulder (ILLUS.) **$175-200**

1970s Black Satin Smock-Style Blouse

Blouse, smock-style, black stain w/pentagonal neck yoke extended to a V in the back, tucked shoulders, long billowing flared sleeves, strip of self-fabric ruffles from neck yoke extending across sleeves in front to neck yoke at back, loose bodice & remainder, labeled "Designed by Ossie Clark for radley - 34," & fabric care label, excellent condition (ILLUS.) **$550-700**

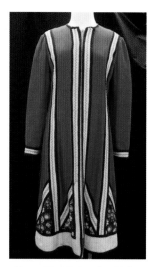

Heavy Red Gabardine Caftan

Caftan, very heavy robe made of red gabardine w/ alternating stripes of white gabardine, trimmed w/dark blue braiding & pink rick-rack, long sleeves w/same white band at cuffs, low hidden on-seam pockets at center front, bottom portion w/insertions of flowered fabric & wide white gabardine band at hemline, center front hidden zipper, lined w/silver silk-like fabric, labeled "Malcom Starr International - Designed by Rizkallah - 14 - Made in British Crown Colony of Hong Kong," good condition, some staining to front (ILLUS.)
. . . . **$350.00**

Rare 1970s Natural Python Coat

Coat, double-breasted, made entirely of natural python skin piece in large panels, convertical wide lapels, long sleeves w/gussets of python skin under the arms, two rows of faux horn buttons down center front, oversized patch pockets at hip level, low waist belt at back w/inverted pleat starting from waist & continuing the length of the coat, decorative buttons on inside, entire coat lined w/grey satin, inside slit pocket trimmed

w/skin, very good condition, some spots of minor discoloration to lining, skin dry in places (ILLUS.)
. . . . **$3,000.00**

Elaborate Foreign Coat & Jacket

Coat, long robe style in black velvet w/elaborate gold braiding & gold thread embroidery accented w/sequins & pear-shaped pearl beads, gold thread-wrapped ball & loop closures down center front, 18" l. side slits heavily embellished w/same embroidery & trim & also w/ball & loop closures, lined w/black lustrous fabric, possibly from Morocco, excellent condition (ILLUS. right with short jacket). **$450.00**

Designer Reversible Patchwork Coat

Coat, reversible patchwork design in black wool crepe w/dolman sleeves, one side w/a collage of patches of brocades, acrylics, knits & metallic threads, reverse side in plain black wool crepe, two hip well pockets, by Koos Van Den Akker, ca. 1979, excellent condition (ILLUS.) **$2,000.00**

Back of 1970s Banded Leather Coat

Coat, slim-fitting design of white & beige leather set in horizontal bands w/a stand-up collar, long slim-fitting sleeves, side slit pockets, oversized white plastic buttons down center front, lined w/cream-colored acetate, labeled "La Flaque de Paris," good condition, some wear & discoloration to leather, one small purple mark on shoulder (ILLUS. of the back) **$400.00**

Rare Valentino Couture Winter Coat

Coat, winter, pumpkin-colored cashmere, double-breasted w/marbleized glass buttons encased in metal, sable fur shawl collar & cuffs, modified saddle stitch long sleeves lined w/pumpkin silk, two on-seam pockets, labeled "Valentino Couture - Made in Italy (in pen) - Mool 230 - 100% cashmere," mid-1970s, excellent condition (ILLUS.) **$10,000.00**

Fancy Ruffled Black Chiffon Cocktail Dress

Cocktail dress, sleeveless style w/black pleated chiffon overlay, high ruffled neck, tucked 3" w. waistband, skirt composed of vertical tiers of the same chiffon w/sculpted wired edges formingg cascades & swirls down the length, center back zipper closure, lined w/black satin, labeled "Travilla - Sara Fredericks," excellent condition, zipper repaired (ILLUS.) **$1,800.00**

1970s Red Velveteen Cowgirl Suit

Cowgirl suit, two-piece, deep red cotton velveteen, shirt w/pearl snap center front closure & deep cuffs, white cotton piping at collar, cuffs & around embroidered & beaded yoke; pleated high-waisted pants tapering at ankles, slit diagonally set pockets at either hip, w/a fabric care label, late 1970s, excellent condition (ILLUS.) **$300.00**

1970s Black Jersey Disco Dress

Disco dress, black polyester jersey w/scoop neck, asymmetrical draped overlay of same fabric, gold-edged "lettuce-leaf" trim, also on hemline, gold braid straps, labeled "California Visionz" & fabric care label, excellent condition (ILLUS.) **$55.00**

1920s-style G. Beene 1970s Dress

Dress, 1920s-style, beige silk chiffon bodice w/low waist, horizontal bands of navy & beige chiffon continuing to

a pleated navy blue skirt, self-fabric-covered buttons down center front & at cuffs, three-quarter length sleeves, scarf of same beige silk chiffon, bands of navy blue & beiges stripes at either end, continuing to large swatch of navy blue chiffon, labeled "Geoffrey Beene," early to mid-1970s, good condition, some discoloration to armscyes (ILLUS.) **$750.00**

Fine 1970s Ronald Amey Jersey Dress

Dress, black jersey, possibly rayon, a mock turtle neck & long tapered sleeves open from shoulder to cuffs & held in place at shoulder & wrist by self-fabric-covered ball buttons & loops, gussets at armscyes, natural waistline w/attached 3" w. self-fabric-covered belt w/same ball buttons & loops for closure, wide skirt w/rolled hem, center back zipper, lined w/black satin, labeled "Ronald Amey New York," & fabric care label, excellent condition (ILLUS.) **$775.00**

Three 1970s Outfits by Mr. Dino

Dress, black shirtwaist style in polyester knit w/red & blue keyhole design, button center front closure, signature in fabric "Mr. Dino," labeled "Mr. Dino - New York Paris - Florence," excellent condition (ILLUS. left with two other 1970s Mr. Dino outfits). **$65.00**

Yellow Wool Dress by Ronald Amey

Dress, bright yellow wool knit, mock-turtle neckline, raglan-type long full sleeves w/openings at the shoulders & tapering athe cuffs w/carved Lucite & gold-rimmed buttons & loop closures, bodice gathered from shoulder yoke & at elastic-covered waistline, attached 3" w. self-fabric covered belt w/button & loop closure, skirt lined w/yellow china silk, rolled hemline, center back zipper closure, labeled "Ronald Amey New York," & a fabric care label, excellent condition, minor pilling mainly at neckline (ILLUS.). **$400.00**

1970s Celine Knit Dress

Dress, crimson-colored pure wool in fine knit weave, stand-up banded collar in contrasting striped weave extending to long ties, long sleeves slightly tucked at shoulder & w/same striped bands at cuffs, shoulder yoke & tiny tucks create fullness at the bodice, small white buttons ending at mid-bodice at center front, elastic waistline & straight skirt ending w/stripes at lower portion, on-seam slit pockets at either hip, labeled "Celine Paris - 100% Pure Wool - Made in Italy - 38," excellent condition, some label discoloration (ILLUS.) **$250.00**

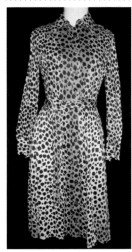

1970s Faux Cheetah Fur Dress

Dress, faux cheetah print in polyester blend knit, pointed collar, center front button closure, self-fabric tie belt, center-back godet, labeled "Avalon Classics - Inc. - Size 12" & fabric care label, excellent condition (ILLUS.) **$85.00**

1970s Paisley Halter Dress with Pom-pons

Dress, halter-style, cotton w/red ground decorated w/paisleys in yellows, greys & pinks, slight V-neck w/tucks on straps creating fullness over the bust, wide tucked straps extending around neck to tie at back, trimmed w/yellow yarn pom-pons, natural waistline continues to slightly gathered & tiered skirt trimmed w/yellow pom-pons, center back zipper closure, lined w/orange cotton, good condition, one small tear on straps (ILLUS., previous page) **$125.00**

1970s Embroidered Cotton Halter Dress

Dress, halter-type, white cotton w/colorful yarn embroidery, Mexican, excellent condition (ILLUS.) **$250.00**

1970s Gernreich Knitted Dress

Dress, knee-length, silver lamé & black yarn knitted to produce a geometric pattern in alternating recessed & raised areas, modified bateau neckline, self-piped, open shoulders, long slim-fitting sleeves widening slightly at the cuffs, center back zipper closure, labeled "Rudi Gernreich Design for Harmon Knitwear - 10," excellent condition (ILLUS.) **$1,500.00**

1970s Floor-Length Lurex Knit Dress

Dress, Lurex knit, floor-length w/orange & gold & yellow subtle striping, low scoop neck, elastic sewn to inside at waist, center back zipper, excellent condition (ILLUS.) **$100-175**

1930s Style Calico Dress from the 1970s

Dress, midi-length 1930s-style, cotton calico in red w/tiny black & beige flowers & yellow dots, ruffles at yoke, scalloped hem w/ruffled flounce w/black piping, center front hidden zipper, back ruffled detail at center waist, excellent condition, perhaps very slight fading (ILLUS.) **$65.00**

1970s Midnight Blue Silk Velvet Long Dress

Dress, midnight blue silk velvet w/wide scoop neck, slightly padded shoulders, long sleeves gathered at shoulders & tapering to wrists w/functioning prong-set rhinestone buttons up the cuff, same buttons down center front of bodice, empire waist w/gathered mid-calf skirt, lingerie straps at shoulder, neckline lined w/blue acetate, excellent condition, lining around neck shows some wear (ILLUS.). **$200.00**

Hand-painted Z. Rhodes Quilted Dress

Dress, of rayon satin, mostly quilted, hand-painted dress & bodice in light peach, quilted squares of curvilinear lines & grids in shades of dark brown w/blue flourishes, brown satin neckline, brown rolled cord laces through brown satin loops, hidden center front zipper skirt falls from rounded princess waist, vertically quilted in light shade of pink, painted w/swirls & lines & stylized leaves in pinks, brown & black, ends in a

V-shaped yoke from which pointed satin pieces fall, underneath is last tier of same quilted satin & designs as bodice, asymmetrical hem, sides 10" shorter than front & back, trimmed w/brown satin piping, back of dress mimics front w/brown satin yoke at center between shoulder blades, entire piece lined w/very light peach colored satin, labeled "Zandra Rhodes - 100% Rayon - 10," excellent condition, some small splotches of colored paint in places original to the piece (ILLUS.). **$3,500.00**

1970s Pink Silk Halston Dress

Dress, pink silk shantung, bias-cut & then pieced, tapered end tie over left shoulder, lined w/pink china silk, labeled "Halston," very good condition, staining to fabric under armscyes, lining restored, late 1970s (ILLUS.) **$900.00**

1970s Oscar de la Renta Shirtwaist Dress

Dress, shirtwaist-style, yellow lining w/chiffon overlay printed w/orange, blue & green swirled lines w/small metallic thread circular brocade, features a wide collar & lapels, long unlined sheer sleeves tapeirng at banded snap cuffs, self-fabric-covered ball buttons down center front continuing to hidden snaps after high waistline, full skirt w/attached 2" w. self-fabric-covered belt w/hook closure, labeled "Oscar de la Renta - 8" & a union label, excellent condition (ILLUS. previous page) **$450.00**

Dress, white polyester knit w/neck yoke of double-ply contrasting color, also at banded cuffs, psychedelic print, "Mr. Dino" signature in print, center back zipper, labeled "Mr. Dino - New York - Paris - Florence" & fabric care label, excellent condition (ILLUS. right with two other Mr. Dino outfits) **$75.00**

1970s Plaid Halter Dress & Shawl

Dress & shawl, halter-style, plaid twilled polyester, halter bodice w/hook & eye closure at upper neck gathered for fullness, darts at bustline, bias-cut wide skirt, zipper down center back, w/matching shawl, labeled "Lillie Rubin," late 1970s, excellent condition, the set (ILLUS.) **$125.00**

1970s Pierre Deux Dress & Purse Set

Dress & purse, both of light blue cotton w/floral & paisley print, dress w/square neckline w/gathered yoke, high drawstring waistline, puffed shoulders & full sleeves tapered to buttoned band cuffs, tiered full skirt, purse w/long rolled self-fabric shoulder strap, ruffled trim & zippered top, labeled "La Provence De Pierre Deux - Handmade Soleiado," excellent condition, the set (ILLUS.) **$350.00**

A Late 1970s Bonnie Cashin Canvas Duffle Jacket

Duffle jacket, light tan canvas w/large shawl collar, raglan sleeves, brass clip & tab closure down center front, vertically set welt pockets at each hip, faced w/beige & white heathered fleece, labeled "Bonnie Cashin Weatherware for Russ Taylor," very good condition, some matting to fleece, late 1970s (ILLUS.) **$200.00**

Burgundy Evening Dress & Capelet

Evening dress & capelet, both pieces of burgundy rayon velvet, halter-necked dress w/smocking of bodice, ruffles around high neckline, armholes & back, 2" waistband, long slim floor-length skirt, deep 7" long flounce at bottom, center back zipper w/single hook capelet cut to accommodate shoulders w/single hook closure at neckline & narrow band of ruffles around edges, lined w/same rubberized fabric, excellent condition (ILLUS.). **$395.00**

Front & Back of Black Wool & Sequin 1970s Evening Dress

Evening dress, black wool jersey, floor-length, round neckline, long sleeves w/zippered cuffs, an application of very small champagne-colored sequins around the neck & continuing in a flaring wide band down the back & ending in points at the upper thighs, labeled "Geoffrey Beene New York," excellent condition, very minor loss to sequins at neck, late 1970s (ILLUS. of front & back) **$1,250-1,500**

1970s Green Chiffon Evening Gown

Evening gown, drab green underdress, sleeveless w/stand-up collar & profuse amounts of Kelly green chiffon overlay, long angel sleeves, slit under arm, darts at bustline, high waist w/gathered self-chiffon fabric cummerbund sash w/purposely frayed edge, rosette on center, center back zipper, hook & eye closure at neckline, labeled "Lillie Rubin," excellent condition (ILLUS., previous page) **$450.00**

1970s Green Sequined Halston Evening Gown

Evening gown, emerald green sequins over emerald green silk chiffon, sequin-covered spaghetti straps, rounded V-neckline, side zipper closure, labeled "Halston," good condition, some sequin loss (ILLUS.)
. . . . **$400.00**

1970s Colorful Organdy Evening Gown

Evening gown, the surplice bodice of green organdy faced w/yellow organdy, long sleeves, self-fabric

gathered waistband w/large bow trim, full taffeta skirt of pink, green, orange & blue madras plaid in eight gored panels, center back zipper closure, labeled "Miss Elliette California - Size 16," & a fabric care label, excellent condition (ILLUS.) **$125.00**

Mink Coat Dyed to Resemble Tiger Fur

Fur coat, mink fur dyed to simulate tiger, wide collar & lapels, hidden hook & eye closure, hip-level slit pockets, lined w/beige satin, inside waist belt, labeled "Boutique Ben Kahn," good condition, some wear visible at collar, some tears in lining (ILLUS.)
. . . . **$800.00**

1970s Satin & Floral Chiffon Gown

Gown, black polyester satin sleeveless underdress w/ floral chiffon overlay, same fabric ruffles around deep scoop neckline & at tapered sleeve cuffs, empire waist w/black satin ribbon belt & bow, center back zipper, labeled "Lot - Size 7-8," excellent condition (ILLUS., previous page) **$150.00**

1970s Yellow Crepe & Chiffon Gown

Gown, bright yellow crepe sleeveless sheath w/same yellow chiffon overlay, embellished w/rhinestones & beading overall, yellow chiffon swath attached at

back shoulders w/hooks & eyes creating a removable watteau train, excellent condition (ILLUS.) . . . **$750.00**

Pretty 1970s Blue Chiffon Gown

Gown, light blue underdress w/double layers of aqua chiffon overlay, asymmetrical neckline & bodice w/one shoulder gathered & pulled up in chiffon bow, acetate-lined bodice, center back zipper, excellent condition (ILLUS.) **$275.00**

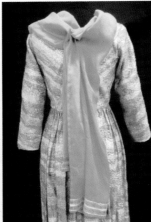

Two Views of a 1970s Brocade Gown by Mary Norton

Gown, brocade w/bands of light green, orange & pale yellow w/silver lame thread running throughout, bodice features a wide V-neckline w/attached light green organdy swatch that drapes around neck & falls down the back, trimmed w/gold-flecked lace, bodice tucked at center for fullness around the bustline w/self-fabric bows at center seam, kimono-style three-quarter-length sleeves w/underarm gussets, high waistline & tucks underneath creating a full skirt, center back zipper, lined w/orange satin, labeled "Mary Norton - Coral Way - Miami, Florida - Bay Harbor Islands-Miami Beach - Main St.-Blowing Rock, N.C.," good condition, some tears along seams, discoloration to lining under armscyes, early 1970s (ILLUS. of two views) **$250.00**

Colorful 1970s Jersey Knit Gown

Gown, polyester jersey knit w/Bohemian eastern print, tucks at shoulders, V-neck w/gold braiding & jewels at empire waistline, bodice lined in orage crepe, center front godets from waistline, center back zipper, labeled "Size 11," good condition, some fabric staining near waist (ILLUS.) **$300.00**

1970s Blue Gown with Floral Overlay

Gown, robin's egg blue sleeveless empire-waisted style w/chiffon overlay in floral print, heavily beaded & sequined collar & waistline, center back zipper,

labeled "Victoria Royal Ltd. - Made in British Crown Colony of Hong Kong - Size 12," good condition, some discoloration on inside (ILLUS.) **$500.00**

1970s Maxi-Gown & Long Vest Ensemble

Gown & long vest ensemble, maxi-length gown w/ bodice of pink acetate w/pink chiffon overlay, mock-turtleneck & sleeveless, attached skirt of pink & green brocade, high self-fabric waistband, straight skirt, slit & center back hem, center back zipper, long vest of same brocade fabric & lined w/same pink acetate, excellent condition, the ensemble (ILLUS.) . . . **$95.00**

1970s Orange Velvet Hot Pants

Hot pants, crushed rayon velvet w/patch pockets & self-belt loops, snap button & fly closure, measures 8 1/2" from waistband to cuffs, labeled "Velpanne - Ameritex," mint condition (ILLUS.) **$50-55**

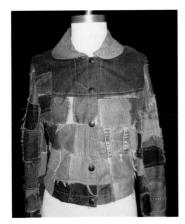

Homemade 1970s Denim Patch Jacket

Jacket, homemade, composed of various denim patches
from numerous sources, features a Peter Pan collar,
overstitching, snaps down center front, excellent
condition, some edges frayed & faded for a desirable
effect (ILLUS.). **$150.00**

1970s Fur Jacket & Shearling Bonnet

Jacket, jacket of unknown real animal fur, long beige
hairs tipped w/brown, high neck, long full sleeves,
two pom-pons of same fur hanging by long suede
strips to tie at neck, hidden hook & eye closures down
center front, lined w/aqua satin, labeled "Echet Petlz
- 40" & fabric care label in German, good condition,
some discoloration to lining (ILLUS. left with shearling
bonnet) **$625.00**
Jacket, short style of black velvet, boxy-cut w/short
sleeves, stand-up collar & elaborate gold braiding
& mostly gold thread embroidery w/some red, blue,
green & pink, long ties of gold thread & braiding form
closure at neck, lined w/black moire fabric, foreign-
made, excellent condition, one long tie at neck missing
(ILLUS. left with views of the long Moroccan coat)
. . . . **$400.00**

1970s Louis Feraud Jacket & Dress Ensemble

Jacket & dress ensemble, both pieces of crepe fabric
w/a black ground printed w/flower-filled baskets in
shades of greens, pinks & browns, the sleeveless
dress w/a camisole bodice w/slight tucks along the
neckline, a natural waistline w/A-line skirt, side zipper
closure, lined w/black acetate; the cropped jacket
w/a slit neckline, wide pointed lapels, slim-fitting
long sleeves 2/3" w. wrapped buttoned cuffs, elastic
waistline w/two wrapped button & loop closures at
center front, labeled "Louis Feraud - Paris - 100%
Polyamid," early 1970s, excellent condition, the set
(ILLUS.) **$350.00**

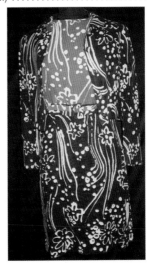

*Early 1970s Hot Pink & Dark Blue Linen Jacket &
Dress Ensemble*

Jacket & dress ensemble, of hot pink & dark blue linen, printed w/white stylized flowers & leaves, the sleeveless dress w/a crew neckline, pink bodice w/a blue skirt w/a fabric-covered belt; the short boxy blue jacket faced w/the blue linen, both pieces labeled "Adele Simpson," excellent condition, belt shows wear, early 1970s (ILLUS. previous page) **$135.00**

1970s Lady's Levi Jeans

Jeans, blue cotton denim w/traditional five-pocket styling, brass rivets, overstitching, zippered fly, labeled "Levis (small e)," very good condition, desirable fading & fraying (ILLUS.). **$225.00**

Jeans, blue denim trimmed w/stripes of gros-grain colorful ribbon diagonally stitched, excellent condition (ILLUS. right with other pair of denim jeans) **$75-125**

Two Pairs of 1970s Decorated Denim Jeans

Jeans, blue denim w/home-made patchwork embellishments on lower flares, five-pocket styling,

perhaps a 'marriage' of two different pairs, excellent condition, intentional fraying of threads & patches, front button missing (ILLUS. left with other denim jeans) **$250.00**

1970s Colorful Jumpsuit

Jumpsuit, bodice of black velvet w/deep scoop neck, cap sleeves, black velvet-wrapped buttons down center front, belt of black velvet cord, attached wide-leg pants of shiny twilled fabric w/colorful print of flowers in oranges, pinks, greens & blues on a black ground, center back zipper, lined w/black crepe, good condition, one stain on pants, some separations at waist seams (ILLUS.) **$45.00**

Early 1970s Parnis Silk Jumpsuit

Jumpsuit, printed solk foulard, a white ground w/red & blue polka dots, the bodice w/a high rollover neckline, full long sleeves w/tapered snap cuffs, high waistline continuing to full wide pants w/oversized polka dot accompanying 2 1/2" w. red & blue striped gros-grain belt w/hidden hook closure, labeled "Mollie Parnis Boutique New York," excellent condition, early 1970s (ILLUS.) **$85.00**

1970s Red & Black Velvet Jumpsuit

Jumpsuit, sleeveless, of red & black velvet w/a high banded neck & slit forming a V underneath, bustline tucked at neck for drape, high waist w/large black & red plastic square buckle, full flared legs, one black, one red, each one faced w/opposite color, hook & eye closure at back of neck & back of waist, center back zipper closure, very good condition, zipper broken, plastic buckle separated from garment in one corner (ILLUS.) **$175.00**

Jumpsuit & coat ensemble, both pieces of thick heavy waffle-knit piqué, the sleeveless jumpsuit w/a Peter Pan collar, set-in pleats from bustline to hemline, straight stovepipe legs, center front zipper hidden under self-fabric center flap, lined w/ivory china silk; the coat of same waffle knit w/color block inserts of brown & red piqué, self Chinese collar, on-seam slit pockets, hidden covered snap closure at center front, lined w/ivory satin, coat in excellent condition, jumpsuit very good w/some areas of discoloration, stains to lower leg, also minor moth holes (ILLUS. of two views, bottom of page). **$400.00**

1970s Colorful Velvet Maxi Dress

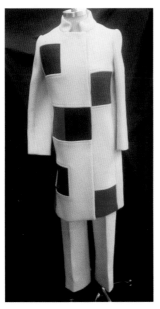

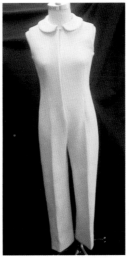

Two Views of a 1970s Jumpsuit & Coat Ensemble

Maxi dress, electric blue rayon crushed velvet w/a turtleneck, long slim-fitting sleeves, the blue ground w/a wild print of pink, orange & white stylized leaves & flowers, center back zipper, labeled "Sarff Zumpano - Erlebacher," excellent condition (ILLUS., previous page)................................. **$95.00**

Colorful 1970s Wool Maxi Dress

Maxi dress, wool w/a light tan ground printed w/a stylized print of flowers, birds & foliage in bright colors, brass gold ball buttons & loops down the center front bodice, contrasting knit waistband, labeled "Goldworm," excellent condition (ILLUS.) **$275.00**

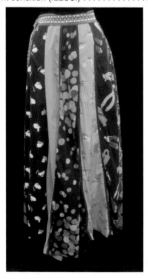

Saint' Angelo Patchwork Maxi Skirt

Maxi skirt, all-cotton, the gored skirt of twelve panels separated by crimson soutache braid, each panel w/a different whimsical print including polka dots, bunnies, toadstools & psychedelic flowers & steeply graduated, a 1 3/4" w. woven & embroidered waistband w/long surplus that wraps around waist finishing w/sash tie, labeled "Saint' Angelo - 10," Giogio di Saint' Angelo, ca. 1976 (ILLUS.) **$700.00**

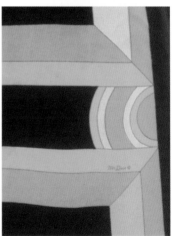

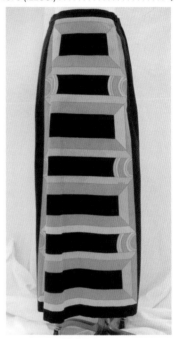

Front & Close-up of a 1970s Mr. Dino Maxi Skirt

Maxi skirt, cotton velveteen, black ground w/large center print of gold geometric shapes in a ladder-like design w/scattered facsimile signature of Mr. Dino, slit up left side w/side zipper closure, labeled "Mr. Dino - New York Paris Florence - 12," excellent condition (ILLUS. of front & a close-up) **$275.00**

1970s Patchwork Maxi Dress & Vest Ensemble

Maxi skirt & vest ensemble, each piece comprised
of various swatches of silk, some printed, some
not, including ones in orange, chartreuse & green
shantung, hot-pink paisleys, orange florals; the short
bolero-type vest edged w/bright yellow silk & lined
w/the same silk; the A-line skirt lined w/lavender china
silk w/23" l. godets at hemline, side zipper closure,
skirt labeled "Made by Calypso - Bermuda - 16,"
excellent condition, the set (ILLUS.). **$300.00**

1970s Mollie Parnis Floral Midi Dress

Midi dress, silk twill w/a bold floral print in shades of pink,
purple, orange & blue on a green ground, V-neckline,

gathered shoulders & full elbow-length sleeves w/
banded buttoned cuffs, decorative wrapped buttons
& loops down the center front, bias-cut flounce added
as insertion on lower skirt, back hemline slightly lower
than front, center back zipper closure, lined w/light blue
lustrous fabric, labeled "Mollie Parnis Boutique New
York," excellent condition (ILLUS.). **$250.00**

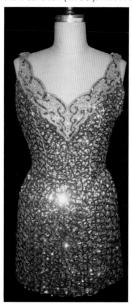

1970s Gold Lamé Sequined Mini Dress

Mini dress, gold sequins over gold lamé, sleeveless,
scalloped V-neck front & back, gold sequins & beading
over nude nylon netting around neckline edge, front
& back, normal waist, center back zipper, lined w/gold
acetate, excellent condition, few beads missing at
back neckline (ILLUS.) **$150.00**

1970s Brown Bell-Bottom Pants

Pants, brown polyester double-knit, elastic waist w/ attached self-fabric wide belt & buckle, widely flared bottoms, excellent condition (ILLUS., previous page) **$65.00**

1970s Crepe Satin Pantsuit

Pantsuit, both pieces of champagne-colored crepe satin, the smock-style jacket w/wide lapels, convertible collar, center front yoke w/tucks underneath, long full sleeves tucked at shoulders to create puffs w/yoke at upper arm, elastic cuffs, three oversized buttons down the front center; the high-waisted pleated pants w/full legs & 1" w. waistband, hidden hook & zipper fly closure, jacket labeled "Beverly Paige" & fabric care label, excellent condition, the set (ILLUS.) **$375.00**

Pantsuit, pink polyester 'crepe de chine,' bodysuit blouse top w/snaps at crotch, pink crystal set buttons down center front & at cuffs, pants w/elastic waist & wide flares, detached self-fabric sash, labeled "Mr. Dino - New York - Paris - Florence" & a fabric care label, excellent condition (ILLUS. center with two other Mr. Dino outfits). **$145.00**

Late 1970s Satin Laurent Peasant Dress

Peasant dress, iridescent rose-colored silk featuring shirred off-the-shoulder neck, full sleeves w/3" w. shirred cuffs, full dress falls from shirred yoke & tight gathers, 13" gathered flounce at graduated hemline, 10" longer in back than in front, labeled "Saint Laurent Rive Gauche - Made in France - Paris - 38," very good condition, some stretching to cuffs & neck, slight discoloration at armscyes, late 1970s (ILLUS.) **$275.00**

Saint Laurent Peasant Skirt & Shawl Outfit

Peasant skirt & shawl, both pieces of silk taffeta, bright pink shawl measures 25" w. & 70" l., edged in ruffles, labeled "Saint Laurent rive gauche - Made in France - Paris," & fabric care label; the floor-length fuchsia skirt w/slightly trained hem, 3" w. waistband in tomato red w/a long sash finish at the side, 8" l. ruffled double-tier at hemline w/a red ruffle behind, side zipper & single hook closure, labeled "Saint Laurent rive gauche - Made in France - Paris - 36," & a fabric care label, both pieces in excellent condition, one small discolored spot on shawl, ca. 1976, the set (ILLUS.) **$2,500.00**

Poncho, bright yellow boiled wool w/sleeves, pink & white rayon yarn embroidery, pink linen piping & bright pink rayon yarn fringe, good condition, some discoloration overall probably due to yarn bleeding, some fraying to piping (ILLUS. left with 1950s wool jacket, page 122) **$65.00**

Two Knitted Wool Ponchos from the 1970s

Poncho, knitted in green & yellow wool yarn, w/a yellow drawstring & pom-pons, yellow yarn fringe, excellent condition (ILLUS. right with white, brown & orange knitted poncho) **$85.00**

Poncho, knitted, white, brown & orange acrylic yarn in a banded design, excellent condition (ILLUS. left with green & yellow 1970s knitted poncho) **$35.00**

1970s Lady's Polyester Shirt

Shirt, thick polyester double-knit in shades of yellow, brown, white & orange, pointed collar, flower-shaped yellow plastic buttons down center front & at cuffs, lined, excellent condition (ILLUS.) **$42.00**

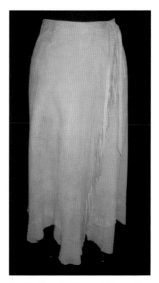

1970s Suede Fringed Wrap Skirt

Skirt, buff-colored suede w/decorative self-fabric stitching at waistline both front & back, wraps around waist w/self-fabric ties, fringed edge, uneven "torn" hem w/same suede tier laced to hem w/suede pieces, excellent condition (ILLUS.) **$350.00**

Fine Chloe Wool Skirt Suit

Skirt suit, two-piece, both pieces of plum-colored lightweight wool, the jacket features convertible rounded side collar & lapels, buttons down center front, long sleeves, seam lines beginning at middle of armscyes continuing to rounded angle-set welt pockets at hip level, back in four panels w/back vent at center, lined w/plum-colored taffeta-like fabric;

the pencil skirt in four panels w/a 1" w. waistband, accompanying belt self-fabric-covered & faced w/ brown leather, a covered oval buckle, jacket labeled "Chloe - Made in France," excellent condition (ILLUS.)
.... **$600.00**

1970s Chanel Chenille Skirt Suit

Skirt suit, two-piece, of viscose, acrylic & wool, both pieces w/bands of chenille stripes in shades of tan, brown & chestnut w/accents of bright blues, greens, pinks & reds, hip-length collarless jacket w/long sleeves, brass-colored metal buttons w/interlocks "Cs" down the center front & on the cuffs, stand pockets at hips, quilted tan silk lining, interior gilt metal chain; the mid-calf-length wrap skirt w/the same buttons at the 1" w. waistband, lined w/tan silk, both pieces labeled "Chanel Creations - Paris - Made in France - 12," & the skirt w/a fabric care & content label, excellent condition, the outfit (ILLUS.) **$800.00**

1970s Michaud Skirt & Vest Ensemble

Skirt & vest ensemble, both pieces of green leather, the vest features vertical stripes of green suede & gold monogrammed buttons down the center front, edged w/decorative stitching, accompanying narrow green leather tie belt, lined w/green lustrous fabric; the straight skirt w/a 2" w. waistband, decorative piece w/monogrammed buckle suggesting a belt at the center front w/same decorative stitching & edging down the center front & arund the waistband, center back zipper, lined w/green lustrous fabric, vest labeled "Andre Michaud - Made in France - Modele Couture," excellent condition, the set (ILLUS.) **$450.00**

1970s Cardinali Brocade Suit

Skirt suit, both pieces of brocaded fabric, golden brown ground & white & black flowers in contrasting weaves & variations, jacket features black velvet insertions on notch collar & lapel, continuing decoratively inside center opening down length of jacket, decorative goldtone & black buttons covering snaps down center front, diagonally set stand pocket at center right, princess seams at back, lined w/white satin crepe, two slit pockets at velvet insertions inside jacket, labeled "CARDINALI," the skirt in slightly A-line style w/2 1/2" wide waistband, hidden snap closure at center left, same decorative buttons covering snaps center front, lined w/gold china silk, labeled "Saks Fifth Avenue," excellent condition, the set (ILLUS.) **$495.00**

Emilio Pucci Sun Dress

Sun dress & scarf, printed w/fanciful floral & leaf design in shades of aqua, green, lavender & baby blue, all on a white ground, facsimile signature "Emilio" in places, dress features 2" wide double-faced yoke band around upper chest, straps of same patterned band w/sewn bows at top of shoulders, lined bodice, same patterned band at drop-waist continuing w/lower skirt w/handkerchief hemline, side zipper closure, accompanying scarf of same design & fabric measuring one meter squared w/hand-rolled & hand-stitched edges, by Emilio Pucci, good conidition, some discoloration at armscyes, one small stain at bottom (ILLUS.) **$800.00**

1970s Hermes Scarf-front Sweater

Sweater, scarf-front style, cream-colored wool & "crylor" yarn finely knit w/a crew neck, the silk scarf front depicting profiles of carriage horses & feathered

headstalls along the front sides w/saddlery straps & buckles down the center, in shades of cream, gold, brown & light blues, knitted round neckline & contrasting knit cuffs, center back zipper, labeled "Hermes Paris Boutique Sport - Crylor et laine - 42," & fabric care label, very good condition, some small spots of discoloration, repaired (ILLUS.) **$450.00**

1970s Gucci Sweater & Skirt Wool Ensemble

Sweater & skirt ensemble, both pieces of wool, the short-sleeves sweater top in cream-colored wool w/a square neckline in conrasting knit w/yellow & blue stripes & contrasting knit on cuffs & 5" w. waistband also set off w/blue & yellow stripes; the A-line skirt w/a 1" w. wasitband of the same contrasting knit, blue & yellow stripe bands around the lower portion, lined w/ white acetate, both pieces labeled "Gucci - Wool 100% - Made in Italy - 48" & a fabric care label, excellent condition, some minor pilling (ILLUS.) **$175.00**

1970s Levi Trousers & T-shirt Outfit

Trousers & tee shirt, Big "E" Levi trousers w/multi-colored woven stripes, two hip slit pockets & two patch pockets at back, center front zipper & brass button closure, labeled "Levi's for Gals - Sta-Prest - Levis;" pink tee shirt w/scoop neck w/raglan cap sleeves, both excellent condition, tee shirt **$38**; trousers (ILLUS., previous page) **$125.00**

MEN'S CLOTHING

1970s Leather Belt with Scenes of Firemen

Belt, brown leather stamped with scenes of firemen in action, stainless steel buckle, good condition, some wear & creasing to leather (ILLUS.) **$55.00**

1970s Beaded Leather Belt with Silver Buckle

Belt, brown leather w/leather appliqués & beaded inserts & cotton thread embroidery details, silver buckle engraved w/basketweave design, good condition, some softening & wear to leather (ILLUS.) **$65.00**

Two 1970s Decorative Disco Jackets

Disco jacket, 100% polyester silver lamé w/silver sequined front, slight padding at shoulders, center front zipper w/metal tassel toggle, elastic at cuffs & waist, labeled "Cervelle - Size XL" w/fabric care label, excellent condition (ILLUS. right with black & gold disco jacket) **$65.00**

Disco jacket, unisex-style, 100% black silk, completely covered in black & gold sequins w/tiger stripe design, center front zipper, large shoulder pads, elastic cuffs & waist, lined in black rayon, labeled "MODI - Size M" & fabric care label, excellent condition (ILLUS. left with silver disco jacket) **$250.00**

Golfing cardigan sweater, 100% orlon acrylic pale yellow textured knit, buttons down center front, full long sleeves, contrasting knit turn-back cuffs, alligator logo over left chest, labeled "IZOD Lacoste - 100% Orlon Acrylic - L," excellent condition, some minimal pilling to yarn (ILLUS. with golfing ensemble). . **$65.00**

Complete 1970s Golfing Ensemble

Golfing knickers, 100% wool in green & black tartan plaid, pleated waist to hem, self-fabric waist belt w/heavy metal buckle closure center front, zipper fly, diagonally-set off-seam slit pockets, tapered cuffs, two back welt pockets, one buttoned, excellent condtion (ILLUS. with golf ensemble) **$200.00**

Golfing polo shirt, cream-colored nylon knit, body & collar of shirt waffle-knit w/weave of contrasting knit over left breast depicting knight chess piece, raglan short sleeves of smooth knit, button front closure, labeled "Brooks Times Square - Fashion Originations - Ban-Lon Full Fashioned - Yarn All Nylon - RN 17547," excellent condition (ILLUS. with golfing ensemble) **$40.00**

Hawaiian shirt, double knit polyester in bold geometric pattern in greens & browns, self-fabric-covered buttons down center front, labeled "Sears Hawaiian Fashions," excellent condition (ILLUS. center left with 1950s & 1960s Hawaiian shirts) **$35.00**

1970s Brown Velvet Jacket

Jacket, brown velvet w/black patterns & squares, wide lapels, singled-breasted w/two carved metal buttons down center front, four small buttons down each cuff, welt pocket at either hip, deep back vent at center lower back, lined w/grey satin, slit pockets in lining, no label although carved metal buttons depict a shield & the word "Salzburg," good condition, some wear under arms (ILLUS.) **$150.00**

Desirable 1970s Man's Levi Denim Jacket

Jacket, cotton denim w/traditional flap patch pockets, overstitching & brass buttons, labeled "Levis (small e)," very good condition, desirable extensive fading & fraying (ILLUS.). **$375.00**

1970s Printed Leather Jacket

Jacket, light brown leather printed w/paisleys, flowers & geometric lines & shapes in shades of beige, blue & light green, full wide lapels, full sleeves w/carved horn buttons at cuffs & two buttons down center front, hip-level welt pockets w/exaggerated flap, center vent at lower back, lined w/beige acetate, labeled "Neiman-Marcus - Genuine Leather - Made in Korea," & fabric care label, excellent condition (ILLUS.) **$450.00**

1970s Jacket, Pants & Shirt Ensemble

Jacket, pants & shirt ensemble, formal yellow shirt of polyester-cotton blend w/tucks & lace on center pront, narrow lace edging at cuffs, labeled "After Six," excellent condition, $55; patterned textured polyester clip-on bow tie, 1960s, excellent condition, $13; plaid trousers of 100% wool w/slight flare at bottom, tab buttoned pocket at right hip, two-inch wide waistband & two-inch wide self-fabric belt loops, top-lined, center front zipper closure & top hooks, excellent condition, $100-125; brown jacket of polyester twill w/satin collar, padding at shoulder, hand-stitched lining, two deep vents at back, center front button closure, excellent condition, jacket (ILLUS. of ensemble) **$150.00**

1970s Leisure Suit with Appliqued Ducks

Leisure suit, beige gabardine, cropped Lindbergh-style jacket w/wide lapels, tabbed buttoned chest pockets & cuffs, buttons down front center, fitted waistband, appliquéd w/flying ducks on the front; the flat front pants w/a 2" w. waistband, on-seam slit pockets at front hips, welt pockets in back, straight trouser legs, jacket labeled "Dallas Unwinders," & fabric care label, very good condition, one small stain on pant front (ILLUS.) **$225.00**

1970s Colorful Corduroy Pants

Pants, cotton corduroy, in shades of orange & yellow depicting tropical foliage & tigers, flat front, 2" w. waistband, slash pockets at hips, welt pockets in back, zipper fly, straight legs, labeled "Lilly Pulitzer Men's

Stuff - Palm Beach," excellent condition, early 1970s (ILLUS.) **$350.00**

Tee Shirt & Pants Outfit, Circa 1970

Pants & tee shirt outfit, tee shirt of peach-colored cotton & polyester blend w/iron-on patch reading "Free Moustache Rides," good condition, some fabric wear & fading, ca. 1970, **$55**; cotton pants (possible blend) in a madras patchwork design in shades of beige, pink, brown & red, two-inch waistband angle set welt pockets in front & straight welt pockets in back, labeled "A JAYMAR SLACK" & fabric care label, ca. 1970, excellent condition, pants (ILLUS. of the outfit) **$175.00**

1970s Pants & Vest Ensemble

Pants & vest ensemble, both pieces of striped polyester & cotton blend, long vest w/patch pockets & self-fabric belt, high-waisted pants, slash pockets, labeled "Sears - The Men's Store - Size Trim Regular," good condition, some fraying along edges of vest, the ensemble (ILLUS., previous page) **$275.00**

1970s Nik-Nik Shirt with Unusual Nudes Design

Shirt, 100% textured nylon, black ground w/smoke & nude prints in pink, browns & grays, center front button closure, buttoned cuffs, labeled "Nik-Nik - 100% Textured Nylon - Made in Italy - Size L," excellent condition w/slight fading (ILLUS.) **$125.00**

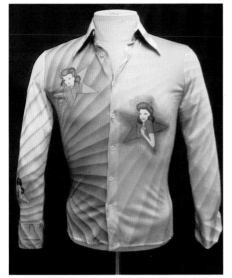

Front & Back Views of 1970s Nik-Nik Fabric Shirt

Shirt, 100% nylon, gray ground w/stage show-themed print in golds, pinks & browns, center front button closure, buttoned cuffs, labeled "Nik-Nik Fabric Hoberu Enterprises Inc. - 100% Nylon Printed in Italy - Size L," excellent condition (ILLUS. of front & back)
. . . . **$175.00**

1970s Oleg Cassini Graphic Shirt

Shirt, polyester w/contrasting black & white graphic print, wide collar w/pointed ends, breast patch pocket, buttoned banded cuffs, by Oleg Cassini, excellent condition (ILLUS.). **$65.00**

1979 Grateful Dead Tee Shirt

Tee shirt, Grateful Dead souvenir-type, 100% cotton w/a tie-dyed effect around a colored silk-screened print on the front, signed "Ed Donahue 1979, " excellent condition, some fabric fading (ILLUS.) **$250.00**

1977 Liverpool Souvenir Tee Shirt

Tee shirt, red polyester & cotton blend w/flocked iron-on letters reading "Liverpool - European- Champs - 77," excellent condition, some fabric fading, 1977 (ILLUS.) **$150.00**

1970s Trousers & Polo Shirt Outfit

Trousers & polo shirt outfit, shirt of cream-colored nylon knit, body & collar of shirt waffle-knit w/weave of contrasting knit over left breast depicting a knight chess piece, raglan short sleeves of smooth knit, button front closure, labled "Brooks Times Square - Fashion Originations - Ban-Lon Full Fashioned - Yarn All Nylon - RN 17547," excellent condition, $40; pants of argyle-patterned polyester double-knit, burgundy, white & gray, back tab patch pockets, front welt pockets, wide belt loops, zipper fly, labeled "100% Polyester Double Knit Slacks" & fabric care label, good condition, some separation of seams at back, pants (ILLUS. of two pieces) **$55.00**

Varsity jacket, orange wool w/black leather sleeves & pocket edging, acrylic knit cuffs & waist, tufted orange & black appliquéd letters reading "FORT LEE BRIDGEMENT 73" in back, gray rayon quilted lining, center snap closure, labeled "Athletic ProLine Sports Equipment," good condition, some drying & cracking to leather, some holes in lining, 1973 (ILLUS. right with 1950s varsity jacket) **$125.00**

PART IV: CLOTHING ACCESSORIES

CHAPTER 11: HATS, CAPS & BONNETS

PRE-1850 CLOTHING

LADIES'

1840s Silk Taffeta Calash Bonnet

Bonnet, drawn or calash-style, burgundy silk taffeta, shirred over thin vertical supports, box pleats at nape of neck, faced w/net, silk-lined, net around front w/bonnet meets forehead, excellent condition, original ribbon tie under chin missing, some discoloration, lining brittle, ca. 1846 (ILLUS.) **$475.00**

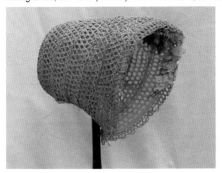

1840s Lady's Straw Bonnet

Bonnet, open-weave straw w/tiny flowers inside the brim, ca. 1840s (ILLUS.) **$175-250**

Early Quilted Silk Lady's Bonnet

Bonnet, quilted purple & green silk, ca. 1830-40 (ILLUS.) **$150-250**

CLOTHING - 1850-1920

CHILDREN'S

Girl's Ivory Straw Fanchon Bonnet

Bonnet, fanchon-style, ivory straw w/blue & ivory striped silk bows & ties, ca. 1860 (ILLUS.) **$100-125**

Boy's French-Made Blue Velvet Cap

Cap, boy's, dark blue velvet w/appliqués & silk tassel, lining w/maker's logo printed in French, ca. 1850s (ILLUS.) **$60-100**

Boy's Straw Hat, Circa 1870

Hat, boy's, straw w/blue cloth band & bow, ca. 1870 (ILLUS.) **$75-100**

LADIES'

Matching 1880s Bodice & Bonnet

Bodice & bonnet, bodice in blue silk faille & fabric alternating stripes of blue silk & gold velvet, buttons w/cut steels, the matching bonnet of blue velvet edged w/large blue buttons & trimmed w/bows of blue silk, gold silk & striped fabric as well as feathers, worn by an 1880s bride, the pair (ILLUS.) **$350-550**

Fancy Black Velvet Bonnet, Circa 1900

Bonnet, black velvet trimmed w/sequins, ostrich feathers & ornate jeweled buckle, ca. 1900 (ILLUS.) . **$250-350**

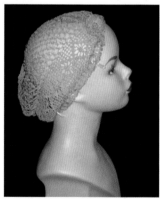

Crocheted Yarn Boudoir Cap, Ca. 1900

Boudoir cap, crocheted tan twisted yarn w/peach silk ribbon running through same yarn sleeves, small self-fabric rosette on either side, excellent condition, 1900-10 (ILLUS.) **$150-200**

1850s Blue Cap with Lilac Flowers

Cap, blue fabric cover w/artificial lilac flowers, ca. 1850 (ILLUS., previous page) $25-40

1860s Lady's White Muslin Cap

Cap, white muslin w/eyelet trim, ca. 1860 (ILLUS.) $30-50

Black Horsehair Hat with Pins

Hat, black horsehair w/rhinestone pins & drawstring lining, ca. 1905-10 (ILLUS.) $125-175

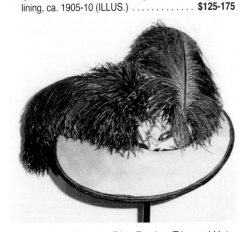

Large Late Victorian Blue Feather-Trimmed Hat

Hat, blue cloth w/black ostrich feathers & jeweled buckle, ca. 1900 (ILLUS.) $200-350

Brown Plush Hat with Ostrich Feather & Velvet Flower

Hat, brown plush w/ostrich feather surrounding crown & teal blue velvet flower, ca. 1900 (ILLUS.) . . . $200-300

1870s Purple Velvet & Feather Hat

Hat, cream felt w/swath of deep purple velvet twisted & piled mostly on crown, slight brim, trimmed w/same velvet & narrow gold cord, bead trimmed white feathers set atop w/one grey of softer variety in between, purple satin ribbon tie, lined w/cream-colored silk, labeled "Winter Importer - 489 Fulton St. - Brooklyn," good condition, some wear & tearing to lining, some beads missing, ca. 1877 (ILLUS.) $375.00

Finely Woven Straw Hat, Circa 1860

Hat, finely woven straw w/wide tiered brim, ca. 1860 (ILLUS.) **$100-150**

Straw Garden Party Hat with Flowers

Hat, garden party-type, straw w/silk band, artificial flowers encircling the brim, drawstring lining, ca. 1900-10 (ILLUS.) **$150-225**

Gold Velvet Hat with Ribbon & Feathers

Hat, gold velvet w/metallic ribbon & ostrich feathers, ca. 1915-20 (ILLUS.) **$75-100**

Fancy Trimmed Green Felt 1890s Hat

Hat, green felt w/printed silk ribbon bows & black ostrich feathers, ca. 1890s (ILLUS.). **$175-250**

Unusual Mink & Mink-Trimmed Hat

Hat, mink trimmed w/mink tails & a flower cluster, ca. 1905 (ILLUS.) **$200-300**

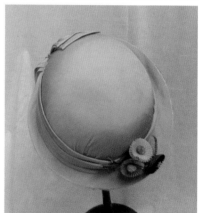

Labeled Lady's Hat of Pink Silk & Flowers

Hat, pink silk w/brightly colored pleated celluloid flowers, inside lining w/label for Carson Pirie Scott & Co., Chicago, ca. 1915 (ILLUS.) **$100-150**

Purple Velvet Hat with Ostrich Feathers

Hat, purple velvet w/purple ostrich feathers, ca. 1880
(ILLUS.) **$100-150**

*Lady's 1860s Gold Felt Riding Hat with
Feather & Bow*

Hat, riding-type, gold felt w/bow & ostrich feather trim, ca.
1860 (ILLUS.) **$100-200**

Flower-Trimmed Silver Straw Hat

Hat, silver-colored straw trimmed w/brightly colored
flowers, ca. 1913 (ILLUS.) **$85-125**

Straw Hat with Feathers, Circa 1890

Hat, tan straw w/ostrich feathers & flowers, ca. 1890
(ILLUS.) **$150-250**

Straw Hat with Wool & Feathers

Hat, tiny bands of peach-colored wool sewn over fine
straw & trimmed w/orange & white ostrich feathers, ca.
1905-10 (ILLUS.) **$125-200**

Ornately Trimmed Lady's Toque Hat

Hat, toque-style, the sides trimmed w/gold metallic
thread, the top covered w/dark green chenille cord,
large buckle & feathers, ca. 1902 (ILLUS.)
. . . . **$150-250**

Tri-Corn Straw Hat with Pulastic Lining

Hat, tri-corn-style, bluish green dyed straw w/large black velvet bow, lining marked "Pulastic adjustable hat lining - Makes any hat fit any head - comfortably," ca. 1915-20 (ILLUS.) **$100-150**

Lady's Hat of White Gathered Net with Blue Puff

Hat, white gathered net w/pale blue chiffon puff, ca. 1890 (ILLUS.) **$100-150**

Large Velvet & Ostrich Feather Hat, Circa 1910

Hat, wide-brimmed oyster-colored velvet w/ostrich feather encircling the crown, ca. 1910 (ILLUS.)
. . . . **$175-275**

Wide-brimmed Feathered Velvet Hat

Hat, wide-brimmed pale bluish green velvet w/a large two-tone blue ostrich feather, ca. 1900 (ILLUS.)
. . . . **$200-300**

Elegant Victorian Lady's Skating Hat

Skating hat, teal blue silk w/wide matching ribbon band & edge w/white fur, ca. 1870-80 (ILLUS.)
. . . . **$100-150**

Decorated Blue Cotton Swim Cap

Swim cap, blue cotton w/yarn flower cluster & bright yellow trim, ca. 1900 (ILLUS.). **$25-40**

MEN'S

Man's Brown Derby, Circa 1910

Hat, derby, brown, ca. 1910 (ILLUS.) **$50-100**

Late Victorian Man's Faux Beaver Hat

Hat, faux beaver w/wide brown gros grain ribbon band & bow, late 19th c. (ILLUS.) **$75-125**

Late Victorian Small Fedora

Hat, fedora, for a small man or large boy, some edge fraying, ca. 1880-90 (ILLUS.) **$50-90**

Simple 1870s Man's Straw Hat

Hat, straw w/simple cloth band, ca. 1870 (ILLUS.)
. . . . **$75-125**

Embroidered Velvet Man's Smoking Cap

Smoking cap, round black velvet w/silk embroidery & tassel, mid-19th c. (ILLUS.) **$85-150**

Man's Collapsible Top Hat, Circa 1900

Top hat, collapsible-type, ca. 1900 (ILLUS.)
. . . . **$100-150**

CLOTHING - 1920-1930

CHILDREN'S

Girl's 1920s Embroidered Cloche Hat

Hat, cloche-style, embroidered geometric design in brown & yellow, ca. 1925 (ILLUS.) **$75-100**

LADIES'

Large Homemade Bonnet

Bonnet, homemade of pink voile fabric covering a padded crown & brim, stuffed perhaps w/wood or straw chips, shallow rounded 2" h. crown w/pale pink satin ribbon around base, pink & blue ostrich plumes sewn to ribbon & graduated brim 4 1/2" w. at front & 2" h. at back, pale pink ruffled edge & same pale pink fabric lining brim, darker pink fabric for crown, pink ribbons used as ties, late 1920s - early 1930s, good condition, execution somewhat sloppy (ILLUS.)
. . . . **$30.00**

1920s Fancy Beaded Bridal Coronet

Bridal coronet, stiffened muslin backing w/glazed white wax flowers & small white beads in varying shapes & sizes, sewn to a clear band w/elastic chin strap, late

1920s, good condition, some loose threads (ILLUS.)
. . . . **$400.00**

1920s Flower-Trimmed Cloche Hat

Hat, cloche-style, black & grey w/flowers & metallic embroidery (ILLUS.) **$75-100**

1920s Embroidered Rose Silk Cloche

Hat, cloche-style, dusty rose silk w/embroidery & a rhinestone ornament (ILLUS.) **$85-150**

Rare 1920s Golden Cloche Hat

Hat, cloche-style, gold guipure lace overstitched w/gold metallic thread & attached to a golden lamé cap decorated w/self-fabric rosettes sewn into clusters, covered w/lace forming flaps on either side of head, lined w/tan-colored silk satin w/a gold gros-grain ribbon sweatband, labeled "Jordan's - Boston - Paris - London," excellent condition, some shreading in lining (ILLUS.) **$650.00**

1920s Colorful Raffia Cloche Hat

Hat, cloche-style, raffia w/slightly open weave, spiraling from center top, 3 1/2" w. central band of multi-colored woven raffia, very narrow band near edge, late 1920s, excellent condition (ILLUS.) **$150.00**

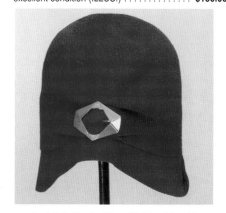

Red Felt Cloche Hat with Metal Buckle

Hat, cloche-style, red felt w/goldtone buckle (ILLUS.) **$65-85**

MEN'S

Man's 1920s Straw Bowler

Bowler, finely woven straw, five-inch high rounded crown w/dark brown gros-grain ribbon around base & side bow finish, 3" w. slightly turned brim, light brown leather sweat band inside, fair condition, straw quite brittle & broken in places, sweatband discolored, late 1920s - early 1930s (ILLUS.) **$22.00**

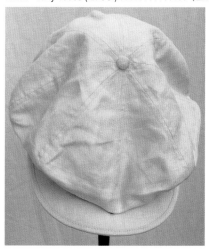

1920s Man's Linen Golf Hat

Golf hat, tan linen, patented by Spalding in 1927 (ILLUS.) **$35-50**

CLOTHING - 1930-1940

LADIES'

1930s Grey Wool Beret

Beret, grey wool, asymmetrical shape falling sharply to one side w/a double row of tiny white buttons secured w/red thread at botton end where hat meets side of face, red gros-grain ribbon sweatband, labeled "Milgrim - 22," includes original hatbox, excellent condition, without hatbox (ILLUS.) **$155.00**

1930s Sequined 'Biggonet' Cap

Cap, 'Biggonet' style, black wool w/black sequined swirls, ends tie under chin, excellent condition (ILLUS.)
. . . . **$175.00**

Green Crocheted Cloche Cap

Cap, cloche-style, crocheted green glazed thread, self-fabric flower at top & side flaps, labeled "Saks Fifth Avenue," excellent condition though thread brittle, ca. 1930 (ILLUS.) **$150.00**

Front & Back Views of 'Baby Doll' Hat

Hat, 'baby doll' style, light blue piqué fabric over a support, resembling a tiny top hat, pink fabric roses & stiff green leaves at front brim & at band, cascading shocking pink net veil attached at back & meant to fall behind, self-fabric wrapped support to secure hat to back of head, black gros-grain ribbon sweatband, lined w/black fabric, labeled "Bloch's Hats of Distinction - 4546 Sheridan Rd.," good condition, minor discoloration, late 1930s - early 1940s, 7" d., 3 1/2" h. (ILLUS. of front & back) **$425.00**

1930s Blue Beret Hat with Fisk Label

Hat, beret-style, navy blue felt, w/a "Fisk" label (ILLUS., previous page) **$25-40**

1930s Brown Straw Hat with Ribbon Trim

Hat, brown straw w/rolled ribbon trim, ca. 1930 (ILLUS.) **$25-40**

Early 1930s Felt & Velvet Cloche Hat

Hat, cloche-style, burgundy felt & velvet, ca. 1930 (ILLUS.) **$25-45**

Black Cocktail Hat with Rhinestone Pin

Hat, cocktail-type, pointed & folded black material w/ lightning bolt rhinestone pin (ILLUS.) **$30-45**

1930s "Empress Eugenie" Feathered Hat

Hat, "Empress Eugenie" style, pink chenille yarn knit in a circle & edges placed over a wire support, subtly peaked crown w/1 1/4" w. mauve satin ribbon at base, profusely layered w/pink, white & mauve ostricyh feathers at front, black & gold-tipped ostrich feathers at back, one spray of short clipped fuchsia-colored ostrich feathers at center back, black rolled elastic band & hair comb at back to secure hat to head, good condition, some discoloration to yarn & ribbon (ILLUS.) **$55.00**

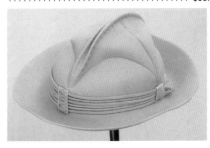

1930s Decorative Grey Felt Hat

Hat, grey felt, paneled crown w/decorative center seam, banded trim (ILLUS.) **$25-40**

Large 1930s Woven Straw Cartwheel Hat

Hat, natural woven straw cartwheel-style, spiral beginning at recessed shallow crown, pink gros-grain ribbon edging at lip w/back bow finish, 5 1/2" w. brim, crown lined w/white satin, pink gros-grain sweatband, fair condition, discoloration to pink ribbons, one large tear in brim (ILLUS., previous page) **$125.00**

Front View of a 1930s Black 'Plateau' Hat

Front & Side Views of 1930s Black Velvet 'Portrait' Hat

Hat, 'portrait' style, black velvet covering entire hat, shallow uneven 3" h. crown, pearl-studded crescent-shaped brooch at center, balck velvet cord around base w/back bow, graduated brim measuring 5" w. at sides & 1" w. at back, front of brim rolled up & secured w/a second pearl-studded crescent brooch, black gros-grain ribbon sweatband, crown lined w/black netting, labeled "22," excellent condition (ILLUS. of front & side view) **$150.00**

Back view of 1930s Black 'Plateau' Hat

Hat, 'plateau' style, black wool felt reaching to a point at the forehead, decorated w/a rhinestone button & continuing to a back w/a large curl finish, black felt strap to secure to head, black gros-grain ribbon sweatband, 3" w. felt piece, 7" across, excellent condition, late 1930s - early 1940s (ILLUS. of front & back) **$150.00**

1930s Wide-Brimmed Black Straw Hat

Hat, ridged fine black straw in a spiral pattern from the center, shallow 2" h. crown made of joined straw spirals w/four spaces between them, black velvet cord around base w/back bow finish, graduated brim 5" at widest to 1 1/2" w. at back, labeled "A Clemar Original by Wesco," excellent condition (ILLUS. previous page)
.... **$125.00**

Two Views of a Late 1930s 'Topper' Style Hat

Hat, 'Topper' style, black wool felt w/crushed 4" h. crown, side of crown tucked to form jagged strip of ruffles down length of hat w/a black tassel at the side, asymmetrical brim 2" w. at widest, black elastic band secures hat to head, labeled "Jeanne Tete - Mandel Brothers Chicago," late 1930s - early 1940s, excellent condition (ILLUS. of front & side view) **$150.00**

CLOTHING - 1940-1950

CHILDREN'S

1940s Girl's Burgundy Felt Hat

Hat, girl's, burgundy felt w/ribbon trim, 1940s (ILLUS.)
.... **$20-40**

LADIES'

1940s Black Beaded Beanie

Beanie, black wool fur felt w/black beads scattered here & there w/rolled black felt creating a tab at center crown, rolled felt edge for brim, black gros-grain ribbon sweatband, labeled "22 M.S.C.," 7" w., excellent condition (ILLUS.)....................... **$55.00**

Black Sequinned Cocktail Hat with Feathers

Cocktail hat, black sequins over black satin w/sculpted & rolled twisted brim, thick sprays of black ostrich feathers at top side, black gros-grain ribbon sweatband, lined in black satin, shredded label reads "...York Creation - 22," late 1940s, excellent condition (ILLUS.) **$195.00**

Red & Orange Floral 'Baby Doll' Hat

Hat, 'baby doll' style, composed of red silk flowers w/yellow & white centers & velvet leaves in gold, oranges & red atop an orange base, two attached combs at the side to secure to head, labeled "Hats By Helyn - Cincinnati," good condition, some staining to underside of base (ILLUS.). **$150.00**

1940s Lady's Fedora

Fedora, black velvet 3 1/2" h. creased crown w/a 1 1/2" w. black gros-grain ribbon around the base & overlapping ends at back, trimmed w/a spray of black & dark green feathers tucked into ribbon at back, 2 1/2" w. rolled brim made from black felt w/velvet back, labeled "Morreton - Made in France," excellent condition (ILLUS.). **$150.00**

1940s Yellow 'Baby Doll' Style Hat

Hat, 'baby doll' style, mustard yellow knitted fabric over a thin pliable base forming a top hat of sorts w/graduated & slightly turned brim measuring 4 1/2" w. at front & 1" w. at back, center back comes to abrupt point, a swath of curled brown feathers set at the front, brown net veil attaches at center back & drapes up sides of crown & falls over brim to cover the face, brown gros-grain pleated ribbon sweatband, brown gros-grain ribbon ties, labeled "New York Creation - Adjustable," excellent condition, very minor fabric wear (ILLUS.) **$400.00**

Rare 1940s Flamingo Hat

Hat, 'baby doll' style, sculpted black velvet-covered base
in a modified tricorne shape trimmed w/two small
flamingoes sitting on top & covered in real feathers,
real feet & glass eyes, the necks entwined, trimmed
w/a black veil, black gros-grain ribbon sweatband,
black elastic cord to secure hat to head, labeled "Bes-
Ben - Made in Chicago (handwritten) - 875," excellent
condition, some tears in veil (ILLUS.)...... **$4,500.00**

'Baby Doll' Straw Hat in Cornucopia Form

Hat, 'baby doll-cornucopia' style, ridged coarse straw
sculpted & rolled to form a cornucopia shape w/
braided black straw forming bows, trimmed w/blue
cotton flowers & green leaves, edged w/black gros-
grain ribbon, good condition, some discoloration to
flowers, ca. 1940 (ILLUS.) **$85.00**

1940s Brown Felt Hat with Mink Fur Trim

Hat, base of brown felt w/2" h. rounded crown covered
w/a wide brown gros-grain ribbon w/the same ribbon
around the base & a bow in the back, graduated brim
3" at widest & 2" w. at back covered w/mink fur, gros-
grain ribbon sweatband, excellent condition (ILLUS.)
.... **$125.00**

Front & Side Views of 1940s Black Organdy Hat

Hat, black organdy woven in a spiral beginning from
top center, organdy-covered wired edge brim,
shallow crown w/ 1 1/2" w. black satin ribbon at base
w/overlapping finish & graduated brim measuring 5"
at widest front to 2 1/4" w. at back, black gros-grain
ribbon sweatband, labeled "New York Creation - 22,"
excellent condition (ILLUS. front & side view)
.... **$150.00**

1940s Black Felt Inverted Tricorne Hat

Hat, black wool felt draped over a round black felt crown piece secured underneath at four points to create an inverted tricorne effect 12" w. from side to side & 12" across front peak to back, black gros-grain ribbon & edged w/black gros-grain ribbon, same ribbon used as a sweatband, labeled "New York Creation - Creations by Lecie Studio," excellent condition (ILLUS.)
. . . . **$165.00**

Two Views of a Large Eliptical Fur Felt Hat

Hat, brown fur felt w/extended nap covering a sturdy diamond-shaped eliptical form, shallow barely 1" h. crown w/brown satin ribbon around base & bow at back, brim measures 2" l. from point to point & 13" w. across center, brown satin ribbon piping around the crown & 1" from edge which issues sprays of ostrich feathers, further brown satin piping along true edge of hat, fur felt-covered support underneath, crown lined w/black satin, late 1940s - early 1950s, good

condition, some wear to feathers & support (ILLUS. of side & back) **$200.00**

1940s Cartwheel-style Hat with Petals

Hat, cartwheel-style, composed of silk petals in shades of purple, lavender, white & grey & sprinkled w/velvet petals on top w/green leaves, secured to a white lace backing over purple velvet-covered wire supports, very shallow crown, labeled "Gimbels New York," fair condition, discoloration & overall wear to petals (ILLUS.) **$175.00**

Large 1940s Straw Cartwheel Hat with Silk Flowers

Hat, cartwheel-style, finely woven straw spiraling from center w/a shallow squared 2" h. crown w/a wide sage green taffeta ribbon around the base, a wide bow at front w/silk flowers, green velvet leaves & a singled green wax bud & brown leaf & stem, 3" w. brim, black gros-grain ribbon sweatband, partial label reads "Adjustable," good condition, flowers discolored in places, ribbon faded (ILLUS.). **$125.00**

Large 1940s Cartwheel Straw Hat

Hat, cartwheel-style, ridged & thin finely woven straw, a recessed barely 2" h. crown w/black gros-grain ribbon around base & surrounded by white cotton petals w/

black edges fanned out & wrapped w/bronze-colorred net veil, 3 1/2" w. brim, velvet-covered side supports to secure to head, black gros-grain ribbon sweatband, labeled "Gage Brothers & Co. - Since 1856 - Chicago New York," excellent condition, some tears to veil (ILLUS.) **$110.00**

Grey Felt Hat with Bugle Bead Trim

Hat, grey felt w/domed crown covered w/black bugle beads (ILLUS.) **$25-45**

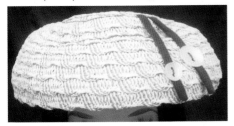

Large 1940s Grey & White Raffia Hat

Hat, grey & white raffia braided & woven spiraling from top center, flat crown & graduated turn-down brim measuring 5" w. at front & 3" w. at back, red velvet ribbon & button detail at front, same woven supports underneath crown to secure to head, labeled "Original by Sherman," mid-1940s, excellent condition (ILLUS.) **$150.00**

Two Views of 1940s Python Skin 'Plateau' Hat

Hat, 'plateau' style, python skin covering a padded disk w/a back support & flourishes covered w/brown faille, labeled "New York Creation - Adjustable - Genuine Python Snake Skin by Phil Berman & Co.," excellent condition (ILLUS. of two views) **$175.00**

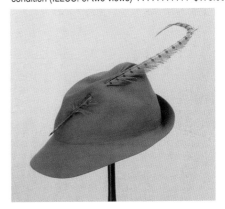

1930s Robin Hood Hat with Feather

Hat, "Robin Hood" style, green felt trimmed w/a pheasant feather (ILLUS.) **$35-50**

1940s Rose Felt Hat with Ribbon Trim

Hat, rose felt w/wide ribbon trim (ILLUS.) **$35-50**

1940s Lady's Stetson-Style Hat in Brown with White Crochet Trim

Hat, Stetson-style, brown felt w/brown & white crochet trim, ca. 1940 (ILLUS.) **$40-60**

Large Fine Woven Straw Hat with Flowers

Hat, very thin straw 'thread' glazed gold & woven into tiny loops spiraling from center top, shallow 1 1/2' h. crown w/a narrow brown gros-grain ribbon around base, covered by cotton flowers, roses, rosebuds, hydrangeas, green stems & leaves at center front & sides, graduated brim from 5" w. to 3" w. at back, black gros-grain ribbon sweatband, unwrapped wire supports at sides under brim, excellent condition (ILLUS.) **$190.00**

1940s Wide-Brimmed Black & Green Hat

Hat, wide-brimmed, black felt w/green crocheted crown & brim band (ILLUS.) **$40-60**

1940s Grey Velvet & Feathers Headband

Headband, dove grey 2" w. velvet band trimmed w/same fabric twisted into a rosette at the top & silvery grey feathers, mid-1940s, excellent condition (ILLUS.) **$65.00**

1940s Black Toque with Bows

Toque, black wool felt w/four bows from thicker cuts of felt, attached at 5" intervalls to the undulating edge, black gros-grain ribbon sweatband, excellent condition (ILLUS.) **$65.00**

1940s Black Straw Flower-Trimmed Toque

Toque, glazed & woven black straw w/burgundy velvet trim, swirl detail at top & same velvet-covered wire supports incorporated into side design, pink silk flower & green leaf trim at top, lined w/navy blue glazed netting, labeled "Kay & Guy Anderson New York - 22 - Ethol Hotelling Kalamazoo," good condition, silk flower slightly withered, net lining torn (ILLUS. of back, previous page) **$65.00**

1940s Toque with Ostrich Plumes

Toque, magenta-colored fur felt w/extended nap & same fabric piping at crown & forming a rolled corded bow at back, trimmed w/pink ostrich feathers cascading from all sides, inside supports covered in fur felt, excellent condition, slight discoloration to edge (ILLUS.) **$200.00**

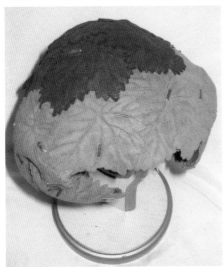

1940s Toque with Flocked Felt Leaves

Toque, purple & mauve-colored flocked felt leaves sewn over a canvas support & spinkled w/clear bugle beads, probably homemade, good condition, some bading to leaves, no lining, not expertly rendered (ILLUS.) **$38.00**

1940s Purple Velvet Toque-Style Hat

Toque, purple velvet w/sculptural bicorne top, self-fabric twisted band & soft vertical folds of same velvet at bottom, goldtone & rhinestone cherry brooch sewn at side, lined w/stiffened purple lace, late 1940s - early 1950s, good condition, some staining, fabric separated slightly from base at front (ILLUS.) **$40.00**

1940s Slouch Toque in Velvet

Toque, slouch-style, champagne-colored velvet sewn into fine ribs, crown 5" h. at highest & 4" h. at front dip w/a tuck at the center, lined w/black satin, labeled "Marion Valle," late 1940s - early 1950s, excellent condition, one small mark in tucked front (ILLUS.) **$125.00**

1940s Purple Velvet Turban with Brooch

Turban, crushed purple velvet tucked to drape from center of crown, purple satin band around the base w/a rhinestone 'snowfalke' brooch at center, purple gros-grain ribbon sweatband, crown lined w/gold lace, labeled "Vogue Mont - Chicago New York," late 1940s, good condition w/some signs of wear & discoloration (ILLUS.) **$62.00**

Two Views of a 1940s Fur Felt Wedding Cap

Wedding cap, ivory-colored fur felt w/extended lustrous nap, self-fabric piping along edges w/side drape & beaded leaf & pearl detail, lined w/brown satin, good condition, nap flattened in places (ILLUS. of front & side view) **$125.00**

MEN'S

1940s Man's Alpine Hat

Alpine hat, tan fur felt w/extended nap, 6" h. creased crown, brown velvet band around base w/vintage souvenir pins, 2" rolled brim edged w/brown gros-grain ribbon, green taffeta sweatband, labeled "Hut Haller - Innsbruck," Austrian, excellent condition, some wear to inside label, pins not original to hat (ILLUS.)
. . . . **$65.00**

Original Stetson Hat and Box

Fedora, Western-style Stetson, stiff taupe wool felt, five-inch high creased crown & sides, three-inch wide brim, gros-grain ribbon edging & band w/bow finish, white satin lining, leather sweat brown band, labeled "STETSON - Twenty Five - John S. Stetson Company - Size 7 1/4 - Oval -EXCEL FRONTIER STORE LUBBOCK TEXAS," excellent condition, minor discoloration to satin lining, w/original box, late 1940s - early 1950s (ILLUS.). **$250.00**

CLOTHING - 1950-1960

LADIES'

Band hat, black velvet undulating base covered w/black-tipped brown & beige feathers, no crown or brim, labeled "Peck & Peck - Fifth Avenue New York," excellent condition (ILLUS. of front & back, top next page). **$50.00**

1950s Black Velvet Beret with Bow

Beret, black velvet tucked from the center allowing for a draped effect over a smaller black velvet band, bow at back w/black gros-grain ribbon, black gros-grain ribbon sweatband, lined w/beige faille, excellent condition (ILLUS.) **$65.00**

Front & Back Views of a 1950s Feathered Band Hat

1950s Givenchy Juliet Style Cap

Cap, 'Juliet' style, tiny white fabric flowers & green leaves covering stiffened brown net w/front comb underneath to secure to head, labeled "Hubert de Givenchy - Made in France," good condition, some wear to flowers & leaves (ILLUS.) **$68.00**

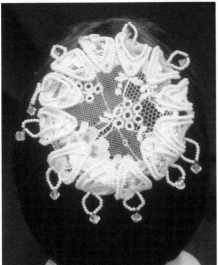

Front & Back Views of 1950s 'Juliet' Cap

Cap, 'Juliet' style, perhaps originally a bridal cap to cover a chignon, features a wire frame covering machine-made ivory lace, draped w/swags of small pearl beads & trimmed w/small dangling crystals, fair condition, some tears to lace, some rusting of frame (ILLUS. of front & back) **$95.00**

Small 1950s Domed & Feathered Cap

Cap, small dome-shaped form covered w/black velvet w/a small black velvet ribbon bow at the back, the front of crown covered w/feathers, mostly in brown & beige & punctuated occasionally by orange, purple & green, black gros-grain ribbon sweatband, two side combs attached w/elastic to secure to head, black silk lined, late 1950s - early 1960s, excellent condtion, evidence of a missing black veil (ILLUS. of two views, previous page)............................... **$68.00**

1950s Purple Fur Felt Casque

Casque, purple fur felt w/extended top, tucked in places to create a draped effect, narrow purple gros-grain sweatband, labeled "Marshall Field & Co., Debutante Room - 22 1/2," excellent condition, 6" h. (ILLUS.) **$85.00**

1950s Circlet with Flowers & Veil

Circlet, narrow ribbons of raffia, folded & arranged resembling rick-rack & then sewn to nylon netting & attached to a wire frame, trimmed w/cotton roses, buds, small white flowers, leaves & stems, veil w/open weave of green & pink threads wrapped around the

hat & trailing in the back, labeled "Stylized by Siegel's - Buffalo," good condition, one flower spray detached, veil torn in places (ILLUS.) **$65.00**

Blue Feathered 1950s Cocktail Hat with Veil

Cocktail hat, blue acetate base w/blue feathers at the front & small peacock eye-style feathers towards the back, dotted w/rhinestones & a feather-covered flourish at the side, backed w/blue velvet, blue velvet-covered supports at side to secure to head, black net veil attached to front, black velvet ribbon ties, good condition, couple of rhinestones missing, veil torn in places (ILLUS.)........................ **$110.00**

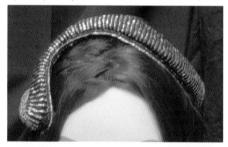

Front & Side Views of a Gold & Black Cocktail Hat

Cocktail hat, ridged circles of fine black straw alternately covered w/gold foil wound in a spiral from the center, rolled at edges w/a side drape, labeled "22MSC," excellent condition (ILLUS. of front & side view) **$65.00**

Two Views of a 1950s Toque-Style Sequined Cocktail Hat

Cocktail hat, toque-style, completely covered w/ iridescent blue sequins, clear-beaded pear shapes w/upright abalone flourishes at each center, sequin-covered side supports & a blue net veil, blue gros-grain ribbon sweatband, crown lined w/blue lace, labeled "Haggarty's - Sequins Stylized and Imported From France," excellent condition, some tears to veil, 8" d. (ILLUS. of front & back) **$125.00**

Front & Side Views of a Green Ribbon & Trimmed Veil Hat

Hat, arched green velvet pleated band trimmed w/a veil of fine green net decorated w/iridescent green velvet leaves & silk-wrapped green stems, late 1950s - early 1960s, good condition, veil torn in places (ILLUS. of front & side view) **$38.00**

1950s Hat with Fluffy Fringe

Hat, base of woven straw covered w/tiers of hair-like fluffy fringe, 3" h. crown w/a white & yellow polka dot ribbon around the base & a bow at back, 4" w. brim, labeled "Rossini - The Genuine Italian," good condition, some discoloration & matting to fringe, late 1950s - early 1960s (ILLUS.) **$65.00**

1950s Blue Velvet & Feather Hat

Hat, blue velvet w/wide feathered border (ILLUS.)
. . . . **$30-50**

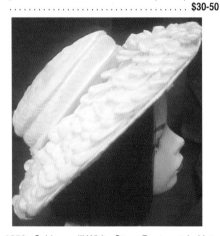

1950s Schiaparelli White Straw Boater-style Hat

Hat, boater-style, woven white straw w/a 2 1/2" h. crown covered in tucked strips of wide raffia ribbon spiraling to the center top, aqua velvet ribbon around the base

w/a bow at back, 3 1/2" w. brim covered w/'fingers' of wide looped raffia ribbon in overlapping circles, crown lined w/stiff netting, white gros-grain ribbon sweatband, labeled "Schiaparelli," good condition, some 'fingers' missing, sweatband stained, late 1950s (ILLUS.) **$155.00**

1950s Hat of Feathers, Velvet Berries & Leaves & a Veil

Hat, composed of cream-colored downy feathers emanating from a center covered w/green & beige velvet berries & leaves w/a cream-colored net veil, excellent condition (ILLUS.) **$75.00**

1950s Hat Composed of Feathers & Veil

Hat, composed of purple feathers & quills emanating from a purple velvet-covered center w/a black net veil, good condition, some feathers & quills missing, discoloration to center (ILLUS.) **$55.00**

1950s Blue Linen Hat Trimmed with Wax Cherries

Hat, glazed navy blue linen faced w/stiffened blue net & navy blue velvet trim & velvet bows around the base, decorated w/red & yellow wax cherries on green wire along the edge, velvet-covered supports at the sides, labeled "Designed by Frances," excellent condition (ILLUS. bottom previous page). **$85.00**

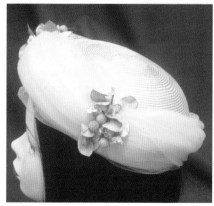

Two Views of a 1950s 'Halo' Style
Tulle-Trimmed Hat

Hat, 'halo' style, ridged finely woven straw spiraling from top center w/a swath of beige-colored tulle wrapped around the base & secured at two points at front & sides w/orange fabric berries, white flowers & green leaves, brown gros-grain sweatband, chenille-covered side supports to secure hat to head, labeled "Vincent De Koven Original," excellent condition (ILLUS. of two views) **$65.00**

1950s Floral & Bow-Decorated Net Hat

Hat, light blue netting w/attached rosettes w/pearl centers, leaves & paper-wrapped stems w/a large organdy bow at the back, late 1950s - early 1960s, excellent condition (ILLUS.) **$35.00**

1950s Hat with Schiaparelli Label

Hat, red knitted jersey stretched over a pliable form, 6" h. crown covered w/red, green, beige, brown & speckled feathers, 1" w. brim slighted turned, crown lined w/black felt, red gros-grain ribbon sweatband, labeled "Made In Italy - Schiaparelli - Paris," good condition, some feathers missing (ILLUS.) **$200.00**

1950s Red Straw Hat with Green Band, Netting &
Birds & Fruits Trim

Hat, red straw w/a wide green band & green netting trimmed w/artificial birds & fruit (ILLUS.) **$35-50**

1950s Hat Decorated with Ivory Silk Calla Lilies

Hat, small ivory silk calla lilies w/tiny green velvet leaves sewn over glazed canvas, a side flourish & white velvet edging, good condition, some discoloration to flowers & trim (ILLUS.) **$65.00**

1950s Round White Rabbit Fur Hat

Hat, white rabbit fur, large round form, carries a Carson, Pirie & Scott label (ILLUS.) **$35-55**

Very Wide 1950s Cream Raffia & Straw Hat

Hat, wide design of cream-colored glazed raffia & natural braided straw, a rounded 2" h. crown & 4" w. brim, small raffia band along inside to secure hat to head w/ two side combs attached by elastic bands, white gros-grain sweatband, excellent condition (ILLUS.)
. . . . **$200.00**

Large 1950s 'Sou-wester' Style Hat

Hat, 'Sou-wester' style, 5" h. crown of lustrous twill in shades of white, black & grey, a narrow red gros-grain ribbon around the base w/loose ends tipped w/black pom-pons, inverted 6" w. brim of ridged & finely woven black straw, black gros-grain ribbon sweatband, labeled "Styled by Coralie," good condition, some warping to brim & fading to red ribbon, late 1950s - early 1960s (ILLUS.) **$75.00**

1950s Yellow Straw Hat with Single Feather Trim

Hat, wide gently pointed yellow straw w/long single feather trim (ILLUS.) **$30-45**

1950s Velvet & Veil Headband

Headband, black velvet-covered wire support in the shape of a bow w/brown dotted Swiss net veil, excellent condition, one small wire tip exposed (ILLUS.) **$45.00**

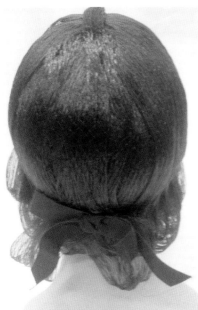

Black Beaded Toque with Marshall Field Label

Two Views of a Lilly Daché 'Wig' Hat

Hat, 'wig' style, made from nylon 'hair' in light brown, looped & swagged around a canvas support cap w/a brown gros-grain ribbon at the back, labeled "Lilly Daché - Paris New York - The French Room - Marshall Field & Company" (ILLUS. of two views)
.... **$650.00**

Toque, black beads in varying shapes & sizes covering stiff black canvas, the brim & sides of the tiny shallow 1" h. crown covered in black net veil, black velvet piping along edge, two side combs attached underneath to secure to head, labeled "Marshall Field & Company - Lemington" & a union label, excellent condition, late 1950s - early 1960s, 7" d. (ILLUS.)
.... **$68.00**

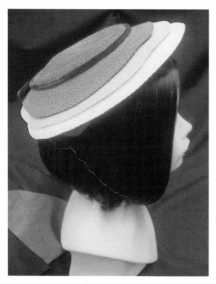

1950s Tiered Straw Toque

Toque, finely woven ridged straw spiraling from the center, a grey first tier w/a 1" h. crown & greyish purple velvet cord around the base w/a bow at back, 1" w. brim overlapping a pearl grey second tier leaving 3/4" base visible, overlapping a bottom white straw tier w/a 1" w. brim visible, grey straw support underneath, grey gros-grain ribbon sweatband, labeled "Jenny - Cincinnati - 22," excellent condition, net veil missing (ILLUS.) **$50.00**

1950s Toque of Raspberry Gros-grain Ribbon

Toque, made entirely of swirled, gored & pleated raspberry-colored gros-grain ribbon over a sturdy base, trimmed w/swirled ribbon rosettes spaced around the edge, raspberry net veil dotted w/flocked points attached at front edge, gold ribbon sweatband,

crown lined w/pink satin w/gold net overlay, velvet-covered side supports also in raspberry, labeled "Saks Fifth Avenue - Millinery Salon," excellent condition, veil torn in places, very slight wear to ribbon fabric (ILLUS.) **$48.00**

1950s 'Pancake' Toque of Velvet & Satin Ribbon

Toque, 'pancake' style, beige velvet w/smooth nearly flat crown trimmed w/beige satin ribbon, bow at back, layers of alternating velvet & satin ruffles around the sides w/a large multi-colored glass bead brooch at the front, beige gros-grain ribbon sweatband, ribbon-wrapped side supports to secure to head, good condition, some discoloration of velvet, staining to sweatband (ILLUS.) **$35.00**

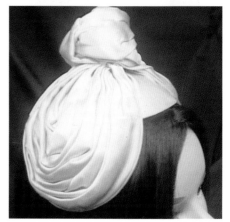

Front & Side Views of a 1950s Edward Paine Toque

Toque, pink satin, swagged & swirled to form a top-knot over a fabric-covered crown & side supports, crown lined w/purple satin, side supports lined w/brown satin, labeled "Edward Paine New York - made exclusively for Bonwit Teller," excellent condition, discoloration where crown meets brown, wear to lining (ILLUS. of two views). **$225.00**

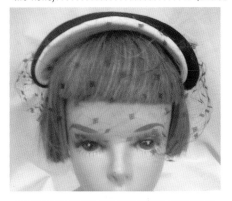

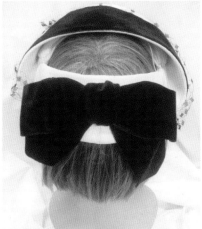

Two Views of a Black & White 1950s Toque

Toque, white linen & black velvet over a sturdy base w/a large black velvet bow at the back, open crown & black veil, white elastic band to secure to head, labeled "Henri Bendel - New York," excellent condition, some tears to veil, elastic band broken (ILLUS. of two views) **$68.00**

Two 1950s Knit Turbans

Turbans, one of knit tan wool yarn, the other of forest green knit yarn, each w/braided twist at center back & a gathered knot at center front, late 1950s, excellent condition, each (ILLUS.). **$45.00**

1950s Ivory Felt & Silk Cord Wedding Toque

Wedding toque, ivory-colored felt w/ivory silk cord & silver beads spiraling throughout from the center, interspersed w/rhinestones, back bow of same ivory felt w/a rhinestone at center, red gros-grain ribbon sweatband, labeled "Kitty Weinstein - 4 West Park Avenue Long Beach," good condition, some beads missing, silk cord w/some wear, back bow resewn to body (ILLUS.) **$95.00**

MEN'S

1950s Dobb's Wool Felt Bowler

Bowler, black wool felt, 5" h. rounded crown w/two inch wide black gros-grain ribbon around base, side bow finish & red feather detail, 1 1/2" w. brim slightly turned, black leather sweatband, pierce-monogrammed "AR," crown lined w/white satin, labeled "Dobb's Fifth Avenue New York - 7 1/8," excellent condition w/original box, lining discolored (ILLUS.) **$300.00**

1950s Black Derby Hat

Derby (bowler) hat, stiff black wool felt, slightly turned brim, gros-grain ribbon edging & band w/bow finish, red feather accent, ivory satin lining, leather sweat brow band, punched w/monogram "TR," labeled "The Aristocrat by Snyder - The United Hatters of North America - Registered - Size 7 1/8," excellent condition (ILLUS.) **$155.00**

CLOTHING - 1960-1970

LADIES'

1960s Crocheted Beanie & Matching Pouch Bag

Beanie & matching pouch bag, both crocheted w/ smooth white yarn & golden thread added for details & edging & an occasional rhinestone or crocheted crescent or star, the bag w/drawstring closure, both good condition, a few loose pieces of yarn, late 1960s, the set (ILLUS.). **$95.00**

French-Made Striped Basque Beret

Beret, Basque-style, 100% heavy wool w/blue ground & black stripes radiating from an all-black center, blue pom-pon at top, lined w/light blue acetate, labeled "Beret Basque - Superieur - Marque D'Origine - Made in France - 100% - Wool - RN2R329," good condition, some discoloration to lining & wear to pom-pon (ILLUS.) **$45.00**

1960s Leopard-Patterned Beret

Beret, of leopard-patterned pile fabric w/self-fabric-covered button at top, brown gros-grain ribbon edging, lined w/black satin, late 1960s - early 1970s, excellent condition (ILLUS.). **$55.00**

Two Views of 1960s Beaded Juliet Cap

Cap, 'Juliet' style, composed of small loops of mulit-colored beads in shades of yellow, mauve, green & blue, sewn over paisley fabric in same colors, lined w/same paisley fabric, labeled "Irene of New York - Stanley Korshak Chicago," good condition, some beads missing (ILLUS. of two views) **$300.00**

Two Views of a 1960s Lilly Daché Wool Fez

Fez, knitted black wool w/a tapered weighted crown & bands of black glass beads encircling the sides, indentation at the brow & slit at center back, crown lined w/black satin, black gros-grain ribbon sweatband, labeled "Lilly Daché Paris - 78 East 56th Street New York," good condition, evidence of missing black net veil, some beads missing (ILLUS. of front & side view) **$250.00**

1960s Mod Brass-Studded Cap

Cap, newsboy-style, brown velveteeen w/a roomy crown & visor-brim, decorated w/brass metal studs, white vinyl sweatband, lined w/tricot fabric in a Mod design, late 1960s, fair condition, signs of wear to sweatband & fabric, some studs missing (ILLUS.) **$38.00**

Maria Pia Ribbon-Trimmed Black Hat

Hat, a blackened stiff canvas base trimmed w/bits of black gros-grain ribbon cut into points, small silk flower buds & stems sprinkled here & there, labeled "Maria Pia - Rome New York," 5" h., excellent condition (ILLUS., previous page) **$275.00**

Double-labeled 1960s Black Velvet Hat

Hat, black velvet w/slouchy 4" h. rounded crown w/a self-fabric rolled ribbon around the base, thick spray of black ostrich feathers at one side, 1 1/2" w. brim, crown lined w/red nylon, black gros-grain ribbon sweatband, labeled "Irene of New York" & "I. Magnin & Co.," excellent condition (ILLUS.) **$225.00**

Large 1960s Black Straw Hat with Silk Flowers

Hat, black woven straw spiraling from the top center, pointed crown covered w/straw 'fingers' simulating grass, dotted w/one spray of wax berries & silk & velvet flowers & leaves of varying types, the crown 3" h., the brim 4" w., braided string underneath ties around chin, labeled "Rhea Brummer Boutique - Worth Avenue - Palm Beach - Hand Woven in Italy," good condition, some flowers missing their bloom (ILLUS.) **$150.00**

Tiger Stripe 'Bubble Helmet' Hat

Hat, 'bubble helmet' style, knitted gored fabric w/tiger stripes, a fabric-wrapped button at top center, lined w/black satin, black gros-grain ribbon sweatband, 7" h., excellent condition (ILLUS.) **$40.00**

1960s 'Bubble Helmet' Hat

Hat, 'bubble helmet' style, stiff beige canvas measuring 34" in diameter, lace at crown & covered w/swaths of beige netting, small beige tricot bow at back of crown, lace-covered support inside fits crown to head, excellent condition (ILLUS.) **$175.00**

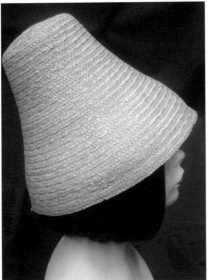

Two Views of a 1960s Italian Straw 'Bucket' or 'Lampshade' Hat

Hat, 'bucket' or 'lampshade' style, finely woven ridged straw spiraling from top center, 6 1/2" h. tapered crown, no brim, labeled "Made in Italy," excellent condition (ILLUS. of two views) **$45.00**

Two Views of a Cone-shaped 1960s Hat with Silk Flowers

Hat, cone-shaped, black raffia ribbon folded to form loops w/white silk flowers & stems, sewn to a black-glazed canvas base, labeled "Marshall Field & Company," excellent condition (ILLUS. of front & side view) **$150.00**

1960s Peck & Peck Cone-Shaped Straw Hat

Hat, cone-shaped, finely woven natural straw w/dark blue yarn in a plaid design, same yarn wrapping edges & yarn tassel hanging from top center peak, labeled "Peck & Peck - Fifth Avenue New York," early 1960s (ILLUS.) **$155.00**

1960s Lady's Derby Hat

Hat, derby-style, crown made from tiny loops of ivory-colored raffia sewn to a sturdy nylon net base, light brown velvet ribbon around the base w/a side bow, a crystal & goldtone pin at center front the 1 1/2" w. brim of lustrous ivory weave & covered wire edge, ivory-colored gros-grain ribbon sweatband, crown 5 1/2" h., excellent condition, some discoloration to sweatband (ILLUS.) **$80.00**

Hat, derby-style, made of bands of ridged finely woven straw striped in shades of olive & light green & white overlapping vertically & meeting at the top of the 4 1/2" h. crown, bands of brown, olive green & yellow gros-grain ribbons encircling the base & slightly turned 1" w. brim w/a blue button detail w/rhinestone center, green gros-grain ribbon sweatband, crown lined w/white satin, labeled "Lilly Daché - DEBS - New York Paris," & a union label, excellent condition (ILLUS. right with other striped Lilly Daché hat, page 225) **$135.00**

Front & Back of a 1960s Domed Jockey-Style Hat in Woven Straw

Hat, domed jockey-style of ridged finely woven straw w/an 8" h. crown, green velvet ribbon around base w/a graduated brim from 2" w. at front to 1" w. at back, plastic hanging stem w/green cotton leaves from top center, green thread bands sewn down length of crown for decoration, very narrow green gros-grain ribbon sweatband, early 1960s, good condition, perhaps missing some leaves, back bow missing (ILLUS. of front & back) **$85.00**

1960s Floppy Leopard Print Hat

Hat, floppy-style, short pile fabric patterned w/leopard spots, 5" h. crown trimmed w/black vinyl bow w/ goldtone tips at center of back base, 4" w. brim, crown lined w/black satin, brim lined w/black canvas, black gros-grain ribbon sweatband, labeled "New York CECILE ORIGINAL," late 1960s, excellent condition (ILLUS.) **$150.00**

Floppy 1960s Hat with Beige Ostrich Plumes

Hat, floppy-style w/peaked crown covered w/gored panels of ivory satin & beige ostrich feathers around the base, some tipped w/brown, brown satin bow at back, 3" w. brown corduroy brim, crown lined w/brown satin, brown gros-grain ribbon sweatband, labeled "Gwenn Pennington Exclusive - New York Paris - 22," crown 5" h., excellent condition (ILLUS.) **$100.00**

Front & Side Views of a 1960s Sheepskin Helmet-Shaped Hat

Hat, helmet-shaped, sheepskin w/long white fleece, two spots of brown fleece at top center, white elastic sweatband, 10" h., good condition w/minimal inside wear (ILLUS. of front & side view) **$85.00**

Front & Side View of 1960s Hat in Early 20th Century Style

Hat, in the style of the early 20th c., black net over a wire base w/narrow braided black raffia insertions in a meandering design, crushed wide crown w/a black velvet ribbon around the base w/large pink silk roses, stiff green leaves & green plastic stems, 5" w. layered brim, black gros-grain ribbon sweatband, labeled "Mme. Poswolsky - New York City," excellent condition, some wear & discoloration to flowers (ILLUS. of front & side view) **$400.00**

1960s Domed Jockey-Style Hat

Hat, jockey-style, cream-coloref wool felt w/domed 5" h. crown, ivory-colored satin band around base w/front gros-grain bow, narrow 1" w. visor brim, cream net veil starting at crown & draping down the sides, labeled "Peachfelt - Henry Pollak - New York - 100% Wool," & a union label, excellent condition (ILLUS.) **$75.00**

Two Views of a 1960s Felt 'Lampshade' Hat

Hat, 'lampshade' style, black felt w/a recessed 4" h. crown w/black gros-grain ribbon at edge, 3" w. light brown gros-grain ribbon around base, turned-down 2" w. brim edged w/ivory gros-grain ribbon, sturdy black net veil emanating from ribbon at crown & covering the sides, black gros-grain ribbon sweatband, labeled "Suzy et Paulette Chapeaux - Paris Chicago - 100%

Wool - Ritz - Henry Pollak, Inc., New York," excellent
condition (ILLUS. of front & side view). **$70.00**

Two Views of a 1960s 'Madeline' Hat

Front & Side Views of 1960s 'Lampshade' Hat

Hat, 'lampshade' style, tightly woven light straw, wide
straight-sided 5" h. crown, a 3 1/2" w. flocked pink
ribbon around the base w/a large bown at the center
front w/a large pink silk rose, leaves & plastic stems,
2" w. brim, w/a union label, excellent condition (ILLUS.
of front & side view) **$65.00**

Hat, 'Madeline' style, rounded crown of black velvet w/
black gros-grain ribbon around the base w/right front
drape finish & red chenille 'bumble bee' trim, turned-
up 2 1/4" w. black felt brim edged in black velvet,
underside of brim also black velvet, black gros-grain
ribbon sweatband, labeled "Corona - Body Made in
Italy - The Gidding Co. Cincinnati," excellent condition
(ILLUS. of two views) **$80.00**

1960s Claret Fur Felt Hat

Hat, muted claret-colored fur felt w/a fluffy nap, 5" h. creased crown w/a red gros-grain ribbon around the base & a bow & large rose made of satin-backed flocked ribbon at the side, graduated felt rolled brim 3" w. at widest point, fur felt on underside, red gros-grain ribbon sweatband, labeled "Alfreda Inc. - Paris New York - Empress Body Made in Western Germany" & a union label, good condition, some wear to nap on brim (ILLUS.) **$75.00**

1960s Tinsel-Covered Pillbox Hat

Hat, pillbox-style, blue & gold tinsel covering the base, w/a blue net veil, good condition, some holes in veil (ILLUS.) **$45.00**

Front & Back Views of a Jan Leslie Pillbox Hat

Hat, pillbox-style, narrow ivory-colored braids sewn around a canvas base w/a slightly 'pop-up' crown, beige net veil attached to base, rolled at edges & secured to brow area w/a beige velvet ribbon w/a bow at the back, beige sweatband, labeled "Jan Leslie Custom Design," 5" h., excellent condition, some tears to veil (ILLUS. of front & back) **$65.00**

1960s Pink Pillbox Hat

Hat, pillbox-style, pink stain w/low rounded sides covered w/pink raffia ribbon, folded & fanned out resembling feathers, pink gros-grain ribbon sweatband, lined in pink fabric, labeled "Marcelle Studio - 22," excellent condition, possibly missing a veil (ILLUS.) **$55.00**

1960s Black Vinyl Pillbox Hat

Hat, pillbox-style, sturdy black vinyl w/narrow sides, black vinyl twist & drape at front, two attached combs at side for securing to head, lined w/ivory-colored acetate, black gros-grain sweatband, excellent condition (ILLUS.) **$65.00**

Two 1960s Lilly Daché Striped Hats

Hat, ridged finely woven straw spiraling from top center, pink, green, beige & orange striped bands around 5" h. rounded crown, 2 1/4" w. band of gros-grain ribbons in pink, brown & beige folded & overlapping around the

base w/an elaborate side knot finish, 2" w. brim slightly turned, brown gros-grain ribbon sweatband, labeled "Dachettes - Designed by Lily Daché," excellent condition (ILLUS. left with green-striped Lilly Daché hat) **$135.00**

Sharply Peaked 1960s Woven Green Straw Hat

Hat, sharply pointed green-dyed finely woven straw spiraling from top center, covered w/green straw 'fingers' simulating grass, elastic band sewn to underside to secure to head, excellent condition, elastic band probably replaced (ILLUS.) **$128.00**

Front & Back Views of 1960s Flowered Aqua Hat

Hat, stiff net crown covered w/stiffened silk flowers in shades of aqua & white, 2" w. aqua velvet ribbon around the base w/bow at back, 1" w. brim covered in aqua metallic fabric, ribbon sweatband, labeled "Individual Le Charme Creations," good condition, some discoloration to brim (ILLUS. of front & back) **$35.00**

Two Views of a 1960s Turquoise Feathered Hat

Hat, wool felt cap completely covered w/turquoise feathers w/long feathers at the top of the crown fashioned into a topknot spray, marked w/a union label, 6" h., excellent condition (ILLUS. of two views) **$275.00**

Two 1960s Rounded Feathered Hats

Hats, wide rounded crocheted cap sewn overall w/dyed feathers, one in mustard yellow, the other in magenta & purple, each (ILLUS.) **$85.00**

1960s Black Velvet Bow Headband

Headband, long black velvet-covered bow on a velvet-covered base on a hard plastic support, excellent condition (ILLUS.)...................... **$25.00**

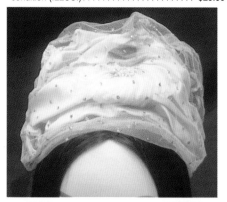

Two Views of a 1960s Dior 'Bubble' Toque

Toque, 'bubble' style, pink satin draped & twisted & trimmed w/pink cotton & silk flowers, green leaves & stems, completely encircled by tulle net sprinkled w/glitter, lined w/pink lustrous faille, labeled "Christian Dior Chapeaux - Paris-New York," 5 1/2" h., excellent condition (ILLUS. of two views) **$175.00**

Front & Back of a 1960s French-Made Ostrich Plume Toque

Toque, composed of long white ostrich plumes radiating from the center & covering a small circular base made from stiffened canvas, white gros-grain-covered heart-shaped wire supports underneath, labeled "Made in France - Exclusively for Lord & Taylor Salon," good condition, some discoloration to canvas base, may have had a detail at top of crown (ILLUS. of front & back). **$150.00**

1960s Italian Satin Turban

Turban, pink champagne-colored satin sewn overall w/tucks, a twist at the front & knot at the back, lined w/ beige satin, labeled "Made in Italy," excellent condition (ILLUS.) **$200.00**

MEN'S

Irish Corduroy Cap

Cap, newsboy-style, tan cotton corduroy w/2" l. visor brim, brown gros-grain ribbon sweatband, lined w/red satin, labeled "Handtailored Blarney Headwear - Made in Ireland - Cotton," good condition, wear visible to lining & sweatband (ILLUS.) **$25.00**

1960s Man's Fishing Hat

Fishing hat, brown, black & white wool yarn knit over a wire frame, 4" h. crown, knit band around base, studded w/fishing lures in various colors, 3 1/2" w. brim, good condition, some wear, late 1960s (ILLUS.) **$30.00**

CLOTHING - 1970-1980

LADIES'

Saint Laurent Conical Beanie

Beanie, conical gold foil-wrapped viscose & cotton weave spiraling from top peak, beige gros-grain ribbon sweatband, labeled "Saint Laurent Rive Gauche

- Made in France - Paris," & fabric care label, 6" h., excellent condition, late 1970s (ILLUS.)
.... **$300.00**

1970s White & Blue Straw Beret

Beret, ridged circles of white glazed straw w/a wide navy blue stripe, a pink gros-grain sweatband, labeled "Frank Clive of Saks Fifth Avenue," excellent condition (ILLUS.) **$48.00**

1970s Silk-Topped Bonnet

Bonnet, multi-colored silk-topped base w/a shallow unlined crown, a large padded graduated brim 4" w. at front & 2" w. at back, self-fabric sash tied in a bow at center back & left to trail w/loose ends, lavender gros-grain ribbon-edged w/purple lace sweatband, labeled "Mr. John," fair condition, sillk brittle, tears along base (ILLUS.) **$48.00**

Bonnet, shearling bonnet w/pom-pons hanging by woven cords to tie under chin, white gros-grain ribbon sweat/brow band, labled "Genuine Tuscan Lambskin Fur - Made in Italy," good condition, visible wear to ties, sweat band & inside suede, original owner's name written inside (ILLUS. right with German animal fur jacket, page 173) **$85.00**

Don Kline Rhinestone-Studded Black Felt Cap

Cap, thick black wool felt heavily studded overall w/various-sized rhinestones in a repeating design, labeled "Don Kline at Saks Fifth Avenue," ca. 1970, excellent condition (ILLUS.) **$750.00**

Two Views of a 1970s Yves Saint Laurent Black Fez

Fez, thick black wool felt w/a short fuzzy nap, black gros-grain ribbon sweatband, labeled "Yves Saint Laurent," 4" h., excellent condition (ILLUS.) **$375.00**

1970s Adolfo Felt & Organza hat

Hat, beige wool felt w/beige silk organza covering the entire hat, softly draped over the 4" h. crown, the 3" w. brim covered w/frayed bits of the same organza & spinkled w/silk roses & buds w/green leaves, red gros-grain ribbon sweatband, labeled "Adolfo II - Paris New York - 22 1/2," good condition, brim separated slightly from crown, wear to sweatband (ILLUS.) **$125.00**

Two Views of a Homemade 'Chandelier' Style Hat

Hat, 'chandelier' style, black velvet stretched over stiff white canvas, trimmed w/mirrored squares & glitter from the top center to front w/appendages of paper-wrapped wire dangling chandelier crystal drops & beads, edged w/narrow black braid, elastic strap at back to hold to head, homemade, no label w/previous owner's name written inside, good condtion, sloppy finishing underneath (ILLUS. of front & side view) **$45.00**

Two Views of a Floppy 1970s Hat with Black Spots

Hat, floppy-style of acrylic pile, the taupe ground w/large black spots, 6" h. crown & a 2" w. black gros-grain ribbon around the base w/a black knot at the front, 5 1/2" w. brim, black gros-grain ribbon sweatband, labeled "Mr. John Jr. - Body Made in Italy," early 1970s, excellent condition (ILLUS. of two views) **$150.00**

1970s Simulated Reptile Skin Floppy Hat

Hat, floppy-style of brown & white woven fabric w/patches of black overweave to simulate reptile skin, black vinyl band around the base & matching bow at back, labeled "Burdines - Sunshine Fashions," brim 4" w., overall 4" h., excellent condition (ILLUS.). **$40.00**

Floppy Hat with Black Braided Trim

Hat, floppy-style of white canvas w/a 4" h. crown, black soutache braided applique on crown, graduated floppy brim 3" w. at front & 1 1/2" w. at back, crown lined w/white satin, white gros-grain sweatband, labeled "Glamor Top Original," excellent condition (ILLUS.)
. . . . **$55.00**

1970s Floppy Orange Felt Hat

Hat, floppy-style of orange pure wool felt w/an orange gros-grain ribbon around the base & a bow at front, black vinyl sweatband, excellent condition (ILLUS.)
. . . . **$45.00**

Black Chenille Hat with Mink Fur Trim

Hat, small peaked domed 5" h. crown of crocheted black chenille w/whimsical feather & quill trim at the front, white mink fur-covered 1 1/2" w. brim w/fur on the underside also, beige gros-grain ribbon sweatband, labeled "Lenore Marshall New York," ca. 1970, excellent condition (ILLUS.) **$300.00**

MEN'S

Italian-Made Straw Boater

Boater, braided straw spiraling from center top, straight sides & 3" h. crown, 2" w. red & blue-striped grosgrain ribbon around base, side bow finish, 2" w. brim, black vinyl sweatband, labeled "Made in Italy - 7 1/8," excellent condition (ILLUS.) **$90.00**

Golf cap, mixed fibers in primarily green tartan plaid, large green pom-pon on top & small attached visor, lined in black acetate, quilted, labeled "Highlands

Arts Scotland," & fabric care label, excellent condition (ILLUS. with 1970s golfing ensemble) **$65.00**

1970s Tyrolean hat

Tyrolean hat, heathered brown thick felt, peaked six-inch crown, twisted green cord around base w/side curl finish, attached kilt pin made from arctic fox paw w/silver tip & amethyst stone in shape of a thistle, 2" w. roled brim, labeled "Dirndle-Ecke Am Platzl - Hindra-Munchen," German, excellent condition, pin not original to hat (ILLUS.) **$75.00**

CHAPTER 12: PURSES & BAGS

CLOTHING - 1850-1920

*Old Tooled Leather Bag with Art Nouveau
Flowering Vines*

Bag, pebble-tooled leather w/hand-tooling at the center featuring an Art Nouveau floral & vine design, brass frame w/delicate twig-like snaps at top, whip-stitched wrist strap & leather pull, chamois-lined, embossed label "Bosca Built," late 19th - early 20th c., good condition, some wear to leather & lining (ILLUS.)
. . . . **$579.00**

Early Reticule-style Crocheted Bag

Bag, reticule-style, golden metallic thread crocheted in an open weave w/intricate openwork & crocheted flowers at the center, delicated looped edging at bottom & side, metallic thread drawstring at top, lined

w/lavender-colored voile, excellent condition, early 20th c. (ILLUS.). **$300.00**

*Early Leather Shield-shaped Bag with
Art Nouveau Designs*

Bag, shield-shaped tooled leather w/Art Nouveau floral & sinuous line decoration, whip-stitched sides & leather strap, nickel-plated frame w/spring-snap closure & loop pull, chamois-lined, loop pull labeled "Turnloc," late 19th - early 20th c., good condition, lining & handle show some wear (ILLUS.). **$300.00**

Early 20th Century Ring Mesh Purse

Mesh purse, ring mesh attached to a simple gunmetal frame w/chain handle, twist knob clasp, indentified stamped mark, very good condition, minor ring loss, early 20th c. (ILLUS.) **$95.00**

Fine Sterling Silver Mesh Purse by Whiting & Davis

Mesh purse, sterling silver, baby fine mesh attached to a filigreed & monogrammed metal frame w/a twist knob clasp, chain handle, marked "Whiting & Davis," early 20th c., excellent condition (ILLUS.). **$600.00**

Miser's purse, blue crocheted silk w/tiny pieces of cut steel used to fashion tassel at the bottom, metal rings sewn to top for drawstring, lined w/blue moiré silk, excellent condition, drawstring missing, ca. 1900 . . . . **$400.00**

Early Chatelaine Purse with Black Jet Beading

Purse, chatelaine-style, nickel-plated frame w/ornate embossed floral designs on the front, spring-snap closure w/attached chain & chatelaine hook w/same metalwork, circular fabric pouch covered w/tiny jet beads on the front, black lustrous fabric on the back,

bottom fringe of loop beaded strands, chamois-lined, for attaching to a belt, good condition, black fabric back replaced, chamois lining w/signs of age & wear, ca. 1900-1905 (ILLUS.) **$500.00**

Early Lady's Leather Purse

Purse, leather w/gathered silk pocket on the back, designed to hang on a chain from a belt, ca. 1860 (ILLUS.) **$125-175**

Late Victorian Petit Point Scenic Purse

Purse, petit point, brown ground w/a scene of a lady & man in a pastoral setting, filigree metal framed w/ stones, brass flower pull, swans atop frame at sides to hold chain handle trimmed w/stones, push clasp, lined w/beige glazed poplin, good condition, some stone loss, some thread fraying, lining torn, chain needs repair, late 19th c. (ILLUS.). **$400.00**

Victorian Purple Plush Purse with Photo

Purse, purple plush, shown w/a period photo of a woman carrying a similar purse, ca. 1885 (ILLUS.)
. . . . **$100-150**

Whiting & Davis Sterling Silver Mesh Purse

Purse, sterling silver mesh w/tiny round silver beads at bottom corners & center point, dome-shaped framed stamped w/a floral & scroll design, cabochon knob clasp w/silver micro-braided adjustable strap handle w/ carved tabs, labeled "Whiting & Davis," ca. 1918-1923,

5" w., 6" l., very good condition, few loops missing on mesh where it meets the frame (ILLUS.) **$450.00**

Early Sterling Silver Purse Frame & Handle

Purse frame, chatelaine-style, sterling silver, stamped relief design w/a mythological scene, chain handle w/a chatelaine clip, marked "Sterling 138" & unidentified company mark, very good condition, ca. 1900 (ILLUS.)
. . . . **$400-500**

CLOTHING - 1920-1930

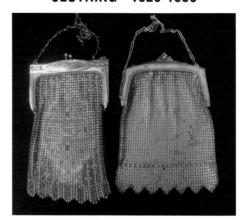

Two Fine 1920s Enameled Mesh Purses

Mesh purse, decorated silver frame, the purse of enameled mesh in light greens & blues w/bright red accents, scalloped bottom, twist knob clasp, chain handle, marked "Whiting & Davis," very good condition, minor enamel wear (ILLUS. left with other enameled mesh purse). **$375.00**
Mesh purse, ivory-colored enameled frame, the purse of light green enameled mesh, scalloped bottom, knob clasp, chain handle, good condition, moderate wear to enamel (ILLUS. right with other enameled mesh purse) **$275.00**

Small 1920s Metal Mesh Purse

Mesh purse, the small bag of square metal pieces linked w/metal links, square embossed metal frame w/chain handle, twist clasp, black-glazed poplin lining, very good condition, some links repaired (ILLUS.)
.... **$150.00**

Mesh purse, white enameled ground w/burgundy & black floral decoration, nickel-plated etched frame w/twist clasp decorated w/blue cabochon stones, chain handle, lined w/grey silk, very good condition, lining torn, some enamel scuffs (ILLUS. left with other white & color floral enameled mesh purse) **$400.00**

Mesh purse, white enameled ground w/red & pink flowers & green leaves, the nickel-plated frame stamped w/a floral & heart design, chain handle, twist clasp, unlined, labeled "Whiting & Davis," very good condition, minor enamel scuffing (ILLUS. right with other white & color floral mesh purse) **$500.00**

Lovely 1920s Petit Point Purse with Ornate Frame

Purse, petit point tapestry pouch in a geometric design in shades of brick red, blue, mustard yellow w/black outlines, the gold filigree frame w/black enamel & encrusted w/coral seed beads, coral cabochon push-botton clasp, ring at top for optional chatelaine, chain handle, lined w/beige poplin, one large compartment w/two inner gathered sleeves, excellent condition, minor coral bead loss (ILLUS.) **$1,500.00**

CLOTHING - 1930-1940

Tuso Beaded Bags

Two Fine 1920s White & Florals Enameled Mesh Purses

Beaded bag, black beaded pouch & handle, brass molded frame encrusted w/silver beads & rhinestones, bag lined w/ivory satin, labeled "Made in France - Hand Made," excellent condition, very minor bead loss near frame, lining w/one or two spots, late 1930s - early 1940s (ILLUS. with top 1950s micro-beaded purse, previous page) **$950.00**

A Rare 1930s Sueded Purse & a Small 1950s Pouch Chatelaine Bag

Purse, dark brown sueded fabric gathered at the finely detailed base-metal frame stamped w/very small leaves, flowers & swags & set w/tiny rhinestones, raised studded hinged clasp, sueded handle, lined w/beige satin, frame engraved "Made in France - E. Gauthier - Rue des Petits Champs Paris," excellent condition, lining soiled (ILLUS. top with small 1950s pouch chatelaine bag) **$900.00**

Rare 1930s Micro-Petit Point Tapestry Purse

Purse, micro-petit point tapestry purse depicting a hunting scene, the gold filigreed frame w/blue, green & enamel, dotted w/cabochon jadeite stones, cabochon twist clasp, lined w/white satin, excellent condition, minor stone loss, lining needs to be restitched to bag, no handle (ILLUS.) **$700-800**

CLOTHING - 1940-1950

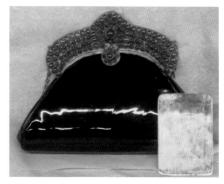

Late 1940s Black Patent Leather Back with Ruby Stones in the Frame

Bag, black patent leather w/a sculpted brass frame encrusted w/ruby-like cabochon stones & a jeweled brass medallion, chain handle, lined w/dark pink satin, accompanying mirror in an inner satin sleeves, excellent condition, minor stone loss, late 1940s - early 1950s (ILLUS.) **$450.00**

Coin purse, frog head, light brown leather w/an actual frog head attached to the front w/its skin & hard brown eyes, zipper closure, very good condition, wear to leather, late 1940s - early 1950s (ILLUS. at right in front of baby alligator purse with other reptile purses) **$95.00**

1940s Beige Enameled Mesh Purse

Mesh purse, beige enamel bag w/a rolled brass filigreed frame encrusted w/prong-set rhinestones, filigreed clasp, snake chain handle, peach poplin lining w/inner sleeves, excellent condition (ILLUS.) **$550.00**

Grouping of Late 1940s Reptile Purses

Purse, armadillo skin, bell-shaped composed of real armadillo w/the head & feet attached, twist brass clasp, lined w/red flocking w/a mirror inside the lid, twisted leather shoulder strap, very good condition, strap broken in one place, some drying to skin, late 1940s - early 1950s (ILLUS. left front with other reptile purses, previous page) **$150.00**

Purse, baby alligator skin, envelope-style, golden brown alligator skin w/a complete baby alligator body w/green glass eyes attached to the front, lift snap closure opening to several compartments, adjustable alligator skin strap, very good condition, one inside compartment needs repair, late 1940s - early 1950s (ILLUS. back center with other reptile purses, previous page) **$125.00**

Purse, baby alligator skin, golden brown skin w/a complete baby alligator body w/green glass eyes attached to the front, brass frame w/hinged brass crescent lift snap clasp, lined w/grey suede, two separate inner compartments w/several inner sleeves, mirror inside the lid, long embroidered strap not original, excellent condition, lining shows some wear, original strap missing, late 1940s - early 1950s (ILLUS. right front with other reptile purses, previous page) **$125.00**

Two 1940s Gold-beaded Box Purses

Purse, box-style, cylindrical, faux tortoiseshell frame & lid, covered overall w/tiny faceted gold beads, wide twisted beaded strap, goldtone metal catch clasp, excellent condition (ILLUS. left with other gold beaded box purse) **$200.00**

Purse, box-style, hexagonal w/a brass frame & twist ball clasp, the flat surfaces covered overall w/tiny faceted gold beads, wide & rolled beaded strap, excellent condition (ILLUS. right with other gold-beaded box purse) **$200.00**

Two 1940s Box Purses with Beading

Purse, box-style, rectangular body covered w/faceted tiny black beads sewn in drapes & folds, wide handle of twisted beaded straps, faux tortoiseshell Lucite frame w/snap-clasp closure, mirror inside lid, lined w/black

faille, excellent condition, inner mirror cracked (ILLUS. left with other Lucite-framed box purse) **$175.00**

Purse, box-style, round faux tortoiseshell Lucite frame w/a beaded bag at the center covered w/faceted tiny black beads sewn in a spiral formation, wide handle of twisted beaded straps, twist ball clasp, lined w/faille, excellent condition (ILLUS. right with other Lucite-framed box purse) **$200.00**

Brown Cordé Purse, Circa 1940

Purse, brown cordé w/unusal designon front flap, concentric circles on the back, goldtone metal pull clasp, lined w/brown watered poplin, small corded handle, excellent condition, ca. 1940 (ILLUS.) **$65.00**

1940s Brown Lizard Skin Purse

Purse, brown lizard skin w/long shoulder strap, 1940s (ILLUS.) **$50-65**

Rare Champagne Bucket Purse

Purse, champagne bucket-form, black sueded fabric over a bucket-shaped supports, decorated on the top w/a tableau of a half-submerged champagne bottle marked "Doux" in gold letters amid stylized melted ice cubes possibly of acrylic, the hinged lid w/a brass lip & snap closure, self-fabric-trimmed brass handle, the sides w/a shield-shaped gold label marked "Champagne - Reims - France," lined w/black satin w/one inner pocket, labeled "Made in Paris," very good condition, some fading to fabric & gold lettering, yellowing to ice cubes (ILLUS. previous page)
. . . . **$2,000.00**

1940s Clutch Purse of Black Cordé Squares

Purse, clutch-style, composed of pieced black cordé squares, a zipper toop closure w/twisted Lucite zipper pull/handle, black satin-lined inner compartment w/three slit pockets, excellent condition, some age-related wear to corners, ends of Lucite slightly darkened (ILLUS.) **$65-75**

1940s Black Crochet Cord-Style Purse

Purse, cord-style, black crochet w/Bakelite frame, ca. 1940 (ILLUS.) **$40-50**

1940s Cylindrical Purse with Compact

Purse, cylinder-shaped frame covered in black faille, coveredd snap lid w/fitted inner mirror & small sleeve holding a round faille-topped compact, self-fabric wrist strap, lined w/red acetate, marked "Made by Lin-Bren in U.S.A.," 5" h., very good condition, minor wear to faille, chipped mirror, some fraying to lining (ILLUS.)
. . . . **$125.00**

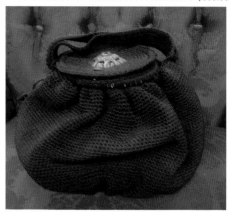

Fine Micro-Petit Point Purse Set

Purse, micro-petit point, the square body w/a beige ground decorated w/purple & pink flowers & green leaves, delicately detailed metal frame w/flowers & vines & small seed pearl-like stones, marcasites & pink stones, hinged floral clasp, lined w/beige satin, w/accompanying coin purse & mirror, chain handle, mint condition, late 1940s, the set (ILLUS.)
. . . . **$600.00**

1940s Black Crocheted Yarn Pouch-Style Purse

Purse, pouch-style, black crocheted yarn in a single-stitch w/a crocheted handle & large pouch body, large round brass brooch at the top w/a tiger eye stone center, lift lid, black cotton lining, very good condition, some fading (ILLUS.) **$250.00**

CLOTHING - 1950-1960

Bag, caviar-beaded black ground w/multi-colored plastic beads, drawstring-style w/black nylon cord handles, excellent condition (ILLUS. left with two other beaded bags). **$50.00**

Bag, gold frame-type covered w/gold metallic yarn & the remainder crocheted w/foil-covered faceted plastic beads, excellent condition (ILLUS. center with two other beaded bags). **$125.00**

Bag, small chatelaine-style w/raised pink pile, elaborate & heavy base-metal frame, lined w/pink fabric, a reproduction of a 1920s era bag, very good condition, chain missing from frame, lining replaced (ILLUS. bottom with rare 1930s sueded purse with fancy frame, page 236) **$175.00**

1950s Plastic-Covered Gold Fabric Bag

Bag, the rectangular body of clear plastic covering embroidered fabric panels of predominately gold thread w/touches of red & green, gilt-metal frame w/small gold wire handle, black flocked lining w/two zippered compartments, very good condition, some lining wear (ILLUS.) **$85.00**

Three 1950s Beaded Bags

Bag, yellow crocheted rayon yarn w/bright yellow diamond-shaped plastic beads, gate top closure, good condition, gate top detached in places (ILLUS. right with two other bags) **$45.00**

Beaded bag, micro-beaded bag w/contrasting beads in a curvilinear design, goldtone metal frame w/a relief floral design, hinged w/a cameo at the center top, black beaded strap handle, lined w/ivory satin, a small interior mirror in a satin sleeves, excellent condition,

slight soiling to lining (ILLUS. bottom with rare late 1930s black beaded bag, page 235) **$175.00**

Two Views of a Finely Beaded French-Made Handbag

Handbag, covered in tiny white seed pearls w/floral tambour-work embroidery, gilt-metal frame w/beaded flat top & cameo-style lift-lock closure, bead-covered handle, lined w/white satin, interior features two envelope pockets, labeled "Saks Fifth Avenue - Made in France," good condition, some yellowing to beads (ILLUS. of front & close-up of closure) **$200.00**

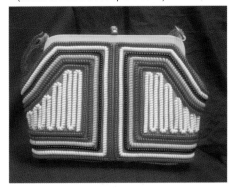

Very Colorful 1950s Telephone Wire Handbag

Handbag, telephone wire construction in primary colors over a red canvas supporting fabric, white plastic frame, brass hinged clasp, lined w/black acetate, very good condition, handles shows wear (ILLUS.) **$95.00**

Purse, beige alligator skin, the gold frame ribbed w/skin, alligator skin strap handle, hinged snap clasp w/pull, lined w/white vinyl, many sleeves inside, labeled "Deitsch," excellent condition, slight soiling & pen marks on lining **$400.00**

Purse, black rectangular leather w/an asymmetrical goldtone metal frame, push ball clasp, tapered leather handle, lined w/beige leather, many compartments & sleeves inside, some moiré lined, labeled "Dorfan," very good condition, minor scuffs, pen marks on lining (ILLUS.) **$200.00**

1950s Black Faille Purse & Accessories

Rare Black Lucite & Rhinestone 1950s Box Purse

Purse, black faille pleated & rounded body w/a rolled filigree metal frame encrusted w/tiny cabochon stones, self-fabric strap, accompanying mirror & faux tortoiseshell plastic comb, the set (ILLUS.) . . **$250.00**

Purse, box-style, oval black Lucite w/the sides covered in rhinestones, handle & arm clasp, large oval mirror inside the flat lid, 6" l., 3" h., excellent condition (ILLUS.) **$900.00**

1950s Black Leather Rectangular Purse

1950s Rectangular Box-Style Lucite Purse with 'Confetti' Decoration

Purse, box-style, rectangular Lucite decorated w/'confetti' of silver glitter & gold threads, nickel bar & ball lift clasp, clear Lucite handles, hinged lid, very good condition, mirror missing & plastic supports holding mirror broken (ILLUS.) **$350.00**

*Three 1950s Box Purses of Basketweave
Metal & Lucite*

Purse, box-style, the rectangular basket-form body of
woven gold metal strips, flat black Lucite lid w/black
wooden handle, brass clasp w/S-hook closure, lined
w/red poplin, very good condition, some wear to lining
(ILLUS. left with two other basket-form box purses)
.... **$175.00**
Purse, box-style, the rectangular basket-form body of
woven gold metal strips, flat black Lucite lid w/clear
Lucite handle, brass ball closure, lined w/peach poplin,
very good condition, some scratches to metal, some
yellowing to handle (ILLUS. center back with two other
basket-form box purses)................ **$175.00**
Purse, box-style, the rectangular basket-form body of
woven silver metal strips, flat clear Lucite lid w/intaglio
flower & clear Lucite handle, brass ball closure,
labeled "by Leslie," excellent condition (ILLUS. right
with other two basket-form box purses) **$250.00**

Butterscotch Lucite & Clear 1950s Purse

Purse, butterscotch Lucite w/carved clear lid, ca. 1950s
(ILLUS.) **$75-100**

1950s Linen & Plastic "Diamonds" Clutch Purse

Purse, clutch-style, black linen w/a thick clear plastic
covering, the linen trimmed w/rhinestones spelling
out "...(diamonds) Are A Girls Best Friend," black
leather covering the metal frame, rhinestone-trimmed

conical snap closure, one slit pocket inside, labeled
"Rosenfeld," very good condition, some clouding to
plastic covering (ILLUS.)............... **$750.00**

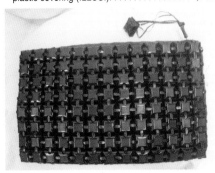

Black Plastic Tile 1950s Clutch Purse

Purse, clutch-style, black plastic tiles joined by black
plastic laces, zipper closure at top w/plastic lace & tile
pull, lined w/black acetate, labeled "Plasticflex," good
condition, tile body intact but zippered top & lining
show wear (ILLUS.) **$95.00**

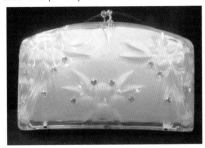

1950s Clear Lucite Clutch Purse

Purse, clutch-style, molded clear Lucite w/intaglio design
of berries & leaves w/scattered rhinestones on the
front, twist snap rhinestone closure at center top,
botton-hinged, lined w/white plastic, 4 x 7", excellent
condition, lining loose on one side (ILLUS.).. **$120.00**

1950s Creamy Ostrich Skin Purse with Coin Purse

Purse, cream-colored ostrich skin, goldtone metal frame
& hinges w/rhinestone press clasp, lined w/white
leather, accompanying coin purse, labeled "Saks Fifth
Avenue - Made in France," excellent condition, leather
slightly soiled (ILLUS., previous page) **$250.00**

1950s White Raffia Purse

Purse, glazed white raffia over a canvas support,
goldtone metal frame & gold looped rigid handle,
blue glass cabochon clasp, lined w/white moiré
fabric, labeled "Made in Italy for Burdine's Sunshine
Fashions," excellent condition, lining soiled (ILLUS.)
. . . . **$55.00**

Gold Leather & Goldtone Metal Cage Purse

Purse, gold leather inside a goldtone metal oval cage w/a
rolled gold leather double strap handle, hinged brass
clasp & lid, over mirror under lid, lined w/peach faille,
labeled "Extra," very good condition, lining slightly
soiled, scuffs to leather, 1955 (ILLUS.) **$110.00**

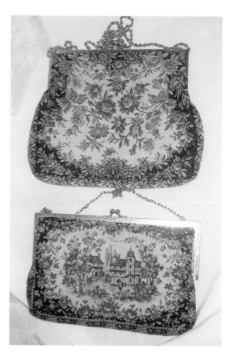

Two 1950s Machine-Made Tapestry Purses

Purse, rectangular machine-made tapestry w/a beige
ground & black edging depicting a scene of country
homes, goldtone metal frame & twist ball clasp, chain
handle, lined w/peach satin, excellent condition, minor
wear to lining (ILLUS. bottom with larger machine-
made tapestry purse) **$38.00**

1950s Red Cloth Purse with Plastic Frame

Purse, red cloth w/clear plastic frame, original tags, ca.
1950 (ILLUS.) **$20-40**
Purse, square large machine-made tapestry w/a white
ground & black trim w/a floral design in reds & yellows,
goldtone metal frame w/chain handle, twist ball clasp,

lined w/peach satin, labeled "Delill - Made in France," excellent condition, minor wear to lining (ILLUS. top with smaller machine-made tapestry purse, previous page). **$58.00**

1950s Black Faille Purse & Matching Accessories

Purse & accessories, black faille rectangular notebook purse w/small metal snap clasp, accompanyed by a gold-edged comb, goldtone metal compact w/mirror, goldtone metal lipstick holder & a black faille-covered card holder, excellent condition, minor wear around clasp, the set (ILLUS.) **$200.00**

Long Gold Foil-Covered Purse & Gold Accessories

Purse & accessories, extra long gold foil-covered purse w/rolled foil-covered handles, gold frame, hinged snap clasp, lined w/beige vinyl, accompanied by a gold foil-covered address book/notepad opening to plastic sleeves & a pair of elbow-length gold lamé gloves, excellent condition, address purse shows wear, the set (ILLUS.) **$175.00**

CLOTHING - 1960-1970

1960s Bag with Tiny Black Beading

Beaded bag, covered w/tiny black beads, some round, some cylindrical, w/a silvered metal frame encrusted w/large faceted rhinestones, square-cut & round, black beaded strap, metall ball & circle clasp, lined w/black satin, labeled "Bags by Josef - Hand Beaded in France," excellent condition (ILLUS.) **$225.00**

Two Views of a Large 1960s Louis Vuitton Garment Bag

Garment bag, Vuitton monogram pattern canvas in beige on chestnut w/light brown leather trim, light brown belt closing strap w/brass buckle, two outer compartments, one zippered & one snapped, zippered larger interior compartment fitted w/hanging rod, lined w/brown linen, Louis Vuitton monogram "LV," late 1960s - early 1970s, good condition, considerable scuffing to light brown trim, lining stained (ILLUS. closed & open, previous page) **$600.00**

Unusual Silver Wire Basket Purse

Purse, basket-style, a woven round silver wire basket w/a center decoration of a gold disk w/an romantic portrait surrounded by faceted stones, old leather hinge & straps, brass twist closure, lined w/ivory satin, good condition, basket bent in places, lining shows wear, ca. 1960 (ILLUS.) **$150.00**

Tapering 1960s Purse of Rose Satin

Purse, bell-shaped, dusty rose satin tapering to the top, trimmed w/a band of faceted copper-colored sotnes, satin double handles, snap closure, lined w/cream-colored satin, labeled "Elizabeth Arden New York Paris," very good condition, some minor scuffs & soiling (ILLUS.) **$350.00**

1960s Black Crocodile Skin Purse

Purse, black crocodile skin w/gold strip frame, black leather handle, brass hinge clasp, lined w/black vinyl, labeled "Meyer New York," very good condition, handle shows some wear (ILLUS.) **$175.00**

1960s Wooden Box Purse with Wishing Well Decoration

Purse, box-style made of bleached wood hand-decorated w/beads & coins in a wishing well design, white vinyl trim w/twist clasp, white plastic handle, large inside round mirror, labeled "Original Box Bag by Collins of Texas," good condition, some damage to vinyl trim, wear to wood, 1966 (ILLUS.) **$55.00**

1960s Silver Lamé & Chrome Box Purse

Purse, box-style, silver lamé fabric over a square support w/riveted chrome corners & trim, molded double chrome handles, top bar & ball clasp, hinges on both sides, lined w/white vinyl, labeled "Fleurette of Miami - Made in Italy," very good condition, lining shows wear (ILLUS.) **$75.00**

1960s Yellow Turtle Skin Purse

Purse, bright yellow turtle skin w/a double handle & goldtone metal press clasp, lined w/ivory leather, accompanying coin purse & mirror, inner zippered compartments & sleeves, labeled "Genuine Turtle - Saks Fifth Avenue," excellent condition, tiny scuffs in hidden places (ILLUS.) **$350.00**

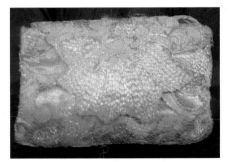

1960s Homemade Blue Lace Purse

Purse, clutch-style, light blue lace over an acetate support, envelope snap closure, lined w/blue acetate, fair condition, homemade bag w/slightly sloppy execution, soiling to lace, fraying to fabric (ILLUS.) **$35.00**

1960s Purse of White Plastic Disks

Purse, composed of white plastic disks on a canvas support, strung together w/metal rings, adjustable chain shoulder strap, lined w/white poplin, good condition, some disks soiled & some unstrung, lining soiled (ILLUS.) **$125.00**

A 1960s and 1970s Robert di Camerino Purse

Purse, dark red velvet w/bands of green & blue for accent, velvet-covered rolled handle & frame, goldtone metal push clasp, lined in black leather, labeled "Made in Italy by 'Roberta di Camerino,'" fair condition, visible wear on exterior & interior (ILLUS. left with 1970s orange di Camerino purse, previous page) . . **$425.00**

Unusual Sponge Purse with Shell Trim

Purse, made from a large loofah sponge, hollowed out & lined w/cream-colored brocade, whip-stitched canvas trim, the lid elaborately trimmed w/a still-life of shells, coral, glitter, tiny binoculars, w/a wrapped button & loop closure, excellent condition (ILLUS.) . . . **$375.00**

Unsual 1960s Yellow Lunch Box Purse

Purse, metal lunch box painted yellow & decoupaged w/flowers & butterflies, rolled & stitched leather handles, wooden tapered feet, lined w/blue felt, signed "Designed for You by Miki," very good condition, minor paint loss (ILLUS.) **$65.00**

Red Plush Italian Purse in the Style of Roberta di Camerino

Purse, mostly red plush velvet w/touches of black at edging & a grey & white plush band at the bottom, thick gilt metal chain w/wrapped bar handle, goldtone metal hinged clasp, lined w/black leather, labeled "Pelletteria - Valigeria - principe - Varese," in the style of Roberta di Camerino, excellent condition (ILLUS.) **$400.00**

1960s Rectangular Beige Leather Purse

Purse, rectangular beige leather w/accordian opening, goldtone metal twist clasp, lined w/cordovan leather, labeled "Rich Craft Bag," very good condition, leather cracked at handle, minor body scuffs (ILLUS.) **$58.00**

1960s Flower-Printed Canvas Purse

Purse, sturdy cotton canvas printed w/red, white, light blue & pink flowers on a light green ground, self-fabric top handles, small brass twist closure, lined w/copper-colored lustrous poplin, labeled "Margaret Smith, Gardiner, Maine," very good condition, some staining to lining (ILLUS.). **$125.00**

1960s Red Textured Leather Purse

Purse, textured red leather w/black bamboo handle & bamboo turn clasp, lined w/black vinyl, labeled "Ronay," very good condition, shows some signs of wear (ILLUS.) **$125.00**

1960s White Ostrich Skin Purse

Purse, white ostrich skin w/ostrich skin-covered metal frame & ostrich skin strap handle, brass hinge clasp w/a heart, lined w/gold faille, two inner sleeves faced w/black fabric, labeled "Block," very good condition, some scuffs) **$400.00**

CLOTHING - 1970-1980

Front & Back of a 1970s 'Magazine' Clutch Purse

Bag, 'magazine' clutch-style, made from rigid molded plastic shaped to resemble a folded magazine w/a photo-print overlay, this issue titled "The Art of Peace," white vinyl strap w/snap closure, lined w/black linen,one large compartment inside w/a small slit pocket, fair condition, some wear to cover, some rusting around snaps (ILLUS. of front & back, previous page). **$125.00**

Bag, 'magazine' clutch-style, made from rigid molded plastic shaped to resemble a folded magazine w/a photo-print overlay, this issue titled "GRAZIA spilla no. 5," leather-studded strap wraps around bag to form closure, lined in bright orange acetate, labeled 'Delill - Made in Italy," good condition, some wear to cover & discoloration to inner lining (ILLUS. of front & back) **$250.00**

1970s Gold Vinyl & Links Pure

Purse, gold vinyl body covered w/circular gold links & woven gold cord, shoulder strap of gold chain & same circular links, beige satin-lined inner compartment w/one small inside pocket, top zipper closure, labeled "Walborg - Made in Hong Kong," excellent condition 6 x 8" (ILLUS.) **$125.00**

Purse, lustrous orange weave w/bands of orange velvet pile suggesting belts & buckles, dark green pile at either side suggesting chain links, chain handle strap, goldtone metal snap clasp w/dangling chain & medallion w/crest, lined w/red leather, inside mirror tucked into a leather sleeves, labeled "Made in Italy by 'Roberta di Camerino' Expressly for Saks Fifth Avenue," excellent condition, one or two snags to weave (ILLUS. right with 1960s dark red velvet di Camerino purse, page 245) **$850.00**

1970s Saint Laurent Colorful Leather Pouch Purse

Front & Back of a 1970s Italian 'Magazine' Clutch Purse

Purse, pouch-style, white canvas duck w/a red leather top, white rope handle & drawstring & tasseled leather ends, composed of squares of red, blue purple & black leather overstitched w/black thread, labeled "Yves Saint Laurent," excellent condition (ILLUS., previous page). **$250.00**

1970s Purse of Woven Gold & Silver Leather Strips

Purse, woven of gold, silver & bronze leather strips, goldtone metal frame & hinged clasp, optional chain handle, lined w/purple satin, labeled "Morris Moskowitz Genuine Leather," very good condition, some leather & lining wear (ILLUS.) **$95.00**

Gucci Monogram Logo Tote Bag

Tote bag, canvas decorated overall w/the interlocking "G" Gucci logo, green & red webbed stripe at center front & back, dark brown trim, corners & double strap handle, top zipper closure, woven lining, one large inner compartment & one zippered sleeve, fair condition, considerable wear to top zippered area, scuffing of leather & soiling of canvas (ILLUS.)
. . . . **$150.00**

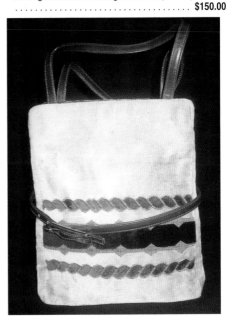

1970s Rectangular Velvet Tote Bag

Tote bag, taupe-colored velvet w/contrasting accents of brown & black velvet bands towards the bottom suggesting twisted ropes, a narrow brown leather strap held by goldtone metal links w/a bold buckle, brown leather straps, top opening faced w/brown leather, remainder of bag lined w/grey faille w/a zippered inner sleeve, labeled "Block," excellent condition (ILLUS.)
. . . . **$120.00**

CHAPTER 13: SHOES & BOOTS

CLOTHING - PRE-1850

CHILDREN'S

Early Girl's Red Leather Boots with Laces

Boots, girl's, red leather w/original laces, ca. 1830-40, pr. (ILLUS.) **$150-200**

SHOES & BOOTS - LADIES'

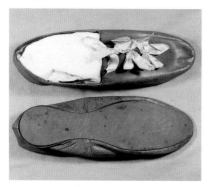

Early Lady's Pale Green Leather Shoes

Shoes, green leather w/silk bows, ca. 1820, pr. (ILLUS.) **$250-300**

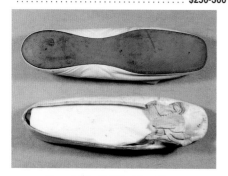

Early White Kid Wedding Shoes

Shoes, white kid wedding-type, labels inside for a Louisville, Kentucky maker, ca. 1840, pr. (ILLUS.) **$250-350**

CLOTHING - 1850-1920

CHILDREN'S

Girl's 1860s Blue Leather Boots

Boots, girl's, blue leather w/front lacing & scalloped top edge, ca. 1860s, pr. (ILLUS.) **$150-200**

LADIES'

Simple Black 1860s Lady's Boots

Boots, black cloth w/low heels & laces, ca. 1860s, pr. (ILLUS.) **$200-300**

High-button Purple Velvet Boots

Boots, purple velvet high-button style, ca. 1910-15, pr. (ILLUS., previous page) **$125-175**

Pumps, brown leather w/silk bows & marcasites, ca. 1890 (ILLUS.) **$250-350**

Circa 1900 Black Lady's Bathing Shoes

1920s Red Satin & Silver Pumps

Bathing shoes, black cloth w/pink stripes, ca. 1900-20, pr. (ILLUS.) **$100-200**

Pumps, red satin w/tiny silver straps & trim, 1920s, pr. (ILLUS.) **$125-150**

Beaded Black Silk Pointed Pumps

Red & Silver Brocade 1920s Pumps

Pumps, black silk w/iridescent glass bead ornaments, very pointed toes, style sometimes referred to as "pickle stickers," early 20th c., pr. (ILLUS.) . . **$125-175**

Pumps, red & silver brocade, gold straps w/jeweled button closure, ca. 1920, pr. (ILLUS.) **$125-175**

Dainty White Silk & Rhinestone Pumps

Late Victorian Lady's Leather Pumps

Pumps, white satin trimmed w/rhinestones, ca. 1915-25, pr. (ILLUS.) **$125-200**

Early 20th Century High-top Shoes

Shoes, dark blue leather high-top button-up style, ca. 1900-10, pr. (ILLUS.) **$150-200**

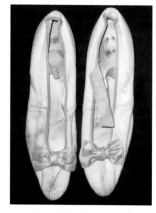

Crocheted Slippers on Early Holder

Slippers, red crocheted yarn, w/slipper holder patent-dated 1888, slipper holder $75-125; slippers, pr. (ILLUS.) **$30-40**

Shoes for Ivory Wedding Dress Ensemble

Wedding shoes, ivory doeskin w/ivory silk bow & elastic strap, one-inch high baby-Louis heel, fair condition, heavily worn toes, elastic stretched, part of ivory silk satin wedding dress ensemble, ca. 1903-10 (ILLUS.) **$85.00**

MEN'S

Ankle-high Men's Shoes from the Early 20th Century

Shoes, ankle-length brown leather, stitching at rounded toe, lace-up style, labeled "The Marlborough Brand - R. Mundy & Sons - Marlborough," fair condition but wearable, ca. 1905-18 pair (ILLUS.)........ **$150.00**

CLOTHING - 1930-1940

CHILDREN'S

1930s White Canvas Mary Jane Shoes

Shoes, Mary Janes, for a teenage girl, white canvas w/rounded reinforced toes, unlined, canvas inner sole, white rubber sole, white button & shank closure, labeled "Cushion Comfort Heel - 5," good condition but extensive age yellowing to sole & canvas, pr. (ILLUS.) **$175.00**

LADIES'

1930s Gold Braid Evening Shoes

Evening shoes, gold braid, bands cross in front w/a peep toe, gold leather heel, braid heel strap & gold leather ankle strap w/rhinestone buckle, lined w/peach satin, gold-covered 3" h. heels, vinyl sole, illegible mark, very good condition, few scuffs on heel, moderate wear to sole & lining, pr. (ILLUS., previous page) **$375-400**

1930s Burgundy Suede Pumps

Pumps, burgundy suede, open strap instep, pair (ILLUS.) **$25-35**

1930s Gold Leather Open-toed Pumps

Pumps, open-toed style w/strap, gold leather, pair (ILLUS.) **$60-90**

1930s Deep Rose Satin Peep-Toe Shoes

Shoes deep rose satin upper w/peep-toe decorated w/pink braiding, open-shank & satin heel back, satin-lined, black leather sole w/satin-covered 2 1/4" h. chunky heel, embossed mark on sole "Comfy Slippers - 295," fair condition, fading to satin, holes & moderate scuffing, pr. (ILLUS.).................. **$275.00**

Scarce 1930s White Canvas Sports Shoes

Sports shoes, white canvas uppers, reinforced toe, front laced w/15 eyelets, unlined, white rubber sole & 1 1/2" h. flat rubber heel, very good condition, some spots on canvas, very minor wear to sole, pr. (ILLUS.) **$350.00**

CLOTHING - 1940-1950

CHILDREN'S

Late 1940s White Leather Mary Janes

Shoes, Mary Janes, white leather w/perforated toes & two-buckle straps at vamps, stitched leather soles, labeled "Friedman Shelby Thrift - St. Louis - Red Goose," late 1940s - early 1950s, good condition, never-worn leather dried & cracked in places, pr. (ILLUS.) **$35.00**

LADIES'

1940s Leather Platform Shoes

Platform shoes, brown suede platform & uppers w/narrow straps at instep, open toe, ankle straps w/buckle, brown leather-lined, brown leather sole, suede-covered 3 3/4" h. boulevard heels, marked "Foot Delight Shoes," excellent condition, moderate sole wear, pr. (ILLUS.) **$350.00**

1940s Brown Alligator Open-toed Pumps

Pumps, brown alligator, peep-toes & thick soles, pair
(ILLUS., previous page) **$75-100**

Late 1940s Faux Snakeskin White Pumps

Pumps, white leather uppers w/embossed insertion over
vamp w/openwork, brown leather lining & inner sole,
brown leather soles, embossed leather-covered 3 1/4"
h. boulevard heels, marked "John Lobb London Paris
New York," soles signed w/customer's name, excellent
condition, late 1940s, pr. (ILLUS.) **$600.00**

*1940s Suede Platform-style Shoes with
Peep-toes & Cut-outs*

Shoes, navy blue suede platform-style w/peep-toes &
cut-outs, pair (ILLUS., previous page) **$75-150**

CLOTHING - 1950-1960

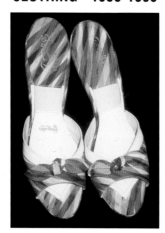

Rainbow-Colored 1950s Open-toed Mule

Mules, rainbow-colored fabric-covered w/open toes
w/knot detail at center vamp, trimmed w/white
leather, fabric-covered 4" h. stiletto heels w/patented

"Springalator" & elastic on white vinyl inner soles,
brown leather soles, labeled "Paradise - Springalator
Pat. Pend. - 8 1/2 N.," very good condition, some
soiling to inner sole, pr. (ILLUS.). **$200.00**

Black Silk 1950s Vivier Pumps

Pumps, black silk peau de soie w/squared toe & oversized
square jeweled buckle, lined w/white leather, black
leather sole, black silk-covered 2 1/2" h. heels w/
triangular bases, marked "Designed by Roger Vivier
Paris - Saks Fifth Avenue - 9AAA," excellent condition,
minor sole wear, late 1950s - early 1960s, pr. (ILLUS.)
. . . . **$700.00**

1950s Roger Vivier Black Silk Pumps

Pumps, black silk w/narrow bow detail at vamp, covered
3" h. spike heel, marked "Designed by Roger Vivier
Paris - Saks Fifth Avenue - 9AAA - #8991," good
condition, some wear to heel fabric, moderate wear to
sold, pr. (ILLUS.). **$400.00**

*1950s White Spike-heeled Faux Snakeskin
Pumps & Box*

Pumps, creamy white spike-heeled faux snakeskin, in original box, pair (ILLUS., previous page) **$40-50**

1950s Saks Gold Glitter Pumps

Pumps, gold glitter w/bronze-colored net overlay, pointed toes w/strap at vamp & small black bow detail, brown leather sole, glitter & net-covered 3 1/2" h. spike heels, satin lining, marked "Saks Fifth Avenue Fenton Last - 9AAA," excellent condition, minor sole wear, pr. (ILLUS.) **$350.00**

Red Leather 1950s Carson Pirie Scott Pumps

Pumps, red leather w/pointed toes, perforation & narrow straps w/buckles on vamp, leather-covered 3" h. spike heels, white leather lining, white vinyl inner sole, brown leather sole, labeled "L. Miller Beautiful Shoes - Carson Pirie Scott & Co.," very good condition, some leather discoloration, pr. (ILLUS.) **$175.00**

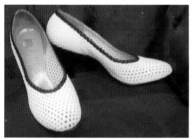

1950s Open Weave White Leather Pumps

Pumps, white strips of leather woven w/an open weave, reinforced leather-backed heels, navy blue braided leather trim, black leather sole & navy blue leather-covered boulevard heels, marked "Shoe Salon - G. Gox & Co. - Hartford, Connecticut - 9AAA --- Designed by Evins," very good condition, moderate wear to sole & uppers, pr. (ILLUS.)................. **$175-200**

Late 1950s Stiletto-heeled Yellow Plastic Pumps

Pumps, yellow plastic w/green curvilinear lines design, pointed toes, lined w/light green leather, brown leather sole, plastic-covered 3 3/4" h. stiletto heels, marked "joseph la rose - exquisite footware," excellent condition, some minor wear, late 1950s - early 1960s, pr. (ILLUS.) **$350.00**

1950s Brooks Brother Black Shoes with Rhinestone Trim

Shoes, open-toed slingback-style, black suede vamps & ankle strap w/almond-shaped Lucite detail at center, studded w/rhinestones, black suede ankle straps w/buckle, lined w/black leather & featuring patented elastic "Springalators" at inside instep, 4" h. Lucite heels studded w/rhinestones, black leather sole, marked "Brooks Brothers Footwear - Chicago - Hubbard Woods - Springalators U.S. Pat. 2001.227," excellent condition, some sole wear, minor stone loss, pr. (ILLUS.) **$500.00**

1950s Shoes with Floral Faille Covering

Shoes, open-toed slingback-style, floral faille covering, featuring clear plastic vamp w/faille rosette & bow at toe, fabric ankle straps & fabric-covered 4" h. spike heels, faille inner sole, brown leather sole, very good condition, some age-related yellowing to plastic, moderate sole wear, pr. (ILLUS.) **$275.00**

1950s Blue Brocade Slippers

Slippers, uppers of peacock blue brocade w/peep-toe, blue poplin piping, lined w/blue satin, brocade-covered wedge & 1" h. heel, marked "Daniel Green - Made in U.S.A.," excellent condition, some minor wear to lining & sole, pr. (ILLUS.) **$120.00**

CLOTHING - 1960-1970

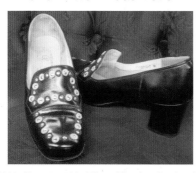

1960s Brass-studded Navy Blue Leather Loafers

Loafers, navy blue leather w/brass studs & red & white suede disks on vamp, leather-covered 2 1/2" h. chunky heels, vinyl inner sole, brown leather sole, labeled "Luana Exclusively Garolini - Made in Italy," excellent condition, some wear to sole, pr. (ILLUS.) **$125.00**

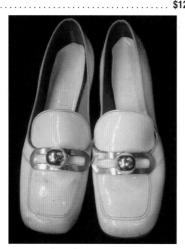

1960s White Patent Leather Loafers

Loafers, white patent leather w/metal buckle & large ball detail, silver foil-covered 2" h. chunky heel, patent leather inner sole, lined w/light green linen, rubber sole, labeled "Carol Brent," good condition, mild scuffing to upper, moderate sole wear, pr. (ILLUS.) **$125.00**

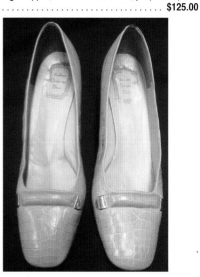

1960s Dior Embossed Beige Leather Pumps

Pumps, beige embossed leather in a faux crocodile pattern, squared toes, raised faux crocodile ridge on vamp w/gold accents at each end, black leather sole, covered 2 3/4" h. heel, marked "Souliers Christian Dior - 6 1/2 A - #273060," excellent condition, very minor sole wear, pr. (ILLUS.) **$125.00**

1960s Saks Embossed Black Leather Pumps

Pumps, black embossed leather in a crocodile pattern, faux tortoiseshell buckle on vamp, 2 1/4" h. covered Cuban heels, marked "Saks Fifth Avenue - Fenton Last," excellent condition, pr. (ILLUS.) **$275.00**

Late 1960s Black Faille Pumps

Pumps, black faille uppers w/lacing over vamp & black faille-covered 3" h. square heels, white kid insole, black leather sole, marked "Miss Bergdorf - 9AA," excellent condition, moderate sole wear, late 1960s, pr. (ILLUS.) **$225.00**

Christian Dior 1960s Black Pumps

Pumps, black satin w/a square toe, gold-stamped tan leather insole, black leather sole, oval-shaped rhinestone buckle on vamp, 2 5/8" h. square heel, labeled "Souliers Christian Dior, 7R, 964710," good condition, slight fading to insole stamp, scuffing on sole, pr. (ILLUS.). **$400.00**

1960s Lustrous Green Pumps

Pumps, bright & lustrous green uppers, pointed toe & fabric-covered 3 1/2" h. stiletto heels, vinyl insoles, vinyl soles, marked "Cameo Room - Narrow Heel Combination Last - Sole of Mand-Made Mat'l - Vinyl Sock," fair condition, moderated soiling to uppers, pr. (ILLUS.) **$85.00**

1960s Dark Green Leather Pumps

Pumps, dark green leather w/perforations at the toes, vamps & sides, small green velvet bow ties low on vamp, black leather sole, stacked wooden 3 1/2" h. spike heels, marked "Michael - 9B," very good condition, some scuff marks on leather & heel, pr. (ILLUS.) **$200-250**

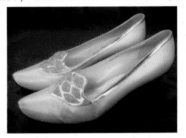

1960s Decorated Ivory Satin Saks Pumps

Pumps, ivory satin uppers w/pointed slightly turned toes & gold beads & gold leather insertion over vamp & gold edging, 1 3/4" h. heels, white vinyl inner soles, brown leather soles, marked "Saks Fifth Avenue Fenton Last - Hand Sewn Made in Italy - 9AA," very good condition, some scuffing on upper, moderate sole wear, pr. (ILLUS.) **$200.00**

1960s Orange Suede Pumps Made in Spain

Pumps, orange suede w/rounded toe, textured 3" h. painted square heels, lined w/white leather, brown leather sole, marked "Pavel Made in Spain - 9B," good condition, scuffing & soiling to suede upper, pr. (ILLUS., previous page) **$195.00**

1960s Silver & Gold Lamé Pumps

Pumps, silver lamé uppers w/silver & gold lamé curlique detail at vamp, brown leather soles, silver lamé-covered 2 3/4" h. spike heels, marked "De Liso Debs," very good condition, minor fraying to lamé along edges of upper, moderate wear on soles, pr. (ILLUS.) **$125.00**

1960s Pink & White Saddle-style Shoes

Saddle-style shoes, pink & white w/perforated squared tooes & backs of heels, silver disk & lace over the vamp, pink covered 1 1/2" h. chunky heels, white vinyl insole, brown vinyl soles, marked "Gaymode - JC Penney," very good condition, some moderated sole wear, drying & curling to insole, pr. (ILLUS.). . . **$85.00**

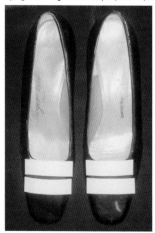

Pair of 1960s Vivier Patent Leather Shoes

Shoes, black patent leather w/white patent leather strips across toes, white patent leather-covered sculpted heels, left shoe labeled "Saks Fifth Avenue," right shoe labeled "Designed by Roger Vivier Paris - 9AAA," excellent condition, probably never worn, the pair (ILLUS.) **$450.00**

1960s Lady's Faux Leather Shoes

Shoes, faux leather w/brown stripe & bow, man-made sole, pair (ILLUS.). **$65.00**

1960s Faux Snakeskin Mary Janes

Shoes, Mary Janes, faux snakeskin, ca. 1960, pair (ILLUS.) **$25-35**

1960s Mottled Brown Leather T-strap Shoes with Original Box

Shoes, mottled brown patent leather, pointed toes w/T-strap & covered 2 3/4" h. stiletto heels, green leather inner sole, brown leather sole, labeled "joseph la rose - exquisite footwear," w/original box, excellent condition, minor sole wear, pr. (ILLUS., previous page) **$250.00**

MEN'S

1960s Men's P.F. Canvas Sneakers

Sneakers, black canvas w/thick rubber sole & rubber toe, round decal on ankle reads "HOOD P-F" w/silhouette of man playing basketball, labeled "P.F. - 7 1/2 - Ventilated Uppers - Washable," fair condition, some age-related yellowing to soles, some cracking around toes, fading to canvas, pr. (ILLUS.) **$55.00**

CLOTHING - 1970-1980

LADIES'

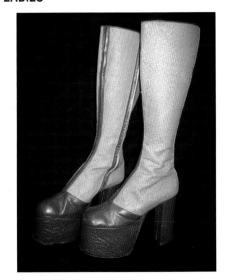

1970s Brown Vinyl Platform Boots

Platform boots, textured vinyl shafts pieced in panels w/ brown vinyl trim, vamps & covered platform heels, very good condition, vinyl over platform wrinkled in some areas (ILLUS.) **$425.00**

Two Views of 1970s Black Suede Pumps with Silver Wedge Heels

Pumps, black suede uppers w/shaped metal wedge & 3 1/2" h. heels, marked "Charles Jourdan - Paris - Made in France - 8.5," very good condition, some wear to uppers, minor wear to sole & heel, pr. (ILLUS. of two views). **$225.00**

1970s Brown Python Skin-covered Platform Pumps

Pumps, platform-style, brown python skin covering the uppers & platforms w/a python skin bow at rounded toe, python-covered 4" h. chunky heel, brown leather sole, marked "Totar - Handemade in Spain," excellent condition, very minor sole wear, pr. (ILLUS., previous page). **$300.00**

1970s Purple Patent Leather Strappy Sandals

Sandals, purple patent leather w/open toe, T-strap & ankle straps, patent leather-covered 3" h. chunky heels, white vinyl inner sole & vinyl soles, marked "Gaymode - JC Penney," excellent condition, some curling & drying to inner sole, pr. (ILLUS.) **$65.00**

1970s Satin "Beatle Booties"

Shoes, "Beatle Booties," black satin w/squared toes, side elastic gores, 3" h. wooden heels studded w/cabochon stones & rhinestones, brown leather sole, marked "Raphael Via Veneto - 37," excellent condition, minor sole wear, some stones missing, pr. (ILLUS.)
. . . . **$225.00**

1970s Blue Suede Shoes with Metal Studs

Shoes, navy blue suede toes & vamps w/open-shank heel backs & ankle strap, upper decorated w/goldtone metal studs, lined w/brown leather, black leather sole, suede-covered 3" h. chunky heel, marked "Milady - Made in Spain," excellent condition, very minor sold wear, pr. (ILLUS.) **$375.00**

1970s Jourdan Biege Leather Platform Shoes

Shoes, platform-style, beige leather straps & platforms, dark brown inner sole, leather-covered 4" h. chunky heels, labeled "Charles Jourdan - Made in Italy - Paris," fair condition, scuffing & cracking to leather, pr. (ILLUS.) **$55.00**

Two Pairs of Platform Shoes

Shoes, platform-style, black patent leather lace-up Oxford style, leather upper & lining w/man-made sole, 3-inch patent leather-covered heel, label illegible w/only "Made in England" remaining, 1970s-style but probably later, excellent condition, pair (ILLUS. left with other platform shoes) **$75.00**

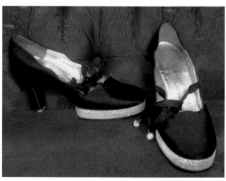

1970s Charles Jourdan Black Satin Platform Shoes

Shoes, platform-style, black satin upper w/scalloped edge, black braided tie w/rhinestone ball ends over instep, silver beaded platform & satin-covered 3 3/4" h. boulevard heels, lined w/silver kid, black leather sole, marked "Charles Jourdan Paris - 5 1/2," excellent condition, moderate wear inside & some scuffing on heel, pr. (ILLUS., previous page) **$350.00**

Shoes, platform-style, chocolate brown velvet lace-up Oxford style, man-made sole, trimmed w/gold cord on vamp & golden metal grommets, brown satin ribbon, 3-inch velvet-covered heels, labeled "Connie," 1970s, excellent condition, pair (ILLUS. right with other platform shoes) **$150.00**

1970s Saint Laurent Slingbacks

Shoes, slingback open-toe style, yellow patent leather woven vamps, open toe, strappy slingbacks w/4 1/2" h. heel w/beige enamel panel, marked "Yves Saint Laurent - Paris - Made in France - 6.5," excellent condition, slight sole wear, some tiny spots on leather, pr. (ILLUS.) **$225.00**

MEN'S

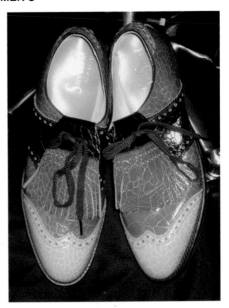

Colorful Golfing Shoes from Ensemble

Golf shoes, crocodile hide-stamped leather in green, yellow, red, black & blue w/red & black feathered tab covering black woven laces, turf cleats on soles, labeled "Sam Snead Golf Shoes - Insole of Man made Materials - 983," mint condition, the pair (ILLUS.) **$400.00**

CHAPTER 14: TIES

CLOTHING - 1850-1920

Large Late Victorian Man's Bow Tie

Bow tie, black w/tiny yellow dots, large, ca. 1880s (ILLUS.) **$25-35**

Patented Man's Victorian Bow Tie

Bow tie, brown w/embroidered green floral design, patent-dated 1874 (ILLUS.) **$25-30**

Victorian Man's Puff Tie

Necktie, puff-style, black w/scattered small white geometric designs, ca. 1890s (ILLUS.). **$25-35**

CLOTHING - 1940-1950

Three Hand-Painted Neckties from the Late 1940s - Early 1950s

Necktie, hand-painted Fiesta pattern, Mexican dancing couple & scattered sombreros on a swirling dark blue & yellow ground, labeled "Moore's 'The Men's Store' - Santa Fe, New Mexico - Holly Vouge," late 1940s - early 1950s (ILLUS. right with two other hand-painted neckties) **$65.00**

Necktie, hand-painted Sea Gull pattern, stylized flying bird in pale greens & brown against a swirling sea green & brown background, labeled "Fred C. Fowler - 'Redlands,'" late 1940s - early 1950s (ILLUS. center with two other hand-painted neckties) **$65.00**

Necktie, hand-painted Starburst pattern, small black stars against a swirling pale yellow & dark blue background, labeled "Lyons - Hollywood - Burbank," late 1940s - early 1950s (ILLUS. left with two other hand-painted neckties) **$65.00**

1940s Necktie with Painted Black Boy

Necktie, hand-painted w/a scene of a little black boy running, label of Mary Vela Art Studio, San Juan, Puerto Rico, Royal Vogue, 1950s (ILLUS., previous page). **$65.00**

CLOTHING - 1950-1960

Three 1950s Hand-Painted Western-Style Bow Ties

Bow ties, hand-painted, clip-on type, Western ribbon-style, in black, red or tan, each decorated w/either horse heads or spurs, unmarked, each (ILLUS. of three) **$35.00**
Bow tie, red & green silk foulard, excellent condition (ILLUS. botton w/three other bow ties) **$18.00**

Group of Four Clip-On Bow Ties

Bow ties, clip-on type, all polyester in different patterns & weaves, all excellent condition, each (ILLUS. of three, above red & green silk bow tie) **$15.00**

CLOTHING - 1960-1970

Abstract 1960s Finnish Necktie

Necktie, bold abstract Mod design in shades of orange, grey & pink, labeled "marimekko - suomi finland," 1966 (ILLUS.) **$75.00**
Necktie, red w/grey stripes, cotton blend, excellent condition, perhaps some slight fading (ILLUS. right with two other neckties, top next page) **$18.00**
Necktie, skinny-style, blue & silver in argyle design of cotton blend, straight ends, excellent condition (ILLUS. left with two other neckties, top next page). . . . **$18.00**
Necktie, skinny-style, dark blue w/red twill, excellent condition (ILLUS. center with two other neckties, top next page) **$25.00**

Three Skinny 1960s Neckties

Two Gucci Neckties in Shades of Black, Blue, Grey & White

CLOTHING - 1970-1980

Three Large 1970s Bow Ties

Bow ties, large wide style, all of polyester in different patterns & weaves, excellent condition, each (ILLUS. of three) **$16.00**

Necktie, black background decorated w/three large blue & white rosettes & a chevron of smaller rosettes at the tip, by Emilio Gucci, late 1970s - early 1980s (ILLUS. right with other black & blue Gucci necktie, next column) **$86.00**

Necktie, black background w/alternating very thin white & red stripes, the red stripes decorated w/tiny white basket-like designs, Emilio Gucci, late 1970s - early 1980s (ILLUS. right with brown striped Gucci necktie, next column) **$65.00**

Necktie, black ground w/diagonal stripes of egg-shaped devices in black, shades of blue & grey, by Emilio Gucci, late 1970s - early 1980s (ILLUS. left with other black & blue Gucci necktie) **$86.00**

Pauline Trigere Necktie

Necktie, bold abstract design of flowers & leaves in dark green & black on a white ground, labeled by Pauline Trigere, late 1970s - early 1980s (ILLUS.) **$55.00**

Front & Back of a Bold Emilio Pucci Tie

Necktie, bold swirling abstract design in shades of blue, purple, white & black, by Emilio Pucci, late 1970s - early 1980s (ILLUS. of the front & back, previous page). **$150.00**

Gucci Neckties in Brown, Tan & Orange or Green & Black

Necktie, brown, tan & orange diagonal stripes edged in looping bands, by Emilio Gucci, late 1970s - early 1980s (ILLUS. left with green & black Gucci necktie) **$150.00**

Two 1970s Yves Saint Laurent Neckties

Necktie, dark blue w/an overall red design of the Yves Saint Laurent monogram logo, late 1970s - early 1980s (ILLUS. left with other Yves Saint Laurent necktie) **$75.00**

Two Late 1970s Striped Gucci Neckties

Necktie, dark brown background w/tan plain & knotted stripes, Emilio Gucci, late 1970s - early 1980s (ILLUS. left with black striped Gucci necktie). **$45.00**

Necktie, skinny style, a stylized diamond-like pattern in shades of light green, black, white & yellow, by Emilio Gucci, late 1970s - early 1980s (ILLUS. right with brown, orange & tan Gucci necktie) **$125.00**

Necktie, wide black background stripes w/alternating narrow red & white stripes, a single Yves Saint Laurent monogram logo near the botton, late 1970s - early 1980s (ILLUS. right with other Yves Saint Laurent necktie). **$45.00**

CHAPTER 15: MISCELLANEOUS ACCESSORIES

PRE-1850 CLOTHING

Ornate Early Cut Steel Hair Comb

Hair comb, cut steel w/ornate pierced scrolls & angled & pointed top, ca. 1820-40 (ILLUS.). **$50-75**

1830s Ivory Handled Parasol

Parasol, cloth cover w/ivory handle, finial & tips, ca. 1830 (ILLUS.) **$125-175**

CLOTHING - 1850-1980

Belt, snake-shaped, dark goldtone metal, reticulated body w/pointed tip, large rhinestone eyes, excellent condition, head slightly tarnished (ILLUS. left with other snake belt). **$85.00**

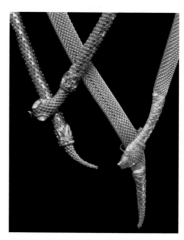

Two 1970s Metal Snake Belts

Belt, snake-shaped, light gold mesh w/coral-colored beads at tail & head, excellent condition (ILLUS. right with other snake belt) **$65.00**

1970s Stretch Metal Snake Belt

Belt, snake-shaped, light gold stretch metal, serpentine w/pointed tip & small turquoise beads for eyes, marked "AccesorCraft," good condition, one loop to fasten belt broken (ILLUS.) **$45.00**

Patented Lady's Victorian Belt Buckle

Belt buckle, silvered metal w/stamped & engraved decoration, opens to attach to a belt, patent-dated 1874 (ILLUS.) **$60-90**

1880s "Bedspring" Style Lady's Bustle

Bustle, "bedspring" style, cloth-covered, ca. 1880s (ILLUS.) **$100-150**

Blue Silk & Ivory Victorian Fan

Fan, blue silk & ivory w/feather-shaped blades trimmed w/small feathers & flat spangles, mid-19th c. (ILLUS.) **$75-125**

Lovely Hand-painted Paper Fan

Fan, hand-painted paper & wood, decorated w/figures in 18th c. costume & ornate gilt scrolls, ca. 1850s (ILLUS.) **$100-200**

Early 20th Century Pink Ostrich Feather Fan

Fan, rose pink ostrich feathers w/tortoiseshell design celluloid sticks, ca. 1915-20, 20" l. (ILLUS. open) **$125-150**

Late Victorian Lady's Silk Fan & Fan Pouch

Fan & fan pouch, hand-painted & embroidered silk fan, ca. 1900, w/matching embroidered silk fan pouch, pouch **$35-45,** fan (ILLUS.) **$100-200**

Late Victorian Fine Lady's Hair Comb

Hair comb, celluloid in a tortoiseshell design trimmed w/solid gold inlay, in original Christmas box, ca. 1900 (ILLUS.) **$100-125**

Decorated Victorian Celluloid Hair Comb

Hair comb, celluloid w/gold & silver inlay & a pearl grape cluster, late 19th c. (ILLUS.) **$100-150**

Set of Victorian Hair Jewelry & Bar Pin with Photo of Original Owner

Hair jewelry, a bead-style necklace w/knob-form drops & matching earrings & a gold-filled bar pin, shown w/a period photo of the young woman wearing the set made from her hair, ca. 1880, the group (ILLUS.) **$400-600**

Lady's Burgundy Silk Parasol, Ca. 1890

Parasol, burgundy silk lined in lightweight orange silk, hooked handle, ca. 1890 (ILLUS.) **$150-250**

Early Folding Carriage Parasol

Parasol, carriage-type, banded tan & brown silk w/silk fringe, folding handle, ca. 1850 (ILLUS.) **$150-250**

Folding Black Silk Carriage Parasol, Circa 1860

Parasol, carriage-type, black silk w/folding handle, ca. 1860 (ILLUS.) **$125-175**

Black Net & Velvet Parasol, Circa 1900

Parasol, gathered black net w/wide black velvet bands, lined w/gathered white net, ca. 1900 (ILLUS.,) **$150-250**

1880s Black Crepe Mourning Parasol

Parasol, mourning-type, ruffled black crepe, shepherd's crook handle, ca. 1880s (ILLUS.) **$125-175**

Striped Silk Parasol, Circa 1900

Parasol, navy blue & white striped silk w/carved wood handle, ca. 1900 (ILLUS.). **$75-125**

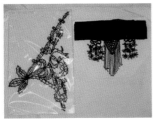

Two Fancy Late Victorian Beaded Passementerie

Passementerie, both pieces of faceted jet beads in various sizes & shapes; at left - one-piece delicately fashioned to depict a nosegay or bouquet, excellent condition; at right - in three sections, on either side iris-like flowers w/cascades of beads flank a central shield shaped piece w/single beaded strands, sewn to a waist belt made of black silk faille w/boning & hook & eye closure, both late 19th century, excellent condition, each (ILLUS. of two). **$200.00**

Scarf, 100% polyester, pink w/large red, gray & white polka dots, machine-stitched hem, printed Vera signature, 1970s (ILLUS. right with three other Vera scraves) **$28.00**

A Selection of Four Vera Scarves

Scarf, 100% wool, striped muffler style w/a black, beige, red & gray graphic print, printed Vera signature, late 1960s (ILLUS. left with three other Vera scarves) **$35.00**

Scarf, lustrous silk crepe, orange w/white borders, hand-rolled & stitched hems, printed Vera signature, 1970s, excellent condition (ILLUS. top center at neck with three other Vera scarves) **$30.00**

Scarf, silk twill, aqua w/blue & green floral print, hand-rolled & stitched hems, printed Vera signature, 1970s, good condition, small stain & pin hole near edge (ILLUS. botton center at waist with other Vera scarves) **$25.00**

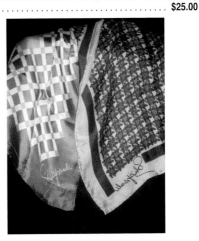

Two Colorful Schiaparelli Silk Scarves

Scarves, 100% silk, each w/a bold colorful diamond lattice design, printed Schiaparelli signature, 1970s, excellent condition, each (ILLUS. of two) . . . **$100-250**

Grouping of Vintage Hermes Scarves

Scarves, Hermes designs, all of silk twill, hand-rolled sewn edges & lavish prints, excellent condition, 1950s-1970s, each (ILLUS. of group) **$250-350**

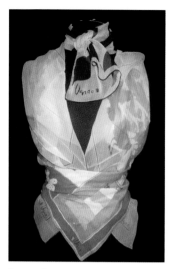

Group of 1960s Vera Chiffon Scarves

Scarves, silk blend chiffon, machine-stitched edges, all signed w/Vera signature & ladybuy logo, excellent condition, each (ILLUS. of several)......... **$28-40**

Two 1960s Signed Vera Scarves

Scarves, silk twill, hand-rolled edges, all signed w/Vera signature & ladybug logo, excellent condition, each (ILLUS. of two) **$35-45**

Jeweled Lady's Shoe Buckles in Original Box

Shoe buckles, lady's, jeweled ornately pierced metal, in original blue velvet-lined leather box, early 20th c., pr. (ILLUS.) **$50-75**

1950s Skirt Hoop in Package

Skirt hoop, cloth & wire, in original package labeled "Hoops! My dear," 1950s (ILLUS.) **$30-50**

Scarce Victorian Lady's Skirt Lifter

Skirt lifter, silvered metal, worn on a belt or ribbon around the waist, clamped onto trailing skirts to lift them off the ground, patent-dated 1870 (ILLUS.) **$150-250**

Two 1920s Beaded Tassels

Tassels, one of clear & silver beads, the other of white & silver beads, covering two spheres & one egg-shaped form, w/long beaded cascades, rhinestone detail strip on egg-shaped forms, excellent condition, each (ILLUS.) **$295.00**

Glossary

Armscyes - opening where sleeve is placed; armhole

Assuit shawl - A garment made of Assuit (also called 'Tulle-bi-telli' that translates roughly into 'net with metal') named after the city in Egypt where the technique originated, these shawls usually are of cotton or linen mesh with folded, cut and hammered silver tape passed through the knots, very popular in the 1920s following the discovery of King Tut's tomb.

Batiste - Fabric made of linen cotton that is lightweight, sheer and delicate of plain weave.

Bateau neck (ba toe) - Wide boat-shaped neckline, high on back and front, close along collarbone, ending at shoulder seams.

Blousoned (bodice) - A term used for style of fullness of fabric from bodice to waist, very billowy, then cinched or gathered at or below the waist

Box pleats - Combination of two flat double pleats in opposite directions, with turned-under edges meeting underneath.

Burnous - a hooded cloak

Canvas duck - Strong fabric made of cotton or linen in plain weave, lighter than normal canvas.

Charmeuse (shar muz) - A satin-finished silk fabric that is lightweight with slight luster.

Day dress - Dress worn for non-formal occasions during daytime, not as elaborate as afternoon dress, with less tailoring made of finer and lighter fabric.

Evening dress - Evening wear that can be worn at formal or semi-formal social affairs, opera, theater etc.

Evening gown - Dress usually made of delicate or luxurious fabric, suitable for activities such as the theater usually décolleté and sleeveless

Faille A soft, slightly glossy woven fabric made of silk, rayon, cotton, wool, or manufactured fibers or combinations of these fibers and having a light, flat grosgrain.

Fanchon (bonnet) - Popular during the Victorian period this bonnet resembles a diagonally folded handkerchief.

Formal - Garments worn on full dress occasions, characterized when men wear white tie and tails, and women wear evening gowns.

Frog closure - Chinese style of closure made of decorative cording or braid. A soft ball of cording or a button is used to complete the closure.

Gazaar overlay - Overlay of gazaar, a medium weight 100% silk fabric from India with a flowing drape and smooth texture, sometimes referred to as 'the cousin to organza'.

Godet - Panel inserted into garment, wider at bottom to add fullness, used with skirts and sleeves.

Panniers - Meaning 'basket' in French gives the effect of draping of the skirt on the sides, similar to the classic peplum look, for an elegant, old-fashioned appearance. The exaggerated panniere, which bought skirts to incredible widths and a narrow front to back came into fashion in the 1730's and lasted until the 1770's.

Passementerie - Trim or adornment on a garment; usually made with heavy embroidery, edges of rich gimps, braids, beads, and tinsel.

Pelerine - Short shaped shoulder cape that is waist-length, usually with long ends hanging down in front, popular in England and Colonial America

Pilling - Small bobbles of fabric that develop on the fabric surface due to general wear and tear.

Piqué knit - A knitting method that creates a firm and fine textured surface that appears similar to a 'birds nest' or 'waffle weave'.

Placket - Slits in upper part of skirt, waist part of dress, neck or sleeve for convenience in putting garment and forming a closure.

Polonaise - Popular during the 18th century a polonaise is a coat like garment for a woman, that buttons down in front, usually short sleeved, has a fitted bodice, with an overskirt drawn back to reveal a colorful underskirt, named after the Polish national costume.

Raglan sleeves - A type of sleeve sewn in with seams slanting outward from neck to underarm. The sleeve continues in one piece to the collar so there are no seams at the shoulder, allowing for ease of movement.

Ruched - Extremely tight gathers used as a decorative top finish to a panel, usually on neck and sleeves.

Shirring (shirrred) - Three or more rows of gathers with stitches done in thread which has an elastic quality to it.

Shrug - A woman's small, waist-length or shorter jacket.

Silk satin surah - Soft, lightweight, twilled fabric of silk or twill

Silk foulard - A light plain-weave or twill-weave silk, (or silk like fabric), usually with a printed design, having dark figures on a light background usually used for dresses, blouses and scarves.

Slubs - A lump or thick place on yarn caused by small lengths of yarn adhering to it during the spinning process.

Surplice neckline - A neckline created by the cross-wrapping of fabric; may be in front or back, and associated with a high or low neckline

Toque - Small close-fitting brimless or nearly brimless hat

Watteau back - having fullness taken in back with box pleat from neck to waistline, and hanging loosely over shoulders.

Welt (pocket) - An inserted pocket, with edged finished, resembling a bound button-hole.

'Weft-ikat' technique (kimono) Ikat or Kasuri fabrics are made by selectively binding and dyeing parts of the warp or weft threads, or even both, before the fabric is woven. For either silk or cotton fabrics, the threads are stretched on a frame, selected design areas are bound, then the hanks of bound threads are immersed in dye pots.